THE NEW COLD WAR

Revolutions, Rigged Elections and Pipeline Politics
in the Former Soviet Union

MARK MacKINNON

CARROLL & GRAF PUBLISHERS
NEW YORK

THE NEW COLD WAR
Revolutions, Rigged Elections, and Pipeline Politics in the Former Soviet Union

Carroll & Graf Publishers
387 Park Avenue South
New York, NY 10016

Copyright © 2007 by Mark MacKinnon

First published by Random House Canada 2007

First Carroll & Graf edition 2007

Library of Congress Cataloging-in-Publication Data is available

ISBN-13: 978-0-7867-2083-5
ISBN-10: 0-7867-2083-2

9 8 7 6 5 4 3 2 1

Printed in the United States of America

To Carolynne. And Odessa.

CONTENTS

LEGEND

Russia-backed
oil pipeline

U.S.-backed
oil pipeline

DRAMATIS PERSONAE

The Russians

BORIS BEREZOVSKY—Reviled "oligarch" who held enormous influence in Boris Yeltsin's Kremlin and who originally backed Putin's rise to power. When Putin, anxious to curb his power, allowed an investigation into how Berezovsky acquired his wealth, he fled to London. He is seen as the main supporter of Russian Pora, a youth group devoted to staging a pro-Western revolution in Russia.

GAZPROM—Giant Russian energy company that supplies gas to most of the former Soviet Union and Eastern Europe. After a series of acquisitions during the Putin era, the company's oil reserves are exceeded only by those of Saudi Arabia and Iran. Under direct Kremlin control, it is often used as a tool to advance Moscow's foreign policy aims.

MARAT GELMAN—A member of Project Putin, the grooming of Boris Yeltsin's successor into a candidate for all seasons. Later, he designed the *temnyki,* a system of government control over the media.

SERGEI IVANOV—Russia's defence minister and deputy prime minister, and, like Putin, a former KGB agent. He is often mentioned as a possible successor to Putin should he step aside in 2008.

MIKHAIL KASYANOV—Prime minister under Putin from 2000 to 2004, when he fell out with the Kremlin over Khodorkovsky's arrest. Now in opposition, he is seen as a potential pro-Western presidential candidate in 2008.

MIKHAIL KHODORKOVSKY—The Russian energy tycoon who ran the giant Yukos oil company and was the country's richest man until he publicly clashed with Putin and began pouring money into opposition parties. He was arrested on fraud charges in October 2004 and later sentenced to nine years in jail in what many called a show trial.

SERGEI MARKOV—Pavlovsky's outspoken sidekick. Once the Kremlin's dominance over Russian political and business life was re-established, he was charged with exporting "managed democracy" to the other ex-republics of the USSR. The goal was to bring them back into Moscow's sphere of influence.

DMITRY MEDVEDEV—Another potential Putin successor, he headed the giant Gazprom energy company—the Kremlin's most effective foreign policy tool—before rising to head the Presidential Administration and then being appointed deputy prime minister.

VYACHESLAV NIKONOV—Another spin doctor who frequently advised the Kremlin and oversaw the rise of United Russia, Putin's chief political vehicle, which some Russians have dubbed "the Communist Party, Part Two."

GLEB PAVLOVSKY—The most prominent of a team of spin doctors who wield enormous power in Vladimir Putin's Kremlin, and the designer of a new system called "managed democracy," which gives individuals freedoms they didn't have in the Soviet years while the Kremlin keeps a tight grip on media and big business. Elections are held every four years, but voters are in reality given no real choice.

VLADIMIR PUTIN—Formerly anonymous KGB agent who became Russian prime minister in 1999, then won the presidency the next year in a landslide victory, capitalizing on his massive popularity after he sent Russian forces back into the breakaway republic of Chechnya. He considers the fall of the Soviet Union a catastrophe and is intent on rebuilding Moscow's influence in the "near abroad." Re-elected in 2004, he is constitutionally barred from running for a third term in 2008, though some expect he'll try anyway.

The Americans

FREEDOM HOUSE—Funded by both the U.S. government and Soros, Freedom House provided support to pro-Western opposition movements in the former USSR. Its long-time head, former CIA chief James Woolsey, was replaced in 2005 by Peter Ackerman, a specialist in non-violent regime change.

THE INTERNATIONAL REPUBLICAN INSTITUTE (IRI)—The international wing of the U.S. Republican Party and an NED grantee, IRI provided funding and training to youth groups intent on overthrowing the established order in former Soviet states. It is headed by Republican Senator John McCain.

MICHAEL KOZAK—U.S. ambassador to Minsk during an abortive attempt to overthrow Belarusian dictator Alexander Lukashenko in 2001, he later became assistant secretary of state for democracy to Condoleezza Rice.

RICHARD MILES—American ambassador to Belgrade during the last years of Slobodan Milošević, he was also ambassador to Georgia when Eduard Shevardnadze was toppled.

THE NATIONAL DEMOCRATIC INSTITUTE (NDI)—The international wing of the U.S. Democratic Party and an NED grantee, NDI would play a key role in marshalling pro-Western forces ahead of the revolts in Serbia, Georgia and Ukraine. It is headed by former U.S. secretary of state Madeleine Albright, who frequently intervened personally in the crises.

THE NATIONAL ENDOWMENT FOR DEMOCRACY (NED)—U.S. government–funded democracy-promotion agency, sometimes referred to as "Project Democracy." It backed pro-Western candidates in elections across the former Soviet Union while also directing funds to get-out-the-vote campaigns, exit polling, independent media and radical youth groups. NED grantees were at the forefront of the revolutions in Serbia, Georgia and Ukraine.

GEORGE SOROS—Billionaire philanthropist who, because of a childhood living under Nazism and Communism, has an extreme distaste for autocratic regimes. He has poured billions of his own money—largely through his Open Society foundations—into supporting pro-democracy groups in Eastern Europe. The Kremlin sees him as the chief ideologist and financier of the pro-Western revolutions that hit Serbia, Georgia and Ukraine.

PAVOL DEMEŠ —A Slovak who headed OK'98, a successful get-out-the-vote campaign that led to the defeat of Slovakia's anti-Western prime minister Vladimír Mečiar in 1998. Backed by American NGOs, he travelled to Serbia, Ukraine and Belarus to train opposition movements there. He is now the director of the Bratislava office of the German Marshall Fund of the United States, a privately funded grant-giving institution that supports pro-Western democracy movements in Eastern Europe.

The Serbs

B92—Rebellious anti-Milošević radio station that mixed rock-and-roll with anti-regime newscasts. Repeatedly shut down by authorities, it repeatedly got back on the air with help from Soros and the U.S. government. Station manager Saša Mirkovic later advised the Georgian opposition.

CeSID—Acronym for Citizens for Free Elections and Democracy, a Western-funded election-monitoring group that revealed efforts by Slobodan Milošević to falsify the country's 2000 election. Marko Blagojevic, a member of CeSID's board of directors, later helped set up similar vote-monitoring groups in other Eastern European countries.

VOJISLAV KOŠTUNICA—Previously anonymous lawyer whom Madeleine Albright convinced the Serb opposition to rally around in 2000.

ALEXANDER MARIC—Founding member of Otpor. Later, American money sent him to Belarus, Georgia and Ukraine to train youth activists in those countries.

MARKO MARKOVIC—Joined Otpor demonstrations against Milošević in the town of Novi Sad. Later he headed the Kiev office of an American-financed group called Znayu, which was charged with carrying out character assassination against Ukrainian president Leonid Kuchma and his chosen successor, Viktor Yanukovych, ahead of the 2004 elections there.

M ILOŠ M ILENKOVIĆ—Founding Otpor member who later helped train student activists in Belarus and Ukraine.

S LOBODAN M ILOŠEVIĆ—Serbian strongman who earned the West's wrath during the Balkan wars of the 1990s. He was overthrown in a pro-Western revolution in 2000.

O TPOR—American-funded Serbian student group that played a cat-alytic role in the protests against Milošević in 2000. Its clenched-fist flag was embraced as a symbol by pro-democracy groups across Eastern Europe. The name means "Resistance" in Serbian.

S RĐA P OPOVIĆ—Self-described "ideological commissar" of Otpor who later helped the Georgian opposition get organized over a series of Soros-funded trips between Tbilisi and Belgrade.

S INIŠA Š IKMAN—Founding Otpor member who later helped train student activists in Belarus and Ukraine.

The Georgians

K MARA—Youth movement created by the Liberty Institute on the Otpor model.

T HE L IBERTY I NSTITUTE—Soros-backed NGO that agitated against the Shevardnadze regime and helped create the Kmara youth move-ment. Co-founder Giga Bokeria was flown to Belgrade by Open Society to study the revolution in Serbia and to help bring it to Georgia.

R USTAVI 2—Soros-backed independent television channel that took a cue from Serbia's B92 and called people into the streets during the Rose Revolution.

M IKHAIL S AAKASHVILI—American-educated lawyer who joined Shevardnadze's government, then went into opposition and led a pro-Western revolution against him in 2003. He was elected presi-dent following the Rose Revolution.

E DUARD S HEVARDNADZE—Former Soviet foreign minister who became president of his native Georgia in 1992. He was seen as a friend of the West until he allowed Russian companies to snap up key commercial assets in Georgia, threatening the viability of a U.S.-backed oil pipeline traversing the country.

ZURAB ZHVANIA—Like Saakashvili, a protégé of Shevardnadze's until going into opposition and becoming one of the leaders of the Rose Revolution and later Saakashvili's prime minister. His cousin David was one of the primary financiers of the Orange Revolution in Ukraine a year later.

The Ukrainians

VLADISLAV KASKIV—An ex-Soros employee who became the leader of Pora, later an adviser to both President Yushchenko and the Belarusian opposition.

LEONID KUCHMA—Quasi-autocrat who was president from 1994 to 2004, winning a pair of elections along the way. Originally viewed as a reformer, he cracked down on the media and drew closer to the Kremlin as a series of scandals soiled his reputation in the West.

PORA—Western-backed youth group modelled on Otpor and Kmara. It led the protests that brought Yushchenko to power.

PETRO POROSHENKO—Key financial backer of the Orange Revolution and, in particular, of 5th Channel, the only pro-opposition television station in the country. The station played the role of B92 and Rustavi 2, calling opposition supporters to join the revolution. Afterward, Poroshenko was made the head of Yushchenko's National Security Council, where he feuded with Tymoshenko.

YULIA TYMOSHENKO—Firebrand opposition leader who stood by Yushchenko's side during the Orange Revolution and later became his prime minister. A post-revolution fallout saw the enormously popular former gas tycoon eventually go into opposition against Yushchenko.

VIKTOR YANUKOVYCH—An ex-convict who was prime minister for the last years of Kuchma's presidency and who won the Kremlin's backing in the 2004 presidential race.

VIKTOR YUSHCHENKO—Pro-Western former central banker who served as prime minister under Kuchma before going into opposition. During the 2004 elections, he called his supporters into the streets to demand a new election after evidence emerged suggesting the authorities had cheated to give Viktor Yanukovych the presidency. He survived a mysterious poisoning episode to become the face of the Orange Revolution.

The Belarusians

VLADIMIR KOBETS—Founding member of Zubr who also took part in Ukraine's Orange Revolution.

ALEXANDER LUKASHENKO—Dictator who has ruled Belarus since 1994, a period that has seen the country plunge into deeper and deeper isolation.

ALEXANDER MILINKEVICH—Pro-Western opposition politician who led a failed revolt against Lukashenko in 2006.

ZUBR—Western-backed youth group founded in 2001, with help from members of Otpor.

The Central Asians

ASKAR AKAYEV—President of Kyrgyzstan (on China's western border). He was seen as Central Asia's most progressive leader until he was deposed in a riot that boiled over into the so-called Tulip Revolution of 2005.

ILHAM ALIEV—President of tiny Azerbaijan, a job he inherited from his father, Heydar. While he spoke of being pro-Western, he used an iron fist to crack down on opposition demonstrations, understanding that the West valued stability in his oil-rich country more than it did democracy.

ISLOM KARIMOV—A one-time American ally who provided a key base for the war in Afghanistan. He fell out of favour after he ordered soldiers to fire on demonstrators in the town of Andijan in 2005.

NURSULTAN NAZARBAYEV—President of vast, oil-rich Kazakhstan. He tilted between policies that were pro-Washington and pro-Moscow while tolerating little dissent at home.

PROLOGUE

Moscow

The forest of nondescript apartment blocks in the town of Ryazan, southeast of Moscow, was an unlikely place for history to pause.

The twelve-storey building that stood at 14/16 Novosyolov Street was the same as tens of thousands of other concrete buildings throughout Russia, structures from the era when Leonid Brezhnev ruled the Kremlin—a time when the state gave you an apartment that was identical to your neighbour's.

On the outside, the buildings were typically grimy, grey and in desperate need of a layer of fresh paint. And while the apartments themselves tended to be warm and kept immaculately clean, the shared stairwells and the elevator were dark and filthy places that stank of garbage and urine. In post-Soviet Russia, the state no longer took care of such common areas, and no one had bothered to figure out whose job it now was. Residents of the building on Novosyolov Street had become used to seeing strangers come and go and to not asking too many questions about them. It was nobody's business.

But in the aftermath of a series of devastating bombings in September 1999 that destroyed a trio of similar apartment blocks—two in Moscow, one in the southern city of Volgodonsk, killing more than three hundred people—there was a renewed communal spirit.

1

Across the country that fall, ordinary people in such apartment blocks formed patrols and neighbourhood watch committees to prevent further attacks.

So when on the night of September 22, 1999, residents of the Ryazan apartments spotted two men and a woman unloading large sacks from a white Zhiguli car they did not recognize and putting them in the basement of their building, they became concerned. One resident, Alexei Kartofelnikov, noticed a piece of paper sloppily pasted over part of the car's licence plate—hiding that the car was not actually from Ryazan, but from Moscow—and called the police.

When they arrived, police found three sacks in the basement, along with a timer, detonators and traces of hexogen, the powerful sugar-like explosive that had been used to bomb the apartment buildings in Moscow and Volgodonsk. The giant bomb had been set to explode at 5:30 a.m. the next day, when most of the building's residents would have been asleep. Police evacuated the area and shut down the entire city in a desperate manhunt for Chechen "terrorists," whom the government had accused of the other attacks. For the next forty-eight hours, Ryazan's airport and train station remained shut, and all roads out of the city were blocked.

Eventually, by tracing a phone call, the police apprehended the two men and one woman—who immediately pulled out badges identifying themselves as members of Russia's Federal Security Service, or FSB, the modern successor to the dreaded KGB. The three were swiftly released.

Nikolai Patrushev, head of the FSB, eventually admitted that agents had indeed been apprehended in Ryazan. But, he claimed, the media had got it all wrong: there had been no thwarted terrorist attack, only a successful FSB training exercise. There had been no explosives in the sacks, he told a TV interviewer, only sugar, though police who had been at the scene continued to claim otherwise in interviews with journalists.[1] Residents of Ryazan, he said, should be applauded for successfully responding to a "test" of their vigilance.

Even before the apartment bombings, fear was already in the Russian air. On August 31, 1999, a blast ripped through the underground Manezh shopping centre in the heart of Moscow, just steps from the Kremlin and Red Square, killing one person and injuring forty others.

That attack had put an exclamation point on the troubles facing Vladimir Putin, the unheralded former KGB agent who had been appointed the country's prime minister just two weeks beforehand.

Putin took office on August 16 with single-digit recognition in most opinion polls, to a collective "Who?" from a Russian public grown weary of President Boris Yeltsin's machinations. In his last two years in office, Yeltsin, ailing but desperately clinging to power, rapidly went through four prime ministers, each one brought in with great ceremony and then quickly disposed of.

But from the moment he took office, Putin assumed the poise of a wartime leader. In the wake of the second Moscow apartment bombings—and while the blast sites were being bulldozed before any investigation could be done—Putin declared Chechnya to be a "huge terrorist camp." The next day, despite repeated denials from the Chechen government that it or its fighters had anything to do with the string of attacks, Putin sent the Russian air force to bomb the breakaway republic, which had just won de facto independence in 1996 from the Kremlin following a bloody two-year war. Within months, the Russian army was once more engaging Chechnya in a full-scale war, one that would win Putin massive popularity, propel him to the presidency and cost tens of thousands of lives. In the eyes of most Russians, this was a just war, begun by the "terrorists" who carried out the apartment bombings in the fall of 1999, and one they trusted their new leader, Putin, to execute.

If the Kremlin's story is to be believed, Russia was a country under assault, attacking Chechnya to protect itself. In that version of history, the public's wholesale embracing of Putin as a man of action in the presidential elections the following year becomes fully understandable. But if the conspiracy theory—that all the bombings were the work of government agents—was right, Russia was backsliding quickly toward autocracy. By using mass murder to convince Russians that they needed to put their trust in the secret agents they had so long despised, the old KGB had effectively carried out a coup in the Kremlin.

The conspiracy theory had two important adherents from the beginning. At the Washington, D.C., offices of the National Endowment for Democracy (NED), a U.S.-government-backed agency dedicated to promoting democracy worldwide—sometimes through funding independent media and trustworthy opinion polls, sometimes through organizing revolutions—senior staff saw the September 1999 bombings and Putin's subsequent war in Chechnya as the end of Russia's flirtation with being a Western-style democracy. They understood instinctively that Boris Yeltsin and the young reformers that NED had worked with since the fall of the Soviet Union in 1991 were no longer in charge. They were back facing their old enemy, the KGB.

American billionaire philanthropist George Soros saw things much the same way. Even before Putin assumed the presidency in early 2000, Soros was warning that Russia was "lost" to the West. And as Putin's Kremlin set out to solidify its grip, first on Russian society, then on the newly independent countries that made up the old USSR, a web of non-governmental organizations financed by NED and Soros worked to stop them. Many of the NGOs were seemingly innocuous groups with stated goals only of providing support to independent media or monitoring elections. But working together, they would effectively undermine Putinism's central concept of "managed democracy"—giving individuals freedom in their personal lives while widening state control over big business and politics—by empowering activist groups that resisted the Kremlin's efforts to introduce a new form of authoritarianism.

While the new Russian prime minister and his team set about using economic levers, political pressure and brute force to bring former Soviet republics like Ukraine, Georgia and Belarus more tightly into the Kremlin's orbit, Soros and NED worked to dismantle the new Russian empire Putin was trying to build. Just a decade after the fall of the Berlin Wall, Washington and Moscow were back at odds, again fighting tooth and nail in an undeclared battle that would bring down at least four governments and influence the development of two major oil pipelines over the course of Putin's presidency.

Unlike the Cold War, which was fought on such far-flung battlefields as Angola and Vietnam, this one would be fought far closer to the Kremlin's doorstep, reflecting the new reality of Russia as a re-emerging power. This battle would also have an ideological overtone, the U.S. once again donning the cloak of defending "freedom" and individual liberties, with Kremlin officials occasionally pining openly for an outright return to the Communist system of days past. But this modern struggle would be as much about competing commercial interests—and the control of the old USSR's vast energy resources—as it would be about political systems or ideologies.

The weapons of this war would be different, too. Nuclear standoffs and proxy armies were gone, replaced by rigged elections, stage-managed revolutions and wrangling over pipeline routes. But it was still Washington versus Moscow. And the peoples of the old USSR— Ukrainians, Georgians, Russians, Belarusians and Central Asians— were the ones caught in the middle.

———

ONE

THE PUPPET MASTERS

Moscow and Toksovo, Russia

Mikhail Pushintsky stands waist-deep in the pit, prodding with a steel rod at the dirt beneath him. A dead silence hangs over the thick forest as he listens for the unsettling sound that's made when metal hits human bone. After a few long minutes, he finds what he already knew would be there: another skeleton, another of Joseph Stalin's nameless victims, summarily executed and then buried in this shallow grave north of St. Petersburg sixty-five years before.

First with a shovel, then more delicately with a brush, Pushintsky begins to reveal the remains. First to emerge is a skull browned with age, the teeth still startlingly white. Beside it, he uncovers a femur, too close to where the skull was found to be from the same person. "At least two more here," Pushintsky solemnly says to his digging partner, Fyodor Drozdov, who is on his hands and knees probing the floor of another pit just a few metres away.

The mass grave uncovered at the Rzhevsky artillery range in the fall of 2002 by Pushintsky and a small team of volunteers from the Russian human rights organization Memorial would eventually prove to hold the remains of tens of thousands of people, nameless victims of Stalin's purges in the late 1930s. How those buried in the shallow pit died is obvious as soon as Pushintsky and his colleagues uncover the bodies: most of the several dozen uncovered so far feature single, clean bullet holes at the base of the skull—the signature execution style of the hated NKVD secret service force, the predecessor of the notorious KGB and its modern successor, the FSB. The pit into which the victims were unceremoniously thrown is hundreds of square metres in size; layers of bodies lie on top of each other in a final indignity.

The discovery of the mass grave at Rzhevsky was greeted with a stony silence from Vladimir Putin's Kremlin. While the Western donors who funded the excavation believed that revealing the horrors of the Communist past was a crucial step in democratizing the world's largest country, Russia's new rulers preferred to focus on the good done by the secret services and the system they served. Many, including Putin, were themselves former KGB agents. Putin wanted to make Russia proud again. The deliberate disinterest in the Toksovo gravesite served a wider government effort to reshape how Russians remembered the Soviet era, an effort that coincided with Putin's rise to power in 2000. Instead of talking about the mass executions, the labour camps and the organized famine that together left 20 million dead, by low-end estimates, the new government stripped the narrative down to this: Russia was once a great empire; Russia can be a great empire again. The type of empire Russia had presided over was not important, and neither were the horrific costs the country's citizens had paid to sustain it.

The fifty-five-year-old Pushintsky dug because of a personal connection to the purges. In 1937, his grandfather's brother disappeared into one of the black NKVD vans that were the harbingers of death during that terrifying period. Drozdov, also fifty-five, had an even stronger tie: he was born in the Siberian labour camp where his mother and father, accused of espionage, were imprisoned. "I've got a score to settle," Drozdov explained to me as he started digging in another part of the forest, trying to determine the extent of the gravesite. "But that's not why I do this. I do this out of compassion for *them*." He nodded his head at another skeleton slowly emerging from the brown earth.

The digging, begun in September 2002, was still going on four years later, largely because the Memorial volunteers were forced to do it alone. Their small team of perhaps a dozen men and women, who drove to and from the site in a pair of rented green vans, worked with only picks, shovels and brushes. With no help coming from their own government, much of what Memorial did was backed instead by foreign donors.

The Kremlin's cool reaction to the dig was symbolic of a struggle that has raged across Russia and much of its former empire throughout Putin's presidency. His Kremlin had been actively restoring elements of the Soviet system of governance, highlighting the achievements of that system while glossing over its terrible faults. Since 1999, when Putin moved from his post as head of the KGB to the prime minister's office—his stepping-stone on the way to the presidency—the government has issued a set of coins commemorating Stalin as war leader and unveiled a Kremlin plaque in Stalin's honour. The heart-pounding tune of the Soviet anthem has been brought back, albeit with new words, and the once-feared red star has been reinstated as the symbol of the Russian military. Statues of Communist heroes, such as the founder of the secret services, Felix Dzerzhinsky, and KGB chief–turned–Soviet leader Yuri Andropov, had been torn down by joyous crowds when the USSR fell to pieces in 1991 but were now quietly replaced with new ones in more discreet locations. It was as if Germany were trying to refurbish the reputations of Hitler, Himmler and Goebbels, and no one called them on it.

Few Russians, however, seemed bothered. A poll conducted around the fiftieth anniversary of Stalin's death found that 36 per cent, the largest share, believed the dictator had done more good than harm to the country. Another 29 per cent disagreed with that statement, while the remaining respondents had such mixed feelings that they couldn't answer one way or the other. Yuri Levada, the country's most respected pollster, told me that the poll was indicative of much of the data he has collected. By 2004, all his research indicated that ordinary Russians had become more, not less, pro-Soviet. Polls he conducted in 1991, at the time of the collapse of the Soviet Union, had showed that 50 per cent of Russians still admired the Soviet system that existed before Mikhail Gorbachev and perestroika. It was a large number, but not unexpected given the indoctrination so many of the respondents had experienced in the Soviet educational system. What Levada was surprised and disappointed to see was that when he put the same question to Russians in 2004—thirteen years later—the number hadn't gone down, as he might have predicted. It had shot up, to 65 per cent.

Asked in the same poll to rank what they most wanted from their government, three-quarters of Russians named the social guarantees that the

Soviet state had once provided, such as free education, medical help and old age insurance. By contrast, only one in four named freedom of speech, and barely one in ten wanted to see their right to freely travel abroad protected. "People like order and strong power, but not individualism, freedom and democracy," Levada said with a long sigh that let on how upset his own data made him. Sitting in his office as a light snow fell on Moscow's Pushkin Square, he admitted that in 1991 he, like many others, had believed that the country was making a conscious decision to leave its terrible and repressive past behind. How so many of his countrymen and women could long for a return was something he could understand, but he could not agree. Levada died in November 2006.

After the chaos of the 1990s—a decade born into idealism but scarred by post-Soviet social collapse, Boris Yeltsin's unpredictable and often inebriated leadership and the 1998 financial crisis—Russians had come to see the words "freedom" and "democracy" as synonyms for poverty and helplessness. It could be argued, then, that President Vladimir Putin was exactly what the Russian people were hoping for. But just in case he wasn't, the Kremlin went to work ensuring there was no one else they could choose.

Managed democracy—a quasi-authoritarian political system camouflaged to look as if it represents the people's will through the window dressing of elections, a multi-party system and a partially free media—was serving Putin's presidency well. First, it increased the Kremlin's control over Russian society while still maintaining the appearance of a democratic state—something that was crucial if foreign aid and investment were going to keep pouring in. Later, once the Kremlin had exported managed democracy to much of the former Soviet Union, it allowed quasi-autocrats in the Putin mould to maintain their grip on power in places like Kazakhstan and Azerbaijan, while also putting them in debt to, and at least partially under the control of, the Russian president and his spin doctors.

The system has its roots in Russia's 1996 presidential election. At that time, an ailing Yeltsin had become deeply unpopular with Russians, who resented the hardships that the first five years of his liberal market reforms had brought them. Polls showed that the people were so disillusioned that they were willing to give up on the project entirely and return the Communist Party, under the leadership of xenophobe Gennady Zyuganov, to power. The Communists had won control of the country's parliament, the Duma, in 1995, and Yeltsin's popularity was mired at less than 10 per cent.

The idea of the Communists returning to power—and possibly renationalizing the recently acquired assets of the country's new rich— appalled the oligarchs, a class of super-rich Russians who had made billions of dollars during the fast-and-loose privatizations of the jewels of the state in the 1990s, snapping up oil companies and media empires for a fraction of their real worth. Unimaginably wealthy, the oligarchs— in particular Boris Berezovsky, who controlled a wide range of firms, from the old state airline, Aeroflot, to the Sibneft oil giant—had also come to wield wide influence in Boris Yeltsin's Kremlin.

For much of the decade, the oligarchs had feuded among themselves. But when faced with a Communist revival, they decided to put aside their differences and work together to ensure a second term for Yeltsin. Meeting on the sidelines of the 1996 World Economic Forum in Davos, Switzerland, Berezovsky, media magnate Vladimir Gusinsky and oil king Mikhail Khodorkovsky agreed to pool their resources for the cause. Berezovsky and Gusinsky controlled ORT and NTV respectively, the two most watched television channels in the country. For the remainder of the campaign the stations would devote much of their airtime to promoting Yeltsin and bashing the Communists. The oligarchs paid US$3 million[1] to Anatoly Chubais, Yeltsin's disgraced former vice prime minister, who was nonetheless renowned as the country's best campaign manager, to get him back in the pro-Yeltsin tent. They sought advice from Dick Morris, Bill Clinton's one-time strategist.[2]

It turned out to be an unbeatable coalition. In the first round, Yeltsin rebounded to win 35 per cent of the vote, nudging out Zyuganov by three percentage points. Then he took the tactical step of appointing General Alexander Lebed, a long-time critic who had finished a strong third, as head of the Security Council. With Lebed's popular appeal added to the oligarchs' war chest, Yeltsin handily won the runoff against Zyuganov, taking 54 per cent of the vote to Zyuganov's 40 per cent.

The West heaved a sigh of relief that the Communists had been defeated. Monitors sent by the Organization for Security and Co-operation in Europe, a body normally quick to point out a flawed election, "congratulate[d] the voters of the Russian Federation for partici-pating in a further consolidation of the democratic process in the Russian Federation." The idea of Russia's ever becoming a real democracy had survived a near-fatal blow, to thunderous applause from the West.

Marat Gelman says almost anybody could have succeeded Boris Yeltsin as president. Even those who were close to the decision making—such as Gelman himself, a bespectacled shock-art collector and Kremlin-linked political strategist—remain, years later, somewhat surprised that the spinning roulette wheel of Russian politics in 1999 and 2000 stopped with Putin. Yeltsin fired the longest serving of his five prime ministers, Yevgeny Primakov, in May 1999 shortly after an attempt by Parliament to impeach the president. He replaced Primakov with Sergei Stepashin, a long-time ally. But the wily Yeltsin never considered the thirty-seven-year-old Stepashin to be successor material. Three months later, Stepashin too was gone and Yeltsin introduced Prime Minister Vladimir Putin to the world. In his memoir, *Presidential Marathon,* Yeltsin says he had been watching Putin for years as he rose through the ranks from his humble beginnings as a KGB case officer in East Germany, through his tenure as an aide to St. Petersburg's liberal mayor, Anatoly Sobchak, and especially since 1997, when Yeltsin had moved him to Moscow to head the Federal Security Service.

Yeltsin writes that he had been impressed by Putin's "lightning reflexes" and felt that Putin was "ready for absolutely anything in life." In reality, Yeltsin's inner circle—known in Moscow as "the Family"—had become increasingly nervous as 2000 approached, and had been desperately scouring the political landscape for a suitable successor. For members of the Family—Yeltsin's daughter, Tanya Dyachenko, his chief of staff, Alexander Voloshin, and tycoons Boris Berezovsky and Roman Abramovich—that meant someone they could trust to protect the wealth and influence they had obtained over the past decade. If the wrong person came to power, a decade of the Family's shady deals and easily made millions could come back to haunt them.

Most analysts believe Yeltsin chose Putin because, given the candi-date's history of loyalty to his superiors, the president felt he could trust him. When Sobchak had faced imminent corruption charges stemming from the privatization of properties, it had been Putin who made arrangements to smuggle him first to Finland, then onward to France, so that he was never arrested. The charges were dropped soon after Putin became prime minister.

After Putin's appointment, and with just months before Yeltsin would have to step down, the Family redirected its efforts into selling the new candidate. This became known as Project Putin, and in the coming elections the man from nowhere would have the full resources of the state plus the considerable influence of Berezovsky and his media empire behind him.

"Honestly speaking, it was just a coincidence [that Putin was chosen]. It could have been someone else. In two and a half years, Yeltsin changed premiers five times. Actually, it could have been any of them that became president," Gelman told me as we chatted years later in the office of his gallery in Moscow's trendy Zamoskvorechye neighbourhood. But, he believes, of the five men who served as prime minister under Yeltsin, only Putin could have fit the public's mood and captured its imagination the way he has.

Born in 1952, the year before Stalin's death, Putin had a personal history that fit the suddenly patriotic times. He was born to a family that had suffered badly during the Nazis' Second World War siege of Leningrad, and he had two older brothers that he never met, one of whom had died of diphtheria during the war. Like most Russians, he had lived much of his life in a communal apartment and had longed from an early age to be counted among the defenders of his country. When he tried to join the KGB at fifteen he was rebuffed as too young, but eventually he was admitted in 1975 to the Andropov Red Banner Institute for future agents. Little is known of his career as an agent after graduation, other than that he was posted to Dresden, East Germany, a relative backwater in espionage terms.

Putin, Gelman added, held some appeal for almost everyone ahead of the 2000 presidential vote. In part this was because he was a blank surface with a murky background that indicated little about his ideology. During the election campaign, Putin went out of his way to keep his intentions a mystery, refusing to campaign or to publicly debate his opponents, claiming he was too busy—as interim president after Yeltsin's abrupt resignation on New Year's Eve—running the affairs of the country to bother with politics.

Russia's liberals looked at his time as Sobchak's aide and concluded he was a liberal who would push through the reforms the country desperately needed. Nationalists, meanwhile, saw his KGB past as a sign that he was going to tackle the oligarchs, confront America and re-establish Russia as a global power. Ordinary Russians simply swooned for this young, fit anti-Yeltsin, even if he didn't tell them exactly what it was he stood for. He seemed likely to bring Russians the one thing they craved after the chaos of the 1990s: *stabilnost*—stability.

"Putin was the answer to several questions at once," Gelman told me. "People wanted someone who was different from Yeltsin—he was the successor, but he was the direct opposite. He was somebody who at least looked like he could solve the Chechen problem."

Gelman was one of those who helped colour in the president-for-all-seasons, and managed democracy was how he and the rest of Putin's cabal of spin doctors did it. There would be elections, but there would be only one serious candidate. There would be independent media companies, but there would be lines those companies couldn't cross when it came to criticizing the president and the country. You could start a business and you could run it freely, so long as you didn't get too big or touch strategic industries like energy or defence.

In 2000, the media, led by the Berezovsky-controlled network ORT, did Putin's campaigning for him, just as it had done for Yeltsin four years before, going harshly negative on Putin's main challengers, Communist leader Gennady Zyuganov and the pro-Western liberal, Grigory Yavlinsky. While Putin pretended to stay above the fray, the major news channels covered his every move and made him look as presidential as possible. The Monday before the vote, every newscast led with dramatic shots of Putin flying into Chechnya in an Su-27 fighter jet. You couldn't buy that kind of publicity.

On March 26, 2000, Putin was announced as Russia's president-elect, having won 53 per cent of the vote, compared to 29 per cent for the second-place Zyuganov. It was a convincing victory—by passing the 50 per cent threshold on the first ballot, Putin avoided the need for a second-round showdown with Zyuganov. Managed democracy had passed its first big test. Putin was inaugurated as Russian president on May 7, 2000, in a lavish ceremony before 1,500 dignitaries in the Kremlin's glistening St. Andrew's Hall. With Yeltsin and even

Mikhail Gorbachev smiling on, it was hailed as Russia's smoothest-ever political transition.

Only months later did the Russian public see evidence of how far the authorities had gone to secure Putin's victory. In October 2000, the English-language *Moscow Times* published the results of a six-month investigation that found evidence of widespread ballot stuffing, vote buying, administrative pressure and intimidation that the paper said resulted in an extra 2.2 million votes for Putin. The paper found significant evidence that thousands of ballots—believed to be in favour of opposition candidates—had been burned in a pit in Dagestan, where Putin had won an improbably large 81 per cent share of the vote. It also seemed incredible, the paper highlighted, that 51 per cent of voters in Chechnya would support Putin, the man who was in the process of bombing the capital city, Grozny, to rubble. [3]

The report, however, was greeted with an almost complete silence. There were no public protests, and most of the mainstream Russian-language media gave the story a wide berth. After only four months of Putin's rule, the vibrant press of the Yeltsin era was already gone. Reporters and editors had seen enough of the new administration to know, from experience, to keep their heads down. [4]

In his first act as president, Putin repaid his debt to Yeltsin by granting him and his relatives immunity from prosecution. But the new head of state soon made it clear that his gratitude didn't extend to all members of the Family.

Under Yeltsin, Boris Berezovsky was considered the Grey Cardinal (others dubbed him the "Godfather") of the Kremlin, and was arguably the most powerful man in the country. At various times, he had been the secretary of the Security Council, the head of the executive committee of the Commonwealth of Independent States and a Kremlin representative in the talks that ended the first Chechen war. But his real influence stemmed from his close relationship with Yeltsin's daughter, Tatyana Dyachenko, and Yeltsin's chief of staff, Alexander Voloshin, a former business partner of Berezovsky.

As soon as Putin came to power, though, Berezovsky found himself under investigation. Prosecutors began investigating fraud and the misappropriation of funds at two of his companies, Aeroflot and the

LogoVAZ automobile manufacturer. Berezovsky was declared a chief suspect in both, and by the end of 2000 had gone into self-declared exile in London, following another media tycoon, Vladimir Gusinsky, whose use of his NTV television network to criticize Putin and the Chechen war had led to the launching of a similar legal assault against his business empire. As soon as he was freed from three nights in jail, Gusinsky fled abroad and NTV was acquired by Gazprom, the Kremlin-controlled energy giant.

It was a startling declaration of the new man's independence. Though he initially hired Yeltsin allies Mikhail Kasyanov and Alexander Voloshin as his prime minister and chief of staff (probably because they had the administrative experience Putin and his cadre lacked), by ousting Berezovsky, Putin had effectively brought an end to the Family's long dominance of Russian politics. In the Family's place rose a new political elite, drawn almost exclusively from the security services and those Putin had worked with in St. Petersburg during the 1990s—people he knew he could trust explicitly.

Putin built what he called a "power vertical"—a top-down chain of command that he viewed as the antidote to Russia's troubles of the 1990s, when, he believed, there had been simply too many cooks in the kitchen, too many power centres besides the Kremlin. "The idea of a vertical power is dear to the heart of every KGB child, of every KGB officer," said Andrei Piontkovsky, a former Soviet dissident whose think tank, the Center for Strategic Research, was one of the first to identify Putin's authoritarian side.

The Kremlin's new power vertical included a group of spin doctors who shared Putin's distaste for ideology—capitalist or communist—as well as his conviction that the Russian state needed to be made strong again. Marat Gelman, Sergei Markov, Stanislav Belkovsky, Vyacheslav Nikonov and chief mastermind Gleb Pavlovsky were unknown names to the outside world, but they were soon among the most influential people in Russia. They were Putin's James Carvilles and Karl Roves, only bound by fewer rules when it came to securing their man's political goals. They spoke in terms of the political "technologies" they were applying—such as the issuing of instructions to the media on how to cover, or not cover, a certain story—and referred to themselves uniquely as "politologists." Rather than just trying to ensure their man won election in four years' time—the normal scope of ambition for a political strategist in the West—they sought to redefine politics in the country, and in many ways to redefine modern Russia itself. It was time, they decided, for a long half-step back.

Sergei Markov, a sharp-featured, short-haired political analyst who speaks almost as rapidly in English as he does in Russian, said the system of managed democracy was developed because he and the others who had influence in the Kremlin had become convinced over the course of the 1990s that Russia was not ready for democracy in the Western sense of the word: "The idea is very simple . . . we should keep stability and we should solve the [country's] problems. If we have no democratic means, that doesn't mean we should give up and not work, we are responsible for the country." Managed democracy, he would tell me four years later, when the last of the political opposition had been marginalized and the last of the major television channels had been brought to heel, was a "success" that was "supported by a majority of the nation."

Once he'd secured the home front, Putin set out to restore Moscow's former dominance over the other republics of the old Soviet Union, whose breakup he has lamented as "the greatest geopolitical catastrophe of the century." He viewed the "near abroad"—the other fourteen countries that had once formed the USSR—as rebellious provinces that had achieved independence through historical accident, rather than equals under international law that were free to set their own course. Where Yeltsin had tried, largely unsuccessfully, to maintain Russian hegemony in the region through the Commonwealth of Independent States, the CIS was in truth little more than a talking shop where leaders met to exchange grievances. Countries like Ukraine, Georgia, Moldova and Kazakhstan paid little heed to Yeltsin and adopted increasingly pro-Western stances, turning to Moscow only when they thought it could help them get attention in Washington. The Baltic republics of Latvia, Lithuania and Estonia never joined the CIS, and were on course to join the North Atlantic Treaty Organisation, viewed by Yeltsin, and even more by Putin, as an alliance with an unreformed anti-Russian bent. Ukraine and Georgia made occasional noises about wanting to travel the same direction.

Russia, under Yeltsin, was a snarly but seemingly powerless bear when dealing with the other former Soviet republics. Nonetheless, it still possessed an array of measures should it choose to rein in the "near abroad," including, foremost, a vice grip on many of its neighbours' supplies of energy and electricity. It could cut the export routes that brought Central Asian oil to markets in the West, or turn off the lights in Belarus and the Baltics. Also, because ethnic Russians had been encouraged to move into the other republics during the Soviet era, and because the Kremlin had sowed discord between the various ethnic groups of the USSR as a matter of policy in order to maintain Moscow's position as arbiter, the Kremlin could also stir up separatist sympathies and create new political movements at will. With limited effort, it could bring Georgia to the brink of civil war, or stir up the bloody Armenia-Azerbaijan conflict of the 1990s. It could rile up the Russian-speakers of Ukraine and Moldova or drive energy prices there through the roof, sparking wider unrest.

Putin planned to remind his neighbours, in a much more direct way than his predecessor had, who was boss in this part of the world. "Yes, Russia has ceased to be an empire," Putin said in an open letter to Russian citizens before the 2000 election. "But it has not lost its potential as a great power . . . It is unreasonable to fear a strong Russia, but she must be reckoned with. To offend us would cost anyone dearly."[5]

As a former head of the Communist Party's Department of Ideology and Propaganda, Alexander Yakovlev was all too familiar with the system that Putin was looking to partially reintroduce. Twenty years before, as an influential member of Mikhail Gorbachev's Politburo, Yakovlev had helped set Russia on what he thought was a better course—designing the ideas of glasnost and perestroika and convincing Gorbachev that the Soviet system was unsustainable and needed dramatic overhaul. But when he warned the current inhabitants of the Kremlin not to turn Russia back, the man who many considered the grandfather of Russian democracy became a voice in the wilderness.

The owl-faced old man spent the last years of his life working to rehabilitate the names of those killed in Stalin's purges. It was a lonely task, one that had been made harder by government obstruction since Putin's rise to power. He was depressed about his country and the direction it was taking. "It's painful for me personally. This glasnost was my project," he said when I met him in his Moscow office, his voice the low grumble of a reliable old car. "I don't want to be disappointed and hysterical, but there are some things with which I must disagree."

Most disappointing for him, he said, was the backslide in freedom of the press, a liberty he had personally worked hard to establish. He told me that newspapers were less free in 2004 than they had been fifteen years earlier, during the last years of the Soviet system. Putin's intolerance of criticism reflected not the strength of the state, Yakovlev worried, but its weakness. "That's more frightening," he said. He compared the war in Chechnya to other historic Russian blunders, including the crushing of dissent in Hungary in 1956 and in Czechoslovakia in 1968 and the invasion of Afghanistan in 1979. And he was deeply offended at the restoration of Soviet-era symbols, such as the old anthem, which should have been hurtful to the ears of those who had grown up in that repressive era but which somehow wasn't. Yakovlev was not so much bothered that the government had erected a new statue of Felix Dzerzhinsky in the town near Moscow still named for the bloody-minded *chekist,* but that there was almost no public outcry when it happened.

Yakovlev had met Vladimir Putin on several occasions and was troubled by what he saw. Putin, he said, reminded him of Soviet leaders he had worked for, from Khrushchev to Gorbachev. When they first came to power, they all listened to the advice of those around them and worried about the implications of their actions. After three to five years, he said, each man would stop listening and start to believe "that he is the only one who knows the truth and what needs to be done. They become deaf to criticism and deaf to real life." He worried that Putin—believing no one else could rebuild Russia—would eventually move to amend the Constitution so that he could remain in power beyond the end of his second term in 2008.

Improbably, the old man, who was still struggling with all his failing might to remind Russia of the dangers of authoritarianism, blamed himself. Fault for the country's backward spiral, he said, lay not with Putin and his cadre of ex-KGB men, but with himself, Yeltsin, Chubais and the other liberals who had flubbed their historic chance to make Russia into a stable democratic state. They had pushed the economic

reforms too far, too fast—something Yakovlev and Gorbachev had actually counselled against—and had created a criminalized economy and
state where residents came to equate terms like "liberal" and "democracy" with corruption, poverty and helplessness.

"We must confess that what is now going on is not the fault of those
who are doing it," he told me in an interview shortly before his death
in the fall of 2005 at the age of eighty-two. "It's us who are guilty. We
made some very serious errors."

TWO

———

PROJECT DEMOCRACY

Moscow, Budapest and Washington, D.C.

[O]ne of the few regular protests against Vladimir Putin and his policies during the new president's first years in office came in the form of a weekly gathering of anti–Chechen war activists on Pushkin Square in central Moscow. During the first Chechen war, Russians quickly grew sick of the unending bloodshed and took to the streets in the thousands until they forced Yeltsin to sign a peace deal, one that gave Chechnya de facto independence, though it remained nominally within the Russian Federation. While the second Chechen war was even bloodier, anti-war sentiment was slow to materialize, in large part because the daily carnage wasn't reported on Russian television (the since-defanged NTV had led the way in showing the deadly toll of the first conflict), and also because a series of bombings and hostage takings had convinced many Russians that Putin was bang on when he described the Chechen separatists as terrorists and criminals who were to be destroyed, not negotiated with.

There were just twenty-one protestors on the square when I dropped by one Thursday night. It was cold and snowy, but the despondent organizers told me that the weather wasn't the problem—twenty-one people was considered a good turnout for an anti-government protest in Putin's Russia. "Fear is back," Valentina Vasilyevskaya, a fifty-nine-year-old retired secretary, said. "We live in the same conditions now that we had in the Soviet Union, when people were of the opinion that there's no use protesting because nothing can be changed. People are tired now. Dictatorship is advancing."

As we chatted, it became clear that the protesters didn't even have the quiet support of many passersby. Most who stopped to read the demonstrators' anti-war placards responded with derision rather than sympathy. "Who pays you to stand here?" more than one person snorted. For many of those standing and shuffling in the snow with placards around their necks, this was a dishearteningly long step backward from 1991, when many of the Pushkin Square protestors rallied to the White House to stand beside Yeltsin as he faced down the coup attempt by Soviet hard-liners and launched Russian democracy. Now they were back in the streets fighting for what they saw as the same cause, but the masses were no longer with them.

Rather than being disillusioned, Svetlana Rud, a fifty-seven-year-old woman bundled up in a winter coat and fur hat, took a longer view of history. "There were just eight people standing on Red Square protesting against the events in Prague," the retired oil-field engineer said, referring to the use of Soviet tanks to crush the 1968 Prague Spring uprising. "This time, there are twenty-one of us."

Following the Prague uprising, dissident efforts to battle an authoritarian Kremlin received financial aid from the West, though covertly. Many of those standing in the snow with Svetlana Rud that night were members of the Committee of Soldiers' Mothers of Russia, and eventually, like many groups battling against Putin and his system, they too would turn to Washington for help.

If Vladimir Putin, a man whose public mask is one of calm and stoicism in the face of his country's many difficulties, were to be shaken awake in the middle of the night and pressed to name the person who represented the single biggest threat to his rule, he would likely name George Soros. The septuagenarian billionaire financier, who shot to fame as the man who "broke the Bank of England" in 1992, was often portrayed in the Kremlin-controlled press as a one-man obstacle to the restoration of a proud and mighty Russia. His hand was seen everywhere, behind political parties opposed to the Kremlin, even behind tiny demonstrations like the weekly gathering on Pushkin Square. It's perhaps unsurprising that a man who devoted much of his time and vast fortune to promoting "open society" would find himself on a collision course with the inventors of "managed democracy."

Even before Putin had completed his rise to the presidency, Soros publicly identified the former KGB agent as an enemy of open society. "Putin will try to reestablish a strong state and he may well succeed," Soros wrote in an article entitled "Who Lost Russia?" for the *New York Review of Books* on the eve of Russia's 2000 presidential election. "But Putin's state is unlikely to be built on the principles of an open society; it is more likely to be based on the demoralization, humiliation, and frustration of the Russian people," he goes on. "Exact predictions are impossible, but it seems likely that the new government will be authoritarian and nationalistic."[1]

It was the opening salvo in a long war that would leave both Soros and his Kremlin opponents bleeding badly. For the next two presidential terms, Gleb Pavlovsky, Sergei Markov and the other Kremlin tacticians would spend much of their time worrying about how to counter, or at least lessen the impact of, Soros's efforts. Intriguingly, many of them had past associations with the Western NGOs they would come to view as the enemy. Pavlovsky had worked in the early 1990s with Soros's Open Society Institute, and briefly served as editor of the Russian edition of the *Journal of Democracy*, a publication produced by the National Endowment for Democracy that would later slam him as a "threat to freedom" to be ranked alongside Venezuelan president Hugo Chavez. Markov, meanwhile, had worked with the National Democratic Institute, effectively the international wing of the U.S. Democratic Party, and had been a fellow at the Moscow office of the Carnegie Institute for International Peace, a think tank that would become one of the loudest critics of Putinism and managed democracy.

Soros made himself into one of the world's richest men through the Quantum Fund, a hedge fund he co-founded in 1969 that became one of the most successful—and controversial—investment vehicles in history. Established with $4 million, it grew at an astonishing pace of more than 30 per cent a year for the next three decades. By 2005, its successor, the Quantum Endowment Fund, was worth $8.3 billion and

Soros himself was ranked by *Forbes* magazine as the twenty-eighth rich-est man on the planet, with $7.2 billion in personal wealth.[2]

Along the way, however, Quantum and Soros became notorious for the role they played in the 1992 re-evaluation of the British currency, when Soros sold short the equivalent of more than $10 billion in pounds sterling and made an estimated $1.1 billion in one day. Five years later he was blamed for the collapse of the Indonesian ringgit. He could move markets even when he wasn't trading; negative comments alone by Soros about the state of the Russian economy in 1998 led to a dramatic plunge in the Russian stock exchange.

Soros, by his own admission, originally got into philanthropy as a tax dodge. But he was soon consumed with passion for the projects he supported through the Open Society Fund, which he established in 1979. By the 1990s, he was giving money away almost as fast as he was making it, pouring upward of $400 million annually of his own money into projects as diverse as funding the Central European University in his native Budapest, giving aid to civilians during the siege of Sarajevo and buying printing presses for opposition newspapers in repressive Belarus. He did it all out of a deep belief in the concept of "open soci-ety," which he had learned at the knee of American academic Karl Popper while studying in the 1950s at the London School of Economics. Open society, Soros wrote, was defined by "the free movement of ideas and of capital."[3] After living as a child under two different forms of totalitarianism, he believed open society was a concept worth spending billions of his own money on.

Soros was born György Schwartz on August 12, 1930, in Budapest and grew up in the city's Klauzal ter Jewish quarter, a thatchwork of streets stretching north of the city's red- and yellow-bricked Great Synagogue, which was then the largest house of Jewish worship anywhere in the world. He was the second son of Erzebet and Tivadar Schwartz.

As anti-Semitism rose in Eastern Europe, the family changed its name to the less Jewish-sounding Soros. It proved to be a shrewd move. In the last days of World War II, Budapest's Jewish quarter became an urban prison. Gates were put up at the neighbourhood's entrances to pen Jews in and keep others out. Jews—initially including Soros and his family—were forced to wear the notorious yellow Star of David. In

May and June 1944, more than 400,000 were deported by trains, most of them heading to Auschwitz.

Just as the mass exterminations were beginning, however, the fourteen-year-old Soros caught a break that would both save his life and shame him forever in the eyes of some of his fellow Jews. As the grandson of a Hungarian government official, he was given a job with the city department responsible for seizing Jewish land. It was a position that alienated him and his family from much of the community, but one that allowed them to strip off the hated yellow stars and avoid being sent to Auschwitz.

The war, and with it the deportations, ended in Hungary in February 1945 when the Red Army rolled into Budapest following a bloody ten-week siege. But Soros's life under tyranny was still only beginning. One of the first jobs assigned to the Soviet units arriving in Budapest was to secure the "political police" headquarters of the Arrow Cross Party on leafy Andrassy Street—with its underground dungeons, torture cells and execution rooms—and to prepare them for use by the Államvédelmi Osztály (known colloquially as the AVO), the hastily organized Hungarian equivalent of Stalin's NKVD secret police. Over the next decade, as a paranoid search for anti-communists and collaborators with the Germans gripped the country, one Hungarian family in three had a relative "disappear."

Soros's father seems to have been quicker than most to recognize that the arrival of the Soviets wasn't the liberation Hungarians had been hoping for: he sent both of his sons abroad, George to London and his older brother, Paul, to New York. But growing up under two separate and brutal totalitarian systems scarred Soros's psyche for life, and would later inspire his thinking and his philanthropy. He had a natural distaste for Europe's new tyrants—Slobodan Milošević of Serbia, Alexander Lukashenko of Belarus, and Putin.

Soros and his money empowered those who would have been voiceless under managed democracy in Russia and in the former Soviet satellites that still deferred to the Kremlin. Even before the fall of the Berlin Wall, he was giving millions of dollars a year to groups that would change the face of Eastern Europe, such as Solidarity (Solidarność), the Polish trade union movement that broke the Communists' hold on power there; Czechoslovakia's Charter 77, the human rights group that led the Velvet Revolution in 1989; and dissidents within the Soviet Union itself. In 1987, the Soros Foundation–Soviet Union opened its doors in Moscow—despite a warning from leading dissident Andrei Sakharov not to bother since Soros's philanthropy would only end up "lining the coffers of the KGB."[4] It kicked off what would be one of Soros's deepest and most vexing investments. After the collapse of the USSR, he poured as much as $350 million a year into Russia, most memorably spending $100 million on salaries for Soviet nuclear scientists when a destitute Yeltsin government no longer could. He spent millions more connecting Russian universities across all eleven of the country's time zones to the Internet and spent heavily to produce new school textbooks free of Marxist ideology. He helped fund Memorial and Alexander Yakovlev's impassioned efforts to rehabilitate the names of all of Stalin's victims. Mikhail Gorbachev even suggested Soros's name for the Nobel Peace Prize.

The election of Vladimir Putin as president in 2000 effectively marked the end of Soros's efforts to cooperate with Russia's powers-that-be in bringing his beloved concept of "open society" to former Soviet soil, and marked the beginning of his new role as a resource for those in opposition to the Kremlin. After pouring more than $1 billion into the country only to see it slide quickly away from the openness he was investing in, Soros would finally shut down his Moscow office in 2003. Russia was rich enough to lift itself up, he said with more than a hint of bitterness.

Soros made no secret of his opposition to Putin and Putinism—he frequently argued in essays and speeches after 2000 that Russia was "lost" and should no longer be treated by the West as an emerging democracy deserving of aid and engagement. But he always claimed to have no personal quarrel with the Russian leader, whom he portrayed as a product of Russia's inherent desire to rebuild its lost empire. "Look, I don't know Mr. Putin, so I don't have any personal impression [of him], but I can guess he doesn't like me," Soros told a Russian reporter during a news conference in the Ukrainian capital, Kiev, in the spring of 2004.[5] It was clear to everyone in the room that the billionaire was a master of understatement as well as of financial markets. It was just as clear that Putin had made himself a dangerous enemy. Soros had become what he himself would dub a "stateless statesman." He had power on the international scene that no other private individual could claim to have.[6]

Strobe Talbott, the deputy secretary of state under Madeleine Albright, described the scope of Soros's influence this way: "I would say that [Soros's policy] is not identical to the foreign policy of the U.S. government—but it's compatible with it. It's like working with a friendly, allied, independent entity, if not a government. We try to synchronize our approach to the former communist countries with Germany, France, Great Britain—and with George Soros."[7]

Putin's "politologists" knew well that Soros, his money and his connections would be an obstacle to the system they were trying to build, and they set out to vilify him in the state-controlled media. And they did it well: the only thing the Kremlin got wrong in its anti-Soros campaign was to put so much of the blame—or credit—on Soros alone. He had a lot of help.

The offices of the National Endowment for Democracy are a surprisingly nondescript affair. In Washington, D.C., a city filled with landmarks that are in turns graceful, audacious and imposing, NED inhabits just a few floors of a grey concrete building on 15th Street. There's no sign on the outside of the building announcing that NED is even there, much less what its staff does. Yet the unknown bureaucrats who work inside have played an enormous role in reshaping the face of Central and Eastern Europe.

NED was founded in 1982 by Ronald Reagan, who set up the government-funded non-profit organization to counter similar Soviet organizations that worked to spread communism. Congress initially approved an annual budget of $18 million for the new agency, which was immediately dubbed "Project Democracy" by Oliver North when he was using it to dabble in the internal matters of Iran. The funding was later upped to $40 million, and then to $80 million a year. Much of that money would be passed on to other American democracy-promotion groups, including the international wings of the two main political parties—the National Democratic Institute and the International Republican Institute—and non-partisan organizations such as Freedom House and IFES, an election-monitoring NGO formally known as the International Foundation for Election Systems.[8]

Theoretically non-partisan, NED nonetheless gained influence following the 2000 election of President George W. Bush (during which there was no outcry from NED about the fairness of the election). NED's long-time president, Carl Gershman, was a neo-conservative who in the 1980s served on the Committee for the Free World, a lobby group headed by the man who would become Bush's defence secretary, Donald Rumsfeld. Secretary of State Condoleezza Rice remains on the editorial board of the NED-produced *Journal of Democracy*, having taken a sabbatical when Bush called her to higher office.

The two main distributors of NED grant money were equally well connected. IRI's chairman was Senator John McCain, the outspoken but respected Republican who had finished a surprising second to Bush in the 2000 Republican primaries and who is a potential candidate for the 2008 presidential race. NDI, meanwhile, was headed by Albright after she finished her term as secretary of state. A personal friend of Soros with a similar life story (she was born in Czechoslovakia just before German troops marched in, and fled to the West with her family as a child) she would assist the democratization efforts of NDI with her mere presence, pressuring the leaders of countries in transition not to interfere with the work being done by the non-governmental organizations. "In a sense, her life story is all about democracy," says NDI president Kenneth Wollack. "She had a lot to do with establishing our mission and our vision around the world."

Though NED operates democracy-promotion programs worldwide, its greatest focus—and its greatest success—has always been in the former Communist bloc. Grantees such as the Andrei Sakharov Institute and the Center for Democracy became places of refuge for Soviet dissidents during the 1980s. NED joined Soros in supporting Solidarity in Poland and Charter 77 in Czechoslovakia, underwriting the peaceful uprisings that brought the end of Communist rule in those countries. Then, as now, NED portrayed itself as a grant-giving operation dedicated to doing good, while effectively serving as a tool for spreading "soft" American power. As Allen Weinstein, the senator who helped design NED, said in 1991 as Project Democracy's grantees were helping tear down the Iron Curtain, "a lot of what we [NED] do today was done covertly 25 years ago by the CIA."[9]

Former CIA head James Woolsey would play a key role in Project Democracy, serving from 2002 to 2005 as head of the board of directors of Freedom House, another key NED grantee. Freedom House, through offices in Hungary and Serbia and in the former Soviet republics of Ukraine, Kazakhstan and Kyrgyzstan, would not only fund revolutionaries, but identify potential target nations with an annual report of what countries it considers to be "free," "partially free" or "not free."

The Berlin Wall fell in 1989 and the Soviet Union crumbled two years later, but NED's role didn't change. Though the countries that emerged from the rubble of the Warsaw Pact were all at least nominally democracies, most retained at least some vestiges of their old authoritarian systems. Troublingly, after initially embracing the West and what could broadly be described as American values, by the mid-1990s many had turned up their noses at them. Economic collapse— which they blamed on Western insistence on "shock therapy" transitions from communism to capitalism—was followed by elections that brought unreformed Communists back to power in several countries, while a surge in Slavic nationalism led to anti-Western, pro-Moscow groups coming to power in several more.

Nadia Diuk, the head of NED's Eurasia program (which funds democracy-building projects across Russia and much of the former Soviet Union), shakes her head now when she contemplates the naivety of U.S. president George W. Bush's decision to embrace Vladimir Putin as a friend and ally. After meeting Putin for the first time in Slovenia in June 2001, Bush declared, "I was able to get a sense of his soul, a man deeply committed to his country and the best interests of his country." He was, Bush said, "an honest, straightforward man who loves his country and loves his family. We share a lot of values." Perhaps only if your dad was once boss of the CIA could you feel so comfortable in the presence of a former KGB agent with a background as nebulous as Putin's. The two men laughed and traded jokes as they strolled around the grounds of a castle that had once been a residence of Yugoslav dictator Marshal Tito.

That initial meeting, with Bush's hearty endorsement of Putin, set the tone for much of what was to follow over the coming years. Putin was the first to reach Bush on the phone to offer his support on

September 11, 2001. Two months later, Bush invited Putin to his ranch in Crawford, Texas, and the two traded amusing anecdotes and slapped each other on the back for an audience of local high school students. The following spring, I sat in the audience under the golden chandeliers in the Kremlin's St. Andrew's Hall as the leaders signed a pact to reduce their stockpiles of nuclear weapons. It seemed then that the Putin era would be one of unprecedented cooperation between his country and Bush's.

Diuk, who has a very different family history than Bush, says she and her co-workers at NED were never fooled. British-born but of Ukrainian descent, she instinctively feared a reborn Sovietism as only the daughter of exiles could. From the start, she looked at Putin and saw an enemy. "When you see a guy who's been trained in the KGB . . . if it is the first thing you learn about a person and that's where his moral values and outlook on the world were formed, and we know that this is a guy who really wanted to be in the KGB and was turned down a couple of times, then you have to be alerted," she told me when we met in the Washington offices of NED, from which she directed funding to anti-Putin groups both inside and outside Russia.

After working reasonably well—making progress in democratizing society, despite setbacks like the 1996 election with Boris Yeltsin and Russia's first post-Soviet government—groups like Open Society and NED that focused on promoting free media and political pluralism and revealing the truth about Russia's dark past found themselves butting heads with Putin's regime almost from the moment it began in March 2000. While Western governments searched for a way to work with Putin, especially in the wake of 9/11 and the "war on terror" that was launched in the attacks' aftermath, Soros, NED and other democracy-promotion groups instantly recognized a man with principles opposed to their own. The former KGB agents in the Kremlin, meanwhile, came to see these Western non-governmental organizations as barely removed from their old foe, the CIA. The National Endowment for Democracy was soon back to Cold War footing.

Diuk says she saw the trouble coming. "What you see with Putin . . . is a prototype dictator who starts centralizing the power," she said. "A crackdown on the media, a centralization of power . . . They took away the political party structure"—in other words, everything NED was mandated to battle against. It wasn't just Russia, of course—neo-authoritarianism was rising across much of Eastern Europe and Central Asia—but the Kremlin was increasingly perceived as Ground Zero, the source of the wider problem.

Funding political turmoil is not a new business for NED. Congress censored the NGO and banned it from directly funding political parties after the media revealed that NED had funded Nicolas Barletta, a candidate favoured by Panama's Manuel Noriega in Nicaragua's 1984 presidential election. While NED is now more restricted in how it meddles in the politics of other countries, it skirts these rules by funding what it refers to as "civil society": non-government organizations and media outlets that are non-partisan on paper but whose activities work to the benefit of a favoured candidate or party.

Outside of Eastern Europe, NED is most heavily involved in Latin America. In the 1990s, it backed groups that worked to topple the regime of Jean-Bertrand Aristide in Haiti and, less successfully, Fidel Castro in Cuba and Hugo Chavez in Venezuela. Following a failed coup in 2002 and a controversial 2004 recall referendum, Chavez blamed NED for funding his opponents, publicizing documents that showed NED had given $31,000 to a Venezuelan election-monitoring NGO called Súmate.

Súmate was actually a carbon copy of groups that NED had been funding for years in Eastern Europe and that had contributed heavily to a series of pro-Western uprisings that were responses to apparently flawed elections. According to NED's Rodger Potocki, NDI and IRI field staff "discovered," while working on Bulgaria's 1996 election campaign, that these NGOs could tilt an election in favour of America's preferred candidate. In Bulgaria, where former Communists had been returned to power, IRI cobbled together a centre-right, pro-Western coalition out of the previously fragmented opposition. Meanwhile, NDI funded an election-monitoring group called the Bulgarian Association for Fair Elections and Civil Rights that would keep the regime honest (or at least make it clear that any fraud would be well publicized) by running a parallel vote count and an exit poll. The 1996 vote saw pro-Western lawyer Petar Stoyanov oust the incumbent president, Ivan Mazarov, to applause from leaders in Europe and America who had almost given in to the idea that people in Eastern Europe enjoyed living under semi-authoritarianism. A year later, NDI and IRI worked together to repeat the success in Romania, using a group called the Pro Democracy Association to play the regime-pressuring role.

"NDI in the early '90s, and IRI in the early '90s, working in Bulgaria and Romania, came up with two key ideas on how you build momentum for democratic change: citizen advocacy and monitoring groups," Potocki said. From those elections, NED spotted the opportunity to encourage "a dramatic wave of change." The NGOs could use the same model in other countries where the United States was interested in ousting a misbehaving regime.

Though in the U.S. the Democrats and Soros (a major backer of the party) rarely saw eye-to-eye with the Republicans and the sort of neo-conservative ideologues who ran Freedom House, in Eastern Europe their aims were more closely aligned. Democrats and Republicans alike wanted to see pro-Western forces triumph and Communist throwbacks like Mazarov defeated. The field offices of NDI, IRI and the other NGOs usually told their political bosses what needed to be done, not the other way around. It was the on-the-ground staff who devised the programs and found the candidates that America would put its muscle behind.

The first coordinated effort to export the techniques discovered in Bulgaria began with a covert meeting at the Vienna International Airport on December 15, 1997. NED flew in Ivan Krastev, a pro-Western Bulgarian political analyst, to meet Pavol Demeš, a leading figure in the pro-Western opposition to Slovak president Vladimír Mečiar. It had been decided in Washington that Mečiar, a former Communist apparatchik whose intransigence (combined with that of Czech premier Václav Klaus) had led to the breakup of Czechoslovakia in 1993, would be the next target for the newly discovered type of regime change—what Demeš would come to call the "electoral revolution."

While the Czech Republic sprinted ahead both socially and economically following the split and by 1998 was on the verge of being invited to join NATO and the European Union, Slovakia stumbled badly under Mečiar's semi-autocratic rule. Bratislava became glittering Prague's ugly cousin, with an unreformed economy and a troubling human rights record, particularly in relation to the country's minority Roma population. Mečiar had also troubled Washington with his outspoken support for the re-establishment of Russian dominance in

Eastern Europe. Secretary of State Madeleine Albright described Slovakia as a "black hole in the heart of Europe." Her words signalled U.S. support for a peaceful change of regime.

Demeš , a fit man with a trim goatee who speaks fluent English and some Russian in addition to his native Slovak, was a close associate of Václav Havel and had served as Czechoslovakia's minister of international affairs. As a member of Charter 77, he had been an indirect recipient of financial assistance from NED since 1987. Demeš returned from the Vienna airport meeting to establish Civic Campaign 98 (better known by its Slovak acronym, OK'98), an eleven-NGO coalition that was modelled on the Bulgarian Association for Fair Elections and that would borrow heavily from the Bulgarian model to run a massive get-out-the-vote campaign aimed at ousting Mečiar—backed by $857,000 in Western funding.

OK'98's donors included the United States Information Service (the "public diplomacy" arm of the U.S. government), Soros's Open Society Foundation, the British and Dutch governments and the German Marshall Fund of the United States, a private, not-for-profit group that was started with German money (as a memorial to Marshall Plan assistance from the U.S. to West Germany) but which now identifies itself as an "American public policy and grantmaking institution." These contributions paid for a massive get-out-the-vote campaign that included thirteen rock concerts, two short films and a series of television commercials in which Slovak celebrities encouraged young people to vote. While none of that is necessarily sinister, neither was it as nonpartisan as both OK'98 and its donors pretended it to be. "Like the majority of our fellow citizens, we feel a deep distrust in our government," read one of the 500,000 election-related brochures the NGO coalition distributed throughout the country. This was a campaign aimed not only at getting young people to vote; it was also aimed at getting them to vote against Mečiar. And it was a massive success: a stunning 84.3 per cent of eligible Slovaks voted in the September 25, 1998, elections, many of them for the first time. Research conducted by IRI showed that almost 70 per cent of the new voters cast their ballots for the opposition, versus 11 per cent for Mečiar's party.

On election day, NED-funded monitors from MEMO 98, an NGO affiliated with OK'98, stood outside polling stations to observe the process and conduct a parallel vote tabulation. PVT, as it's known, is a simple but effective tactic: monitors at each polling station (or at a random sampling of polling stations) obtain a copy of the official vote count at the source, before any central authority has a chance to tinker with it. By putting the PVT results out to the media quickly, suspicion is instantly raised should the government choose to announce altered numbers.

Mečiar didn't. The official results were largely the same as the PVTs: he had been defeated, though narrowly. His Movement for a Democratic Slovakia had won the largest share of the votes, 27 per cent, but the opposition collectively had won enough seats to form a nearly two-thirds majority in Parliament around the pro-Western Mikuláš Dzurinda. It looked to the world like democracy was blooming in Slovakia—and to a certain extent it was. But NED's behind-the-scenes machinations tell a different story. Mečiar had been toppled by American-supported NGOs as much as he had been voted out of office. Though pro-democratic in their stated intent, the NGOs had demonstrated their potential to dramatically affect the outcomes of elections. Their proponents would later argue that they were only counterbalancing the efforts of neo-authoritarians like Mečiar and, later, Putin.

"We developed a civic software of how to deal with neo-authoritarianism," Demeš acknowledged years later, when we met at a democracy-promotion conference in Istanbul. That software, he explained, was used in a string of what he called "electoral revolutions" that would roll across Eastern Europe over the next eight years, altering the region's political landscape and ousting several other leaders who, like Mečiar, had an authoritarian streak and an aversion to the post–Cold War American influence over the region. In their place rose a phalanx of new prime ministers and presidents who, like Dzurinda, would owe thanks and allegiance to the West.

The revolution-makers targeted Croatia next, where in 1999 strongman Franjo Tuđjman was facing re-election. Though Tuđjman's death on the eve of the vote would alter the political landscape, the system worked again, using an OK'98-style NGO, Citizens Organized to Monitor Elections (better known by its Croatian acronym, GONG). As in Slovakia, record-high voter turnout and a Western-funded advertising campaign against the old regime resulted in a pro-EU coalition of opposition parties ousting Tuđjman's nationalist bloc from power.

Demeš, who helped train GONG, would go on to make something of a career out of being a revolutionary. In 2002 he became the director of the Bratislava office of the German Marshall Fund. In effect, he would be responsible for doling out money to NGOs trying to replicate what he and OK'98 had accomplished in Slovakia. And unlike others involved in the uprisings who disingenuously argue that Western money was a minor factor in what were domestically driven efforts, he is blunt about the role foreign money played: "External funding for these civic campaigns is critical. Without external support, they wouldn't happen."

THREE

PROXY FIGHT: THE FALL OF MILOŠEVIĆ

Belgrade

To people watching on CNN as hundreds of thousands of protestors took over the streets of Belgrade, the Serbian Revolution of October 5, 2000, came almost out of nowhere. Until the day before, it had seemed to most casual observers that Milošević's hold on Yugoslavia was unbreakable. The strongman had remained at the top of Serbia's power structure for a dozen years, weathering the breakup of the country, a succession of wars, indictment as a war criminal by an international tribunal and a seventy-eight-day NATO bombing campaign along the way.

But October 5 was in fact the result of a long American-orchestrated campaign, run in its later stages from their embassy-in-exile, the Office of Yugoslav Affairs, some 450 kilometres up the twisting Danube in Soros's hometown of Budapest. From the moment that office was opened in August 2000, the diplomats stationed there had one task—to overthrow Milošević, something Secretary of State Madeleine Albright would describe in her memoirs as a personal goal of her own last months in office.

The Serb-dominated Yugoslavia (at this point consisting, out of the original six republics, of only Serbia and the much smaller Montenegro) that emerged from the Balkan wars of the 1990s was not the outright dictatorship it was often portrayed in the Western media to be. In fact, it was more like an early version of the "managed democracy" that Pavlovsky and the other spin doctors would later bring to Putin's Russia. Free media existed—and loudly railed against the regime—even if they struggled to find advertising revenue; businesses knew that placing a spot in the anti-Milošević media could mean a retributory visit from the tax police. Opposition parties could hold mass demonstrations, though police frequently broke the rallies up. Everything was at once both possible and forbidden.

This veneer of freedom gave Milošević's rule a sheen of legitimacy in the West, at least until his role in the bloody Balkan wars ate it away. He could also point to his genuine popularity among Serb nationalists as evidence that he was not an outright tyrant (his regime tolerated— and survived—several waves of dissent), but that in fact he represented a significant portion of the population.

In the winter of 1996–97, tens of thousands of demonstrators filled Belgrade and other Serbian cities day after day to protest a government decision to annul more than a dozen local elections that had been won by the opposition that November. The protests were encouraged from outside by supportive words from Bill Clinton, and inside by the covert support of the U.S. ambassador, Richard Miles, a veteran diplomat who made the embassy into a haven for the opposition and its supporters. Milošević's opposition united for the first time under an umbrella group called Zajedno (Serbian for "together") and forced him to admit the fraud. Opposition leader Zoran Đinđić was sworn in as mayor of Belgrade on February 21, 1997, a victory tainted by the fact that Milošević had been caught red-handed perpetuating a massive fraud and yet remained firmly in power.[1]

It was during those same protests that a seventeen-year-old named Marko Markovic got his first taste of activism. With a Serb mother and a Croat father, Markovic's family had been traumatized by the internecine wars of the 1990s, fleeing Croatia in 1991 to the relative safety of Novi Sad, in Serbia's northern province of Vojvodina, in time to experience the economic fallout of Milošević's wars. United Nations sanctions targeting Serbia as the aggressor, applied shortly after the out- break of fighting in Croatia, had a crippling effect on life in a country that was already struggling economically. Inflation in Serbia zoomed to an unfathomable 600,000 per cent. At one point in December 1993, prices were changing at 3 per cent an hour. Stores kept employees whose only job was to apply new price stickers to items on the shelves, and the panicked central bank was forced by desperation to introduce, first, a 50 billion dinar note, and then, a week later, a 500 billion dinar note. The morning the latter note, with its eleven zeros, came into circulation, it was worth $6. By the time Serbs were settling down to staggeringly expensive dinners the same night, it was worth $3.

While many Serbs bought into Milošević's rhetoric and blamed the outside world for their troubles, Markovic and his family had seen enough to understand that their president was ultimately the one responsible for the country's dire situation. "I was really unhappy the entire time I lived in Serbia . . . all those wars, the sanctions. No one normal would want to live in those conditions," the handsome, chisel-featured Markovic told me. When the 1996–97 protests broke out, his entire family joined. "My parents were so pissed off. My mom was on the streets, my dad was on the streets, my brother was on the streets. The mood was so positive. We had a strong belief in victory."

From the moment B92 radio was granted a temporary broadcast licence in May 1989, the student station was headed for a clash with the authorities. Its first broadcast was a critique of the lavish ceremonies the Milošević government had arranged to mark Tito's birthday, eight years after the strongman's death.

The government had given the station a fifteen-day licence on the 92.5 FM frequency and a small studio in downtown Belgrade, which the students were amused to find crammed with long-forgotten minutes from a meeting of the Communist Party's central committee. And when their fifteen days were up, the students decided they were having too much fun to stop. Their formula of the latest in alternative rock plus hard-hitting hourly newscasts that challenged the regime had shocked a public accustomed to getting information only from state-controlled newscasts. But with Eastern Europe's political landscape changing at breakneck speed in 1989, culminating that autumn with the fall of the Berlin Wall, the government initially paid little heed to the tiny station and its growing following.

Those who listened to B92 were primarily university-educated, Western-looking youth who were despairing that their country—once the most open and advanced in the Communist East—was falling behind its neighbours, succumbing to the charms of its retrograde socialist president at a time when anti-Communist icons Lech Wałęsa and Václav Havel were winning elections in Poland and the Czech Republic. While folk songs lauding the military life and Serbian nationalism dominated the rest of the state-controlled airwaves (which Milošević saw as an antidote to the spread of popular Western music), along with "turbo-folk"—a bizarre fusion of those same nationalistic folk songs and revved-up techno music—B92 proudly played American and British acts like Massive Attack, Nirvana and the Clash, plus the latest Serbian rock. Songs about sticking it to authority were in the heaviest rotation.[2]

The station finally gained the attention—and the animosity—of the government two years later, during the 1991 street protests against Milošević. The government realized that opposition supporters were turning to B92 not only for newscasts critical of the government, but when they wanted to know where and when the next demonstration would be. Milošević briefly ordered the station closed. "We were a thorn in Milošević's eye, a pain in the ass for the regime," Saša Mirkovic, the station's co-founder, recalls proudly with a wide grin. When the station returned to the air, it refused to compromise; among the first songs it played was Public Enemy's anti-establishment rap anthem "Fight the Power."

In 1991, as Mikhail Gorbachev's transformative years in the Kremlin wobbled to an end, Serbia experienced another, less publicized event, which would shape its future. On June 17, nine days before the outbreak of the first of Yugoslavia's wars, the Soros Foundation opened its first office in Belgrade. The foundation's mandate, as elsewhere in Eastern Europe, was to seek out, fund and support the development of "pro-democratic" institutions and non-government organizations. B92 fit the bill perfectly, and the billionaire financier soon adopted it almost as his own.

"Mr. Soros was personally interested in B92," said Jadranka Jelinčić, a program manager for the Soros Foundation who later became executive director of Soros's Fund for an Open Society–Serbia. "B92 was one of these independent, autonomous institutions of high importance that had high credibility with the Serbian public. It was one of the few channels to inform the public about what was going on inside the country and outside the country . . . The state media was just propaganda for the regime."

B92, Mirkovic readily admits, was dead set against Milošević from the beginning. So too was every other Serbian organization Soros funded in the early and mid-1990s. Jelinčić says the design was never to foment unrest, but she acknowledges that the money Soros—the only major international donor operating in Belgrade for much of the 1990s—poured into civil society and independent media during the decade created "a kind of anti-regime league." In 1996, the regime began to perceive Soros's efforts as a threat to its well-being. In February of that year, a Belgrade court forced the foundation to close over a technicality in the way it had registered in 1991. It reopened in June as Open Society–Serbia.

Jelinčić said that during the 1990s the Soros Foundation's Belgrade office and its successor gave $108 million to democracy-promotion and human rights NGOs and to independent media companies. That figure, however, doesn't include money given to the same projects via the foundation's Budapest and New York offices. Jelinčić says even she doesn't know the full amount of aid Soros gave to the Serbian opposition. "We were not aimed at changing the Milošević regime," she insists. "The philosophy was aimed at helping build those institutions that were pertinent to democratic society." However, she admitted that she and others working for Soros at the time understood well that for a democratic society to emerge, Milošević would have to go.

By 1996, B92 had grown from a tiny underground radio station into a multimedia force. The station set up Serbia's first Internet service provider, and when the government forced it off the air again for calling people into the streets after the municipal election fraud that year, the station simply switched to publishing its news bulletins on its website, maintaining its attack on the regime. Two days later, under intense international pressure, Milošević—who had his own persecution complex and viewed the station as a foreign tool—allowed it to resume broadcasting. B92 gained more clout than ever, as radio stations in the municipalities won by the opposition in the 1996 elections began playing its news broadcasts at the top of every hour.

Station manager Mirkovic, a genial, bearish man with cropped black hair, developed a personal relationship with Soros during the billionaire's two visits to Belgrade in the 1990s. He believes Soros developed a distaste for Milošević that evolved from genuine horror at the images Soros had seen on television of the Serb atrocities committed in the Balkan wars. "Soros was fed up with war," Mirkovic said, "and was always upset, as a member of the Jewish community who left Hungary, by the photos of the massacres on the territory of the former Yugoslavia. They reminded him of what he saw when he was young."

Other foreign donors—primarily the American taxpayers (through the United States Agency for International Development, USAID) and the National Endowment for Democracy, as well as the European Union—eventually came on board and backed B92 because, as Mirkovic put it, "they saw in our editorial content an agenda they wanted to support." That agenda, he says openly five years after the fact, involved toppling Milošević, and the money came in large enough amounts that it eventually allowed B92 to open a television station at a cost of millions of dollars.

Other donors were largely headquartered in Budapest and, in the case of the EU, took so long to process funding requests that the money often arrived too late for the recipient project. But Open Society was in Belgrade, and Soros was effectively willing to pay whatever it cost to keep B92 and other anti-Milošević media, like the scrappy *Vremya* and *NIN* newspapers, operating.

"Soros came to this country several times and spent a lot of money, really huge money, because he had a dream," Mirkovic said. That dream involved building a democratic, free-market, Milošević-free Serbia. "There was nobody on the media scene in Serbia back then who was against Milošević and didn't have contacts with Soros."

By the late 1990s, Soros's effort was starting to pay off. The 1996 protests proved to be a watershed for Serbia, Jelinčić said, proof that the majority of Serbs did not support Milošević or his bloody-minded policies. They also showed that Serbs were not so cowed by fear that they couldn't be mobilized to oppose him. "It proved that what we did, what we promoted, found fertile soil in Serbian society," she said.

Now all Serbian society needed was a little direction.

In the fall of 1997, Soros backed another key project, a group called CeSID, the Serbian acronym for Citizens for Free Elections and

Democracy. Though they would dub themselves "independent elections monitors," this group of university students and their professors fed up with the regime had a single, very partisan goal—to catch Milošević in the act if he ever again tried to manipulate the results of an election. Jelinčić proudly says that Open Society helped CeSID "immensely" in the early days, though she again shied away from saying how much money Soros gave them.

The group took on two main tasks, the first being to lead the get-out-the-vote campaign for the 2000 elections. Western donors and Serbian NGOs felt that the silent majority in Serbia disapproved of Milošević and his policies; if they could be persuaded to cast ballots, the opposition would win. CeSID's second job would be to monitor each and every polling station in the country and to carry out a parallel vote tabulation, funded by a $75,000 NED grant. Immediately releasing a credible PVT to the media on voting day would be crucial for convincing the crowds that they had again been spectacularly lied to by the authorities.[3]

Open Society paid the startup costs for CeSID, but the group soon gained a second powerful backer in the National Democratic Institute. NDI, which at the same time was putting money into various anti-Milošević political parties—parties that any parallel count would theoretically benefit—paid to send CeSID staff to Bulgaria to observe the 1997 elections there, and helped arrange contacts between CeSID and their colleagues from GONG in Zagreb. Recalling how the NDI funding came about, Marko Blagojevic, a founding member of CeSID, says, "We didn't approach them, they approached us."

By this point, the NDI's erstwhile rival, the International Republican Institute, and Freedom House were also pouring money into anti-Milošević political parties, media and NGOs. Soon, donor coordination meetings were necessary to ensure that the various Western government agencies and NGOs weren't tripping up each other's work in the push to oust Milošević from within.

Otpor, which means "resistance" in Serbian, was founded in October 1998 by a group of students who were veterans of the 1996–97 protests and who wanted to finally cut out what they saw as a cancer at the heart of their country: the rule of Slobodan Milošević and his cadre. There was no foreign backing at the very beginning, just eighteen fed-up young people brought together at Belgrade's Greenit café by Srđa Popović, a wiry, intense twenty-five-year-old who became, in his own words, the group's "ideological commissar."

Siniša Šikman, one of the leaders of the 1996–97 protests, initially stayed out of Otpor, believing that whatever movement materialized to face Milošević, it had to be more broadly based than the students who made up the group. But on November 4, 1998, following the first police crackdown on Otpor, he quickly dropped his qualms and joined the group. Four students were arrested that day, and Šikman's subsequent enlistment highlights a pattern that Milošević repeatedly failed to grasp: the more he persecuted his opposition, the more credibility he gave it both on the streets of Belgrade and with foreign donors.

The November 4 arrests were for spray-painting walls with the black clenched fist that was to become Otpor's ubiquitous symbol. The design began as a sketch on a café napkin by founding Otpor member Nenad Petrovic to impress his girlfriend. But it proved easy to replicate and struck an immediate chord with ordinary Serbs. They didn't have to say that they were against Milošević, or explain why—they just had to wear a T-shirt emblazoned with Petrovic's fist.

The group was deliberately kept leaderless. They had learned in 1996 and 1997 that naming one or even several leaders meant providing the regime with someone to target, persecute, blackmail or corrupt. With no leadership structure, no matter who the security services threw in jail, Otpor could carry on. The group backed no candidate or idea in particular. They were simply against Milošević.

Open Society–Serbia took an immediate interest in the student movement, whose founding members had already become mini-celebrities in Belgrade from the 1996–97 demonstrations. In the fall of 1998, several Otpor members, including the charismatic Ivan Marovic—as close to a public face as the group would ever have—went to the Open Society offices, tucked in an alley off Belgrade's Zmaj Jovina Street, and asked for some startup cash. Both Marovic and Jelinčić claim they can't remember the amount, but they agree that it was small. "They did ask for money for office space, one or two computers so they could communicate and some money for printing pamphlets," Jelinčić recalls. "The grant was very, very modest, not a big one . . . In the very beginning, I didn't think they'd turn into such a big organization, or have such a big impact. In the beginning, you never know what the potential is."

Using the money from Soros, the group rented office space at 49 Prince Mihailo Street, a cobblestoned lane lined with nineteenth-century buildings, the main pedestrian shopping stroll in the heart of Belgrade. The location gave the group high visibility and made it easy to manage the regular demonstrations that took place a short walk away at Students' Square, a one-time Turkish graveyard that was paved over into a café-lined marketplace after the Ottomans were driven out of the city.

Perhaps the most crucial—and controversial—thing Open Society did for Otpor was to pay for cans of spray paint. From the start, graffiti was Otpor's weapon of choice for attacking Milošević. Soon the walls of Belgrade and other Serb cities were covered with the group's ubiquitous fist symbol and its anti-regime slogans.

Drawing on the lessons learned in the 1996–97 protests, Otpor initially organized a series of actions designed to be at once light-hearted and non-violent and to draw maximum media attention to their cause. They played mock soccer games on the streets of Belgrade, ending each match by asking for the coach's resignation, a metaphor pointed straight at Milošević. They set up an effigy of the president on a busy Belgrade sidewalk and offered passersby the chance to punch it for a dinar.

They dealt with the police similarly, forcing them to crack smiles behind their riot shields whenever they were set to disperse the troublesome students. When an edict was issued mandating that anyone wearing an Otpor symbol was to be arrested, the organization responded on National Security Day—a holiday to honour the police and army—by sending attractive flower-bearing young women wearing Otpor shirts to visit police stations across the country. "Were they really going to arrest pretty girls who are smiling and handing them flowers? Of course not. They laughed and kissed the girls," Popovic said. He called the stunt a "dilemma action," meaning that whatever the police did in that situation—whether they arrested the women or decided to ignore their orders and accept the flowers and kisses— Otpor would score points against the regime.

Otpor's dilemma actions were modelled on Gandhi's simple and symbolic 1930 salt march, which effectively dissolved the British Empire's hold on India. It was the sort of action that the organization perfected—making a mockery of Milošević's heavy-handedness. Marovic, who was repeatedly arrested and interrogated in 1998 and 1999, said the regime's use of the police to suppress the group actually backfired, since it allowed police to see first-hand that the students weren't violent and that they posed no threat to anyone but Milošević. A cheerful, broad-shouldered twenty-six-year-old at the time, Marovic says he got to know—and befriend—many of the police officers who were assigned to harass Otpor. Over time, he could feel their sympathies for the regime fade and their affection and respect for this plucky student group grow.

"They would bring us in for interrogations—one hour, two hours, twelve hours—then, most often they would just release us," Šikman, who was also arrested several times, recalls. "The police would just be going through a printed list of questions. Number one was 'Who is financing you?' Number two was 'We know that you are working for the CIA. Why are you betraying your country?' Even then, the police officers would say to us, 'We are with you. We're just doing our jobs.'"

In October 1998, sensing that Milošević's grip had sufficiently weakened, Otpor went public with its manifesto, publishing an ad that ran in white letters on a black background under the group's white clenched-fist symbol, in the *Nedeljni Telegraf* newspaper. "Resistance is the answer! There will be no other way!" the ad read. "It will be [too] late when someone you know starves to death. When they start killing in the streets, when they put out the last light, and poison the last well . . . It will be [too] late! This is not a system, this is a disease! Fight the system! Get a grip, live the resistance!"

The time was right, Otpor thought, for the final push. But then Milošević led Serbia into even deeper chaos.

On March 19, 1999, Richard Miles lowered the American flag outside the imposing brick building of the U.S. embassy on Kneza Milosa Street. War was in the air. NATO was threatening military strikes if Milošević didn't withdraw his soldiers from the Muslim region of Kosovo, and the U.S. embassy in Belgrade was closing indefinitely. It was a portentous moment for the diplomat, who had gone from seeing Milošević as a force for stability in the Balkans in the early 1990s to being an ardent supporter of the burgeoning opposition. Miles had turned the embassy into a haven for the opposition during the 1996–97 protests. Those had failed, and now America was resorting to force to deal with Milošević.

The Kosovo crisis caught many in the West, who had hoped that the Dayton Accords would put an end to the Balkan bloodletting, off-guard with its sudden ferocity. The tipping point for NATO was the massacre of forty-five ethnic Albanians in Račak, a small town in southern Kosovo that was known as a stronghold of the Kosovo Liberation Army. In early January 1999, KLA fighters struck twice at Serb forces in the area, apparently retreating each time to Račak. On January 15, Serb forces surrounded the town and kept international monitors away. After shelling it for several hours, troops entered the town and executed dozens of men in their homes and on the streets outside. When the monitors were allowed in the next day, they saw forty bodies (five others had already been removed by their families), including those of three women and a twelve-year-old boy.

Though Milošević's government, which carried out its own investigation of the incident, found that the attack on Račak was a justifiable police operation and that the vast majority of those killed were KLA "terrorists," the international community reacted swiftly. Within days, the United Nations Security Council had condemned the killings and the United States and NATO were preparing for war.

February talks aimed at a negotiated solution to the crisis quickly died. The proposed solution, which would have effectively restored the pre-1990 balance of an autonomous Kosovo within the republic of Serbia, was rejected by both sides. Madeleine Albright, who had spent so much of her time as secretary of state trying to pacify the Balkans, decided it was time for Milošević to go. "I believed in the ultimate power, the goodness of the power of the allies and led by the United States. We were dealing with such a basic evil, that could not be tolerated," she later told a BBC interviewer. "Milošević was the same, evil Milošević who had started this whole thing actually in Kosovo by denying them of their rights. And we just had to stand up."[4]

The seventy-eight days of NATO bombing that followed are often described in the Western press not as war, but as "pinpoint strikes" that sought only to knock out the regime. Grainy video on CNN showed missiles slamming into their carefully chosen targets but leaving the buildings around them intact. To ordinary Serbs, however, there was no question that the West had declared war on their nation. Tomahawk cruise missiles destroyed targets of questionable military value—and obvious civilian use—targets such as bridges over the Danube, heating and power stations, the Hotel Yugoslavia and the busy headquarters of Radio Television of Serbia (RTS), the country's largest television station. The strike on the RTS building alone left sixteen people dead and eighteen injured; it was later referred to The Hague for investigation as a war crime.

The attacks inspired a wave of nationalism that translated into increased support for Milošević. Otpor activists, B92 journalists and foreign NGO workers all agree that the opposition had had Milošević on the ropes before the bombings began and that the attacks extended the strongman's hold on power by an extra twelve months. The popularity of any politicians or groups associated with the West plummeted, while the standing of Russia—the only major power to show any kind of support for Serbia during the period surrounding the war—rose measurably. "During the NATO bombing we had to stop all of our activities because Milošević was stronger than ever," Otpor's Siniša Šikman remembers. "It was very dangerous to go against him at that time."

The pro-Western, democratic opposition was left in tattered confusion by NATO's decision to bomb Serbia. "When you feel war on your skin, you instantly become a very patriotic person," said Markovic, the Croatian Serb dissident. "I had friends who started protesting against NATO and yelling slogans in favour of Milošević. I didn't feel that way, but a lot of people did."

Among the minor tragedies caused by the war was the temporary split-up of Mike Staresinic, an employee of the Freedom House office in Sarajevo, and his Serbian girlfriend, Nevena Antonijevic, who left him and returned to Belgrade after a fight over whether NATO's actions were justified. Days after the last of NATO's bombs fell on Serbia, Staresinic went to Belgrade to see her. He was nervous about returning, not just because he was uncertain about whether his relationship could be rescued, but also because he knew he could be thrown in jail by the regime as a "Western agent" or targeted by an anti-American mob.[5]

Things went well with Nevena, but Staresinic stayed on an extra day before returning to Sarajevo, to meet with various Serbian opposition groups who were perplexed at the U.S. strategy. In their eyes, America had shattered Belgrade and punished ordinary Serbs but had left Milošević and his regime standing. They knew Staresinic from his old job working for Ronco, a Belgrade front company that before the war had covertly handed out USAID grants to anti-Milošević groups. "Since the U.S. had just finished bombing the heck out of the place, there was a sense of 'what the heck do we do now?'" Staresinic remembers. "They were open to new ideas." There was also a renewed enthusiasm for opposition, he said, driven by Madeleine Albright's vow that Slobodan Milošević would be forced from office before she was. That meant before the end of 2000.

From the moment it opened in Budapest in August 2000, the Office of Yugoslav Affairs—effectively the exiled American embassy to Belgrade—had no contacts with Milošević's government, only with the opposition. The office was headed by William Montgomery, who had been quickly reassigned from his previous post as ambassador to Croatia, where he had liaised with GONG during that group's successful push to oust Franjo Tuđjman's regime. Here he was charged with a clear mandate: a month before the Office of Yugoslav Affairs opened, both *Time* and *Newsweek* reported that President Bill Clinton had authorized the CIA to start working toward toppling Milošević. Making the West's overt and covert push for change in Serbia easier to justify, Milošević had been charged with war crimes by the International Criminal Tribunal in The Hague.[6]

With Montgomery's arrival, Budapest became a hive of revolutionary activity. A stream of Serb dissidents was invited to the OYA's nondescript offices to brief the American diplomats and agents and to receive money and advice from their American patrons. "In Budapest back then, you could see people from every corner of Serbia. You had to go there to access bank accounts and to meet with foreigners and NGOs," said B92 manager Mirkovic.

Perhaps the most difficult task for the Office of Yugoslav Affairs was to unite Serbia's fractious opposition around a single person, a crucial step if Serbian voters were to be convinced that they really had an alternative to

Milošević. In October 1999, diplomats from the mission, together with the NDI, organized a highly secret meeting of twenty opposition figures at which they were shown an in-depth opinion poll conducted by the American firm Penn, Schoen & Berland Associates (the same group that would later conduct the controversial exit poll that showed Hugo Chavez had in fact lost the recall referendum in Venezuela) asking 840 Serbs about their feelings toward the country's various politicians.

The message drawn from the results was a compelling one: Milošević could be beaten in a fair election. Some 70 per cent of voters had negative feelings about the man who had put them through four wars, turning their country into a pariah state along the way and exposing it to crippling economic sanctions that had left store shelves bare. Gasoline was scarce, especially through the Kosovo crisis, and the city's bus system, prevented by the sanctions from acquiring the spare parts it needed to service its aging fleet, had all but stopped running. The only problem for Montgomery was that the two most prominent opposition politicians—Zoran Đinđić and Vuk Drašković, who for years had battled each other as well as Milošević—rated almost as poorly as the president.

Doug Schoen, the pollster who ran the seminar at the Budapest Marriott, a massive concrete structure overlooking the restaurant boats that float idly alongside the banks of the Danube, offered an alternative: a mild-mannered lawyer named Vojislav Koštunica, who was considered a moderate nationalist and no friend of the United States. Such a candidate might be more palatable to Serbian voters still bitter over the NATO bombing campaign. Schoen's numbers showed that Koštunica was well known and that he elicited few negative emotions among voters—a trait that distinguished him from Milošević, Đinđić and Drašković.

In December 1999, while leaders of the world's richest nations were gathered in Berlin for a G8 summit, Đinđić and Drašković were summoned to the InterConti hotel, on Budapest Strasse in the German capital. There, in a small, windowless room, they were given their marching orders by a stern-faced tag team of Madeleine Albright and Joschka Fischer, the German foreign minister. Koštunica, they were told, would be the sole opposition candidate in the coming elections. They were to gracefully bow out and throw their support behind him.[7]

Neither Đinđić nor Drašković, both proud politicians, was thrilled with the decision, but Đinđić—by far the more influential of the two on the streets at that time—agreed and joined the emerging coalition, known as the Democratic Opposition of Serbia, that would back Koštunica. Drašković didn't join DOS but did agree not to run against it.

From that point on, the money was handed out in gobs, with Otpor the leading recipient. Through USAID-funded grant-giving groups such as NED, Freedom House, NDI and especially IRI, American tax-payers gave a combined $2.5 million to the student group. IRI led the way, paying directly for some five thousand more cans of spray paint that were used to emblazon Belgrade's walls with the group's clenched-fist logo and "*gotov je*," Serbian for "he's finished," the ubiquitous catch-phrase of the group's anti-Milošević campaign.[8]

Srđa Popović (a biology graduate who was one of Otpor's founders and informal leaders) and Đinđić were invited by Bill Clinton to the annual National Prayer Breakfast in Washington, D.C., in February 2000. The act was meant as a deliberate snub of Milošević, and Popović says that representatives of American organizations like NED, IRI and Freedom House agreed to give Otpor everything he asked them for. "It was easy to raise money," he recalled as we sat in a trendy outdoor café on Belgrade's Republic Square, the site of many of Otpor's rallies. "I just convinced them that it was all for the cost of one day of bombing."

Freedom House paid for the establishment of several regional offices for Otpor outside Belgrade. NED directly contributed $137,390 to Otpor in order "to educate and encourage citizens to take an active role in the political process," according to the organization's 2000 annual report. NED also paid $150,000 for B92's Rock the Vote concert series, modelled on Slovakia's successful MTV-inspired campaign two years earlier. It would see top Serbian acts tour the country encouraging young Serbs to vote—and not for Milošević.[9]

Popović and other Otpor members were among those who repeatedly shuttled back and forth between Belgrade and Budapest in those days, meeting with their donors and with representatives of Montgomery's Office of Yugoslav Affairs. And it wasn't just for funding.

B92 had been shut down during the war. It re-emerged briefly as B2–92 in August 1999, using a borrowed signal and premises, only to be closed again in early 2000. Fortuitously, Mirkovic was already in Budapest when he heard that B2–92 had been forced off the air. He went to the Office of Yugoslav Affairs, briefed Montgomery on both B92's plight and the wider crackdowns inside Serbia, and asked what should be done next.

The Americans were in no mood to cut Milošević any slack, and they knew well that B92 was going to be central to any effort to depose the strongman. Montgomery promised Mirkovic his full support, and together they devised a plan that would see the station's staff continue to produce news reports from a collection of ten "safe" apartments rented around Belgrade. The newscasts would then be sent out of the country over the Internet and broadcast back into Serbia from transmitters stationed in neighbouring Bulgaria and Romania. The Americans paid for the transmitters and took care of the dodgy diplomacy. "It's not easy to put up transmitters that will effectively be jamming local signals," Mirkovic said. "They were not 100 per cent legal, so the Americans had to prepare the conditions for that." The task was likely simpler in Bulgaria, where Milošević's old nemesis, Richard Miles, had reappeared as the U.S. ambassador in Sofia.

The most radical step Montgomery's office took was to organize a four-day training seminar, from March 30 to April 3, for Otpor activists at the Hilton in Budapest. Retired U.S. Army colonel Robert Helvey, a veteran of two tours in Vietnam who later worked as military attaché to the U.S. embassy in Rangoon, Burma, headed the seminar. Helvey had studied successful methods of non-violent resistance worldwide and had spent time on the Burmese-Thai border training supporters of Aung San Suu Kyi's National League for Democracy. He was a disciple of Gene Sharp, an American academic who had published several essays on how to gain political power without the use of violence.[10]

Helvey talked to twelve Otpor members who attended the session about the various "pillars of support" that the Milošević regime relied on—the media, police, military, church and civil service—and taught them how to go about undermining these pillars, or at least winning them over so that when the now-inevitable crisis broke they would side with the opposition. And he directed the Otpor members to what was

THE NEW COLD WAR 51

to become the bible of the revolution-makers, Sharp's essay "From Dictatorship to Democracy: A Conceptual Framework for Liberation," which outlined 198 methods of non-violent resistance. The whole Hilton session was paid for by the International Republican Institute.

"He's my hero," Popović said of Helvey. "He is the Yoda master of our Jedi order. He's the best trainer I've ever seen." He can still recite Helvey's opening words: "Removing the authority of the ruler is the most important element in non-violent struggle."

Helvey had essentially devised a five-point program for disposing of an unwanted anti-American dictator, and Otpor was putting it into practice with the help of Soros and the USAID-backed NGOs:

- Get the opposition to unite around a leader—not necessarily the most popular, but the most electable.
- Promote "independent" (that is, pro-opposition) media that will get the anti-regime message out. Newspapers are fine, but can't do the trick on their own. A muckraking television station with a national reach is best.
- Pour money into NGOs that will raise awareness of the election "issues" (namely the problems with the power-that-is, as defined by the groups' Western sponsors).
- Pay for election observers and exit polls that (it is expected) will show the election was a fraud, and that the "democratic" opposition candidate is in fact more popular than the strongman clinging to office.
- Have a dedicated, militant youth group ready to play a front-line role in the street protests that the opposition leader will call for. The kids must be funny, dedicated to non-violence and ready to be arrested or beaten for the cause, if it comes to that.

Serbia, by the summer of 2000, had done all five. "These trainers and donors knew very well what the preconditions for a revolution are," B92's Mirkovic reflected. "They knew you need strong NGOs, you need an organization like Otpor, you need an opposition united around one leader and at least one independent television or radio station." In the fall of 2000, this model for revolution was ready for its first test. OK'98's Pavol , who met repeatedly with Otpor and CeSID in both Bratislava and Belgrade during that time, said the message he was passing on was simple: "You need to adopt [what OK'98 did] for your own situation, but at the end of the day it's doable."

Inside Belgrade, word went around that the American government, postwar, was now keen to fund "election projects" targeted at deposing Milošević through the coming presidential and parliamentary polls. Regular donor meetings were hosted inside the Canadian embassy in Belgrade (Canada had been one of the first Western countries to reopen its mission after the Kosovo war). Otpor remained a favoured recipient. But rather than take money directly, which the Otpor leaders feared might corrupt those who handled the financial side, they asked donors to back specific campaigns. "We didn't say 'Give us money,' we said 'Buy us T-shirts,'" Šikman said. Between them, NDI, IRI and NED fronted the $2.5 million cost of Otpor's *Gotov je* campaign and its parallel, more positive, *Vremya* ("It's time") campaign, dedicated to boosting voter turnout.

"For the Americans, it's part of their global strategy to spread their values around the world," Otpor member Miloš Milenković shrugged. "But I don't believe it was in anybody's interests to have a black hole in the middle of Europe . . . Unfortunately, there was no one locally who could [put up the money] during the Milošević regime."

On the day Serbs were to vote, September 24, Soros was attending a joint conference of the World Bank and the International Monetary Fund in Prague. Asked by reporters there what he thought of the voting in Yugoslavia that was just getting underway, Soros predicted that Serbs would take to the streets if Milošević tried to deny Koštunica the victory that Western-backed polls were by then predicting. "We will all be surprised by the mobilization of society," the billionaire said. He spoke with the confidence of a man who knew exactly what was going to happen next.

While the funding agencies' activities could be construed as a very undemocratic, American-led plot to oust Milošević, there's no doubt that Milošević was a tyrant who sowed the seeds of his own undoing. No matter how much American money was poured into the election, Serbs could not have been prodded into the street if the previous decade hadn't provided them with so many legitimate grievances against the regime.

Milošević had called the September 24 presidential election primarily to show to the West just how popular he was at home. He never expected to lose. Only when it was too late did he recognize the size of the threat posed by Otpor and Koštunica, and he responded just as they expected him to—by cheating like mad in a desperate bid to hold on to power.

CeSID had prepared for exactly this move, however, and assigned a total of ten thousand monitors to every polling station in the country, except in Kosovo, where it was impossible for them to go. Two weeks earlier, authorities had given notice of what kind of tactics the regime would use when police raided CeSID's offices and confiscated the computers that were crucial to assembling and publicizing the parallel vote count. Potentially crippled, CeSID turned to its donors, who facilitated a fail-safe election-day plan. "We had headquarters in ten different offices in Belgrade. Each was a substitute for the other," CeSID member Marko Blagojevic recalled. "If one office fell, we had another duplicate. If all ten fell, we had an office in Budapest. It was a foolproof system. Even if everything got shut down, we still had results."

On election day, the regime banned CeSID from entering polling stations, so instead the monitors interviewed voters on the way in and out about their voting intentions and the conditions in the stations. Polling station clerks made CeSID's work much easier when they posted the results on the doors for all to see. All CeSID had to do was record the numbers from each polling station and tally them up. "The election results were never manipulated at the polling stations," said Blagojevic. "It's always higher up." In another early sign of the cracks emerging in the regime, Nikola Denić, a district court judge in the city of Nis, resigned three hours after the polls closed, complaining that security guards had prevented judges from examining the ballots, as the judges were constitutionally required to do.

Within hours, CeSID had compiled its tally. Fifty-seven per cent had voted for Koštunica, and just 33 per cent for Milošević—results that were quickly broadcast into Serbia by B92's transmitters-in-exile. It was a first-ballot victory for the opposition, one that brought cheering crowds of twenty thousand onto Belgrade's streets.[11]

Milošević, though, hadn't given up. The Federal Election Commission that he had stacked over the years with loyalists worked for the next forty-eight hours to doctor the numbers. It finally decided that while it couldn't claim that Milošević had won the vote, it could torque the figures so Koštunica would receive less than the 50 per cent required for a first-round victory. The black hole where large-scale doctoring of the results could take place was Kosovo, where there were almost no election monitors. The official numbers gave Milošević an improbable win there after the last-minute appearance of what CeSID called "phantom votes." Election-day tallies submitted by the various polling stations showed just 45,000 people had cast ballots in Kosovo. But when the official results were released on September 26, the number had somehow ballooned to 145,000. The commission announced that Koštunica had received 48.22 per cent of the vote, to Milošević's 40.25. Koštunica immediately said he would boycott the runoff, set for October 8.

Three days later, Đinđić called a general strike that shut down schools, factories and mines. Serbia, having been convinced by B92 and Otpor how to lose its fear, was hurtling toward open rebellion.

Miloš Milenković was all nerves the morning of October 5, 2000, as he surveyed the crowd outside the Plato Café on Belgrade's Students' Square. It wasn't that the carefully crafted plan was falling apart, as he had feared might happen with so many things to organize that day. Quite the opposite, in fact—things were going too well, and he was suddenly struck by an overwhelming sense of responsibility for the fates of the tens of thousands of people he was going to lead on the two-kilometre march to the parliament building.

"Fear is not a good enough word to describe what I felt," the charismatic Otpor leader, just twenty-two at the time, told me later. "It is an extremely high responsibility to lead a column with forty thousand young people behind you . . . I was frightened to death, not for myself, but for all those people walking behind me."

October 5 had dawned cold and grey in Belgrade—an icy wind known in Serbian as a *kosava* was blowing in from Ko   to the south—and Otpor's complicated plan to seize the centre of the city was going perfectly. Columns of protestors were making their way toward the capital from every corner of Serbia, along five roads, occasionally using fists and sticks to bash their way through police roadblocks that had been set up along the way. Other demonstrators were holding back and staging smaller rallies in their home cities, a tactic meant to tie up local police units so that Milošević couldn't call them all to Belgrade.

But one huge question mark remained: no one knew how Milošević would respond to this massive effort to force him from office. All the protest leaders—and all those up the river in Budapest—were quietly terrified that the Butcher of the Balkans would not hesitate to call in the army. At the very least, they were certain, his police would use gas and batons as they had so often before to disperse opposition rallies.

Ivan Marovic, an Otpor founder who was drafted into military service just ahead of the uprising, was stationed with his unit in Montenegro on October 5. He said the soldiers expected to be sent in that day to quell the protests but the order never came. "No officers talked to us," he recalls. "They were just panicking, running around trying to figure out what to do." While they waited for instructions, they talked amongst themselves and discovered that, almost unanimously, they sided with the crowds, not with Milošević. "Some of the soldiers were saying, 'We're going to drop our weapons and go to Belgrade.' Others were saying, 'We're going to go to Belgrade with our weapons and join the protest,'" Marovic said.

Milenković remembers a "dead silence" falling over the crowd on Students' Square as medical students explained to demonstrators how to counter the effects of tear gas. He worried for a moment that such a graphic description might cause some to think better of marching on Parliament. But no one left. After the disappointments of 1991 and 1997, there was a sense that—one way or another—this day was going to be a decisive one in the country's history. "There had been lots of protests in the 1990s, but this one was different. There was a strange determination in people's eyes," Milenković recalls. "We couldn't ask them to come back another time. There weren't enough police in the country to defeat this energy."

He was right. By mid-morning, hundreds of thousands of people from all over the country had arrived in the centre of Belgrade. Anger over the lost wars, over the tiny repressions and Yugoslavia's backward slide—from being the most economically developed corner of Eastern

Europe to the point where Belgrade was ranked the twelfth worst city on the planet to live in (worse than Lagos, Nigeria)—had reached, and passed, its boiling point.

Just after noon, as Milenković's column marched east from Students' Square to Republic Square—pausing occasionally according to Otpor's delicately arranged traffic plan to let other columns through intersections ahead of them—and then up King Aleksandar Boulevard toward the parliament, Popovic peeled away from the main march and joined a smaller group of five thousand people headed toward the old B92 headquarters.

The crowd converged on the station, expecting a battle, but there was no one left to guard it. Milošević's security services were already sensing the changing tide and worrying about who their bosses might be the next morning. Within hours, Popovic's group had seized the B92 building and Miroković and his staff were back broadcasting on their old frequency, 92.5 FM. Later that day, B92 television broadcast for the first time, and the state-controlled Radio Television of Serbia—nicknamed "TV Bastille" because of how voraciously the regime had defended it during the 1991 protests—had also been taken over by the opposition, which started broadcasting its own message after a brief pause.

Things had swept rapidly out of control yet somehow remained almost bloodless. By 3 p.m., upwards of 100,000 people were gathered on King Aleksandar Boulevard in front of the Yugoslav parliament. Within an hour, demonstrators—some of them eschewing Otpor's calls for non-violence and fighting their way in with clubs—stood inside the green-domed building, having crashed through a thin police line that never got the reinforcements it had requested.

Šikman, who as the oldest of the Otpor veterans had been stuck guiding traffic from the organization's headquarters on Prince Mihailo Street, ran out of the offices to see for himself what was happening. Upon reaching Parliament, he noticed the two flagpoles in front and decided someone should raise Otpor's clenched-fist flag. As he was running back to headquarters to retrieve the flags, he glanced back and came to a dead halt. Behind him, the parliament was burning.

Slobodan Milošević didn't concede the election to Vojislav Koštunica until the evening of October 6. But his "pillars of support," as Gene

Sharp had branded them, had collapsed at least thirty-six hours before that.

First to go were the courts. At 10 a.m. on October 5, while the hordes of demonstrators were still gathering at their meeting points around the capital, a group of domestic NGOs arrived at the City Magistrate's Court to present a petition demanding that the court stop its practice of dispensing summary justice and of jailing regime opponents without advising those individuals' lawyers or families. To their shock, the NGOs—who had approached the court in pairs to avoid attracting the attention of security guards and getting themselves jailed as well—were greeted by a smiling judge who told them immediately that their request had been granted. Everyone walked away from the meeting confident that Milošević would be removed from power in days, if not hours.[12]

Next was the media. From the moment B92 was back on the air, and with RTS disabled, Milošević and his regime had lost control of the message for the first time. (By evening, RTS was back on the air as New Radio Television Serbia.) Then, as more demonstrators surged toward the parliament in the minutes after the doors were first breached, Milošević's last line of defence, the security apparatus that had served him unquestioningly for so long, disappeared.

At 4:17 p.m., police tapes recorded a call from headquarters for all available units to redeploy to Parliament and retake the building. There was no response from the units in the field, many of whom had already gone home or defected to the opposition. Thirteen minutes later, a police helicopter flying over the city centre received an order from headquarters to drop tear-gas canisters into the crowd below. Tear gas had already been used by police in a failed effort to disperse the crowd, but firing into the thick masses now could have caused a panicked stampede and resulted in the day's first deaths. The order was ignored, as was another directive given three minutes later, at 4:33 p.m., for officers defending Parliament to "take further action"—something policemen later admitted was a coded instruction to fire on the demonstrators. "There was one moment where the police officers who were standing in front of the parliament, they just put down their shields and their weapons and joined the protestors," said Milenković. "That's when I knew he really was finished."

The last pillar to go was Milošević's backing from Moscow. Vladimir Putin's government had remained silent throughout the crisis that followed the September 24 vote, drawing criticism from the Russian press (a rare thing) that Putin's inexperience was showing through, that he was not doing enough to defend Russia's "friend" from the American-backed effort to oust him.

In her memoirs, Albright says she was frequently on the phone to her Kremlin counterpart, Igor Ivanov, trying to convince him to join the international consensus against Milošević. "Our cell phones mysteriously seemed to lose their connection whenever I mentioned Serbia," she wrote. "'You have got to tell Milosevic to give up,' I told him. 'Your own credibility with the Serbs depends on it.' More than once Igor responded, 'Madeleine, Madeleine, I can't hear you Mad-el-eine.'"[13]

Too late, the Kremlin realized that even a strongman like Milošević could be defeated from within. It decided to cut its losses and recognize Koštunica's win only on October 6, after the matter was settled and when there was nothing more for Moscow to gain from supporting the regime. Even then, the Russians tried to convince Koštunica to accept a deal that would have made Milošević prime minister, thereby handicapping the reformers and preserving much of the former president's old authority.

On November 21, 2000, Richard Miles, the victor, returned to Belgrade to raise the flag once more over the reopened American embassy. Standing beside him outside the scarred and graffiti-covered building—down the road from the Defence Ministry, still a pile of rubble after having been levelled by a Tomahawk missile during the NATO air strikes—was William Montgomery, who had closed the now superfluous Office of Yugoslav Affairs and would succeed Miles as ambassador. Miles didn't remain in Belgrade long after the revolution—just enough to say farewell and soak up the moment of victory. December parliamentary elections would sweep the opposition coalition to power and give Đinđić the prime ministership. Seven months later, Slobodan Milošević would be in The Hague.

Miles headed back to Sofia to begin making preparations for his next posting, in another of Eastern Europe's "problem" states: the former Soviet republic of Georgia. Coincidentally, that tiny corner of the South Caucasus Mountains was exactly where George Soros would also soon be turning his attention.

FOUR

THE REVOLUTION-MAKERS

Minsk

Days after the revolution in Serbia, the phone at Otpor's Belgrade offices began to ring. Pro-Western activists in several other post-communist states had watched the uprising with envy and wanted to know if Otpor thought their techniques were exportable. The answer, Otpor's informal leadership decided, was yes—so long, of course, as the Western NGOs were willing to put up the money.

Just as they had learned from Slovakia's OK'98, from veterans of Poland's Solidarity movement and from the Croatian activists who had opposed Tuđjman, the Otpor leaders set out to teach others how they had brought about Milošević's fall. "Many groups from non-democratic countries were looking at Serbia's example because it was so dramatic and so well presented on CNN and different global networks. We were well sold," said Srđa Popović. "They were like Christians looking for Jerusalem . . . Immediately after the year 2000, the various groups coming from all different parts of the world, I can name you eleven countries to which I've communicated or been in touch." He made a list: "Georgia and Ukraine are pretty obvious. Belarus, Colombia, Venezuela in Latin America, Zimbabwe in Africa and even North Korea." He stopped at seven, but we both understood that he'd just named some of the most entrenched opponents of U.S. global hegemony.

"The Belarusians were first, in the beginning of January 2001. They were the first to make contact after the revolution with anybody," activist Miloš Milenković remembers. Later that month, he, Slobodan Djinovic, another Otpor member, and CeSID's Marko Blagojevic made a trip to Minsk that was funded by Freedom House. "We shared our experience with these people who shared our backgrounds as Slavic peoples and from our common, communist past," Milenkovic says. "We tried to help them, as our colleagues from Poland, Slovakia and Croatia helped us. To choose their direction."

For years, the National Democratic Institute and the International Republican Institute had been active in Belarus, funding opposition parties and civil society groups opposed to President Lukashenko. After the success in Belgrade, the revolution-makers made the Belarusian regime its next target. In August 2001, ten months after the ouster of Slobodan Milošević—which Lukashenko condemned as "scandalous, abnormal and undemocratic"—hundreds of teenagers emerged from an underground walkway in central Minsk wearing T-shirts emblazoned with the words "Time to choose." Police arrived within minutes, beat several protestors and loaded about twenty of them on a bus to be charged.

Stanislau Shushkevich doesn't look like someone who helped shape the history of Europe. He pads around his wood-walled dacha in a lumberjack shirt and suspenders. His thick fingers are dirty from a morning spent working around the small countryside cottage, and he has to clear tools off the kitchen table to make space for us to sit and talk. Though few outside his native Belarus—a country wedged uncomfortably between Russia and the expanding European Union— know his name, he's considered here to be the founder of the independent Belarusian state.

In December 1991, the former physicist invited Boris Yeltsin and Leonid Kravchuk, the future presidents of Russia and Ukraine, to a dacha in the Belovezhskaya Pushcha nature reserve in western Belarus. There, after a few drinks, they dissolved the Soviet Union.[1]

Shushkevich, as head of the new republic's Supreme Soviet, became the country's first modern head of state. He led the country for its three wobbly years of independence—a time when the Belarusian economy was bloodied by the economic shock therapy of its transition from communism to capitalism. Three years later, in 1994, Shushkevich was such an unpopular figure that a forty-year-old populist former collective farm director named Alexander Lukashenko thumped him resoundingly in the country's first presidential election.

Now sixty-nine, Shushkevich has a lot of time to reflect on his role in history, and recounting it at speeches to foreign universities is one of his chief sources of income—Lukashenko has slashed the former leader's government pension to the equivalent of just $1.50 a month from the $200 to which he is legally entitled. He is denied permission to work in his own country, and drives a battered red Russian-made Zhiguli sedan that looks at least twenty years old.

Lukashenko, a towering, athletic man with broad shoulders, a balding skull and a thick moustache, won the presidency in 1994 by promising a people fed up with post-Soviet chaos that he would restore order to their country. He openly admired Joseph Stalin and, as Vladimir Putin would later, spoke about the collapse of the Soviet Union as a preventable tragedy; he was a reactionary figure for a reactionary time.

While all fifteen post-Soviet republics struggled to find their feet after the system shock of 1991, Belarus—still recovering from the fallout of the 1986 Chernobyl disaster—was among the worst affected. As Shushkevich listened to his Western advisers and dutifully began mass privatization of the economy, jobs disappeared and inflation soared. Soviet-era factories were shut and 50 per cent of economic production disappeared, as did the social guarantees the Communist system had provided.

Lukashenko, the man who was to become known to Belarusians simply as Babka—"father"—entered public life in 1990 as a member of the Supreme Soviet. He founded a faction called Communists for Democracy and was the only member of the chamber to vote against ratifying the December 1991 agreement to dissolve the Soviet Union. In 1993, he was elected chair of a parliamentary anti-corruption committee and turned his rhetorical guns on Shushkevich, accusing the president of stealing state funds for personal use—including a box of nails for his dacha. Shushkevich considered the charges beneath him and refused to answer. His silence was a huge political mistake: voters interpreted it as a sign of guilt. In the first round, Lukashenko surprised everyone by capturing 45 per cent of the vote, triple that of the second-place candidate and embarrassing Shushkevich, who garnered just 10 per cent. In the second round, Babka won a resounding 80 per cent. Even his harshest critics concede that result was likely accurate, such was the hard-liner's popularity at the time.

Once in office, Lukashenko immediately set out to rebuild what he blamed Shushkevich for destroying: the stable, ordered system Belarus had known in the Soviet Union. Democracy had failed, he believed, and it was time to roll back the clock. Within six months of Lukashenko's coming to office, four Belarusian newspapers went to press with blank space on their pages in a desperate protest against a presidential order banning reporting on the widespread corruption within the presidential office. Within two weeks, the editors of all four were fired by Lukashenko's decree, and two of the newspapers were banned from using the state-owned printing presses, effectively damning them to extinction.

After taming the press, Babka turned to eliminating symbols of the country's hard-won independence. Lukashenko, whose terrible command of Belarusian (he almost never speaks it) was a source of ridicule among his country's intelligentsia, pushed a referendum in 1995 that once more made Russian an official language. Belarusian, he told his countrymen in a televised address, was an "impoverished language" in which "you cannot express anything of significance."[2]

Next he turned on the country's flag—a horizontal red stripe running between two white ones—which had been the banner of Belarus both since 1991 and in 1918, during the country's first brief period of independence, before the Red Army marched in. Declaring that the flag belonged to "fascist sympathizers" (it was hoisted by Belarusians who fought alongside the Nazis in World War II, hoping to escape Stalin's murderous rule), Lukashenko banned it and brought back the red and green banner of the Belarusian Soviet Socialist Republic, minus only the hammer and sickle in the corner. In 1996, Lukashenko and Russian president Boris Yeltsin began negotiations toward creating a "union state" between Russia and Belarus, one they hoped would eventually include Ukraine and other former Soviet republics.

When Putin came to power, he considered Belarus the heart of the "near abroad," over which he believed Russia should again hold sway.

Belarusians, after all, look and speak like Russians. Furthermore, Russians and Belarusians don't need a visa—or even a passport—to travel between the two countries, only their regular internal travel documents. Most Belarusians, in fact, still use their Soviet passports as identification, never having fully believed that Belarus was a country in its own right. Flights from Moscow to Minsk take off from the domestic terminal of the Russian capital's Sheremetyevo airport.

A granite statue of Lenin still stands in front of the parliament buildings on Minsk's central square, where the sprawling offices of the KGB (as it's still called in Belarus) dominate the city's main drag, Francyska Skaryny Street. Across the wide road in a small park is a bust of "Iron" Felix Dzerzhinsky, the man who founded the Soviet secret services, and one of history's most notorious murderers. The atmosphere of fear and paranoia that Iron Felix brought to Bolshevik Russia still hangs thick in the Belarusian air.

Most troubling for Russia's liberals, Putin's new Kremlin seemed to admire what Lukashenko had accomplished: a functioning police state with order, clean streets and no dissent. Worried that Putin would pursue what they dubbed a "Belarusification" of Russia, pro-Western politicians like Boris Nemtsov and Vladimir Ryzhkov built links with their Belarusian counterparts, seeing the struggle to free Belarus from Lukashenko as part of their own battle to regain control of Russia's direction. "Russia is now a virtual democracy, becoming more and more authoritarian. Nobody knows how far it can go," Ryzhkov, one of the few independent deputies remaining in Russia's State Duma, told me. The nightmare scenario, he said, was a Belarus-style regime in the Kremlin—equipped with nuclear weapons and Russia's vast oil resources.

Belarusian nationalists also found Lukashenko's crackdown unthinkable. Not understanding how far the president would go to recreate the Soviet system, seventeen deputies from the Belarusian National Front—the party that had led the push for Belarus's independence from the USSR—staged a sit-in in the country's parliament in April 1995 to protest the plan to bring back the old Soviet flag. Unmoved, Lukashenko sent in machine-gun-wielding riot police, who beat the lawmakers with batons before dragging them out of the building. From then on, anyone defiantly displaying the white-red-white banner became a target for police harassment.

Lukashenko pressed on, ordering schools to bring back Soviet textbooks so that children would grow up as he did, understanding that duty to the motherland comes first and that the country was surrounded by enemies. They were also told to teach all classes in Russian, something most schools had stopped doing after the Soviet Union fell. Years later he would complete the trip backward by restoring "ideology" classes in schools and workplaces. The only difference from the old days was that instead of reading the works of Lenin, Marx and Engels, students would read the writings of President Lukashenko.

Belarusians initially supported Lukashenko's efforts, which did have the effect of returning some of the stability they'd known in the Soviet era. But then they got a reminder of the totalitarian system's darker side.

The first to disappear was Yuri Zakharenko, a former interior minister who broke with Lukashenko over policing tactics and became an outspoken critic of the president. His wife says he went missing one evening in May 1999 on his way home from work and hasn't been heard from since. Four months later, the opposition's de facto leader, Viktor Gonchar, and businessman Anatoly Krasovsky, a friend of Gonchar's, were snatched from outside a *banya* (steam bath) in Minsk and never heard from again. The following July, television journalist Dmitry Zavadsky—once Lukashenko's personal cameraman—disappeared after a falling out with the president.

Though the regime has denied any knowledge of what has happened to the four men, there is evidence they were executed by a purple-beret-wearing special forces unit called Almaz. The charge is based largely on an investigation conducted by two Belarusian police investigators. Dmitry Petrushkevich and Oleg Sluchek, who released a report pointing to the involvement of senior figures in the Interior Ministry in the disappearance and apparent deaths of the four men. Petrushkevich and Sluchek then fled to the United States, believing their lives were in danger.[3]

"I still don't know what happened to him, and I don't know what to do about it," Gonchar's wife, Zinaida, told me, her brown eyes glowing with anger almost five years after her husband's disappearance. She was certain that her husband had been under KGB surveillance, and that nothing could have happened to him without their knowledge and connivance. "There are, of course, people who know what happened," she said. "You should ask Lukashenko."

It was a measure of how far the country had slid that the conversation we were having—five people gathered around a bare kitchen table in a small, nondescript Minsk apartment—qualified as an illegal gathering. The meeting had been arranged by Viasna, an association of human rights lawyers that had been banned earlier that year by the government. Throughout the afternoon, there was palpable fear in the room that at any moment the KGB—who kept an office across the parking lot— might come crashing through the door and end the conversation.[4]

Most Belarusians knew nothing about the disappearances. Like Vladimir Putin, Lukashenko has long been obsessed with maintaining a tight control over the flow of information. He confronted the Soros Foundation in 1997, recognizing quickly (more quickly than Milošević) that its work promoting entrepreneurship and free media was anathema to authoritarian rule. Soros, the president told deans and professors at Minsk University, "not so much helped us, as worked out programs to overthrow the government and president." Either Soros or the regime, Lukashenko astutely surmised, would have to go.

In March 1997, the head of the Belarusian Soros Foundation, Peter Byrne, landed at Minsk airport, where he was arrested, held for several hours and then expelled on complaints he had attended opposition rallies. A week later, the first secretary at the U.S. embassy, Serzh Alexandrov, was expelled for the same reason. A month later, the Soros Foundation was charged with tax fraud, had its bank accounts seized and was fined the equivalent of $3 million, which an indignant Soros refused to pay. Four years after the foundation was effectively forced out, authorities seized a Soros-funded printing press as collateral on the unpaid fine. Magic, as the press was known, had been the main printer for opposition papers. Once it was shut, the remaining independent press had to cooperate with the state if it wanted to be printed in Belarus.

"They have simply restored what existed in the Soviet Union, making people into zombies," Svetlana Kalinkina, editor-in-chief of *Belorusskaya Delovaya Gazeta*, told me one afternoon as we sat in her paper's cramped and grungy offices near the centre of Minsk. Kalinkina's newspaper remained editorially independent but was barely hanging on financially. Denied access to both the state-owned printing presses in the country and the state-run newspaper kiosks, *Delovaya Gazeta* was reduced to being printed in the western Russian city of Smolensk— where at least the free market prevailed—and smuggled back into the country each day for direct delivery to the paper's dwindling base of loyal subscribers who wanted to know what was really happening in their country.

"They're telling people that everything is good in Belarus, and that everything is going bad in Poland, bad in the Baltics, and that it's only good in Belarus because we have Lukashenko. It's becoming the same as in Soviet times, when people honestly believed there was no better country than the Soviet Union," Kalinkina sighed.

Shushkevich believes he left Belarus on a democratic path, having introduced the legal concept of private property and having presided over a period that saw the birth of a range of political parties. The country had good relations with the West and had begun implementing a deal with the U.S. to remove all nuclear weapons from its territory and ship them to Russia to be destroyed. He blames the country's long, hard fall since then entirely on Lukashenko, a man he labels "obscene."

"I don't know of anyone else like him—maybe Gadhafi or Kim Jong-il, but those people are smarter," he says, opening a bottle of homemade red wine early in the afternoon. At the end of our conversation, he makes a plea for the West to help Belarus, comparing the political climate in his country to the one faced by his friend Lech Wałęsa, who led the Solidarity movement in Poland in the late 1980s. "The situation is worse now than in Poland," he says. "What we need is for the West to support us the way they supported Solidarity."

In the two years preceding the 2001 presidential elections, the U.S. spent some $50 million on "democracy-promotion" initiatives in Belarus. It's a pittance compared to the money Washington throws around in other parts of the world—the Middle East, for example— but in a country where the average monthly wage was just $77 a month, it empowered the opposition to challenge the status quo.

That $50 million was just the overt spending. American money funded about three hundred non-governmental organizations, some with such clear links to the opposition that many observers considered them to be one and the same. In the clearest sign that the State

Department saw Belarus in 2001 as being ripe for a repeat of Belgrade, the U.S. funded the creation of Zubr ("bison" in Belarusian), a radical youth group dedicated to Lukashenko's non-violent overthrow, and one consciously modelled on Otpor—the Serbian student organization that led the anti-Milošević demonstrations in 2000. Like Otpor, Zubr was an American invention from day one.

It sprang from a January 2001 trip to Minsk, paid for by Freedom House, that brought Otpor veterans Miloš Milenković and Slobodan Djinovic, along with NGO representatives (including Marko Blagojevic of Serbia's Centre for Free Elections and Democracy), to the capital to see if they could help stir up Belarusian dissent in the same way they had at home. They met with leaders of the Belarusian opposition at the Hotel Planeta, a run-down Soviet-style hotel just outside the city centre done up to look newer than it is, with a garish neon facade and lobby that have all the taste and class of a Las Vegas casino, that is nonetheless considered one of the most fashionable places to stay in Minsk.

In the Hotel Planeta lobby, Otpor and Zubr made their first acquaintances. Djinovic was sitting in his dowdy room when he got a call asking him to come downstairs. In a scene right out of a Cold War spy movie, he saw a young man sitting in a chair, his face hidden behind a newspaper. As he passed, the man lowered his newspaper, stood up and tapped the Serb on his shoulder. "Are you Slobodan?" he asked. When Djinovic nodded, the man said brusquely, "Follow me," and headed out into the street.

The mysterious stranger led Djinovic to a nondescript apartment block that was to serve as Zubr headquarters. Members sat Djinovic down and asked him where to begin. He and Milenković returned frequently after that. "I think I made another twenty trips to Belarus," Milenković told me.

In later years, anxious to debunk the "American agents" label that Lukashenko's regime had quickly pasted on them, Zubr activists became reluctant to discuss how they were funded. But in the heady days of 2001, with the presidential election drawing near and the growing feeling that Lukashenko might be in trouble, they weren't so cautious. "They transfer the money into European banks in Poland, and we bring it in from there," twenty-two-year-old Zubr organizer

Alexei Shydlovski told the *Wall Street Journal.* In another interview, he admitted that Zubr had "relations" with Western embassies in Minsk. "We tell them what we're doing and planning," he said.

Zubr tried to execute the Otpor playbook page by page, and telegraphed its intentions by posting a copy of Gene Sharp's "From Dictatorship to Democracy" tutorial on its website. Mimicking the public-awareness stunts performed on the streets of Belgrade in 2000, masked Zubr activists announced the group's formation with acts of street theatre. One day they'd be standing silently with photographs of the missing Zakharenko, Gonchar, Krasovsky and Zavadsky; the next they'd be clowning around with a mustachioed blow-up doll that looked remarkably like the country's dictatorial ruler. Minsk and other cities were soon covered with stickers of Zubr's orange bison mascot and anti-Lukashenko graffiti. One stunt that caught the public eye—and led to arrests for defaming the president—involved four Zubr activists in doctors' gowns chasing a fifth dressed up as Lukashenko. They appealed for help to amazed bystanders: "Have you seen our patient? He has escaped from a mental hospital!" Even the police sent to break up the demonstration couldn't help laughing into their megaphones.

In February 2001, the State Department stepped it up a notch, funnelling money through IRI to pay for a trio of Otpor leaders, led by Belgrade veteran Siniša Šikman, to travel to Minsk and meet with Shydlovski and other Zubr members. The conversation was to the point: the Otpor members told their new comrades that they believed the Belgrade formula was exportable, and that Lukashenko could fall just as Milošević had. "These guys were our mentors. We learned a lot from them," Zubr's genial leader Vladimir Kobets told me.

Soon after this, Trygve Olson, head of IRI's Belarus section, oversaw Otpor-led training camps for the Belarusian opposition in Vilnius and Bratislava, where Zubr activists learned Sharp's principles of non-violent resistance. NDI paid for the next session, in Poland. At each training camp, activists were drilled on the tactics of street demonstration and on how to respond if the police decided to disperse the crowd.[5]

Despite the repressive state machinery and Zubr's lack of access to the mainstream media, momentum seemed to be on the young activists' side. The Internet and mobile phones made mobilizing resistance far easier than it had been in the Soviet era, and each opposition rally seemed to be bigger than the last. By summer 2001, advance preparations were already being made for a "victory rally" in central Minsk the day after the September presidential vote. The opposition knew well that the official results would show Lukashenko had won, and they were preparing to force him from power.

Under heavy pressure from the American embassy, the Belarusian opposition united in 2001 behind Vladimir Goncharik, a former trade union leader. It had been a tortuous process—the opposition had previously been fractured into five groups with little in common besides a distaste for Lukashenko. But the embassy controlled the purse strings, so they had to go along with the plan. Goncharik was far from an easy choice. IRI polls found that because of the state's tight grip on the media, the public knew few politicians besides Lukashenko and none of the others had any substantial popularity. Goncharik represented the least radical choice, and was therefore considered the most likely to draw support from Lukashenko's legitimate, largely rural constituency, who shared his nostalgia for the Soviet Union.

The presence of U.S. ambassador-designate Michael Kozak in Minsk was no coincidence. Appointed in 2000, Kozak had made a career of being backstage when "regime change" was happening on the streets. He was working for the State Department in Nicaragua in 1989–90 when the leftist Sandinistas were unceremoniously booted from power. He was the man Ronald Reagan sent to Panama to offer Noriega a $2 million retirement package in Spain that, had the strongman taken it, would have spared the U.S. the trouble of invading the country a year later. Before being posted to Belarus, he was assigned to joust with Fidel Castro as the U.S. envoy to Havana.[6]

From the outset, Kozak made his intentions in Belarus clear. Belarus was the "Cuba of Europe," and may have been selling Soviet weapons to Iran and Iraq, he told the U.S. Senate Foreign Relations Committee that approved his posting. He proposed to treat Lukashenko the same way he had treated Castro—to work toward his ouster. In a letter published in the *Guardian* just before the September election, Kozak put it bluntly, and in the process coloured himself as more of an agent than a diplomat. The American "objective and to some degree methodology are the same" in Belarus as they were when he was posted to Nicaragua in 1989–90, he wrote. As if the message wasn't clear enough, the U.S. State Department brought its Serbia and Belarus experts together at a joint strategy session soon afterward.

Unsurprisingly, the Belarusian government saw Kozak's appointment and Senate committee testimony as an American declaration of war on the Lukashenko regime. The local KGB and the Russian FSB, who had spent long decades going head to head with the CIA on a global scale, knew what a looming *coup d'état* attempt smelled like, and the regime began to fight back. For months, Lukashenko sat on Kozak's papers to keep him out of the country. He delayed and denied visas to election observers sent by the Organization for Security and Co-operation in Europe, believing that the OSCE's ambassador, Hans-Georg Wieck, was also knee-deep in the conspiracy to topple him.[7]

Putin's Kremlin may not have been as keen on Lukashenko as Yeltsin's had been, but after Belgrade it was nonetheless loath to see further Western encroachment in the "near abroad." There's a Russian proverb that says "he may be a son of a bitch, but at least he's *our* son of a bitch." It was often used in Moscow to describe Lukashenko. In the Kremlin, where few in the political elite had ever accepted the notion of an independent Belarus, Lukashenko's talk of a "union state" and the need for "Slavic unity" was intoxicating. Dreams of empire were being reborn.

Lukashenko's public deference to the Kremlin following his election in 1994 further reinforced these aspirations, as had his push to join the two countries in a union state that would obviously be dominated by Moscow (though Lukashenko likely envisioned himself as president of the joint federation). There have, however, been drags on the relationship, particularly since Putin's ascension to the presidency in 2000. Unlike Yeltsin, who would get drunk at meetings with Lukashenko (the latter, like Putin, is a health nut, and much more cautious in his imbibing) and talk of the seemingly inevitable rejoining of Russia and Belarus, Putin never liked Lukashenko. He treated him for what he was: a collective farmer turned despot who had to be tolerated but who could also be treated roughly because he had nowhere to turn if he ever lost favour with Moscow.

But there was no question that Moscow was more comfortable having Babka in Minsk than another pro-Western Vojislav Koštunica.

In the wake of Milošević's fall, Russia quickly recognized the danger Lukashenko was facing as Western pressure mounted to oust the man dubbed the "last dictator in Europe."

Unable to match the West's money, Minsk and Moscow fought back the best way they knew how, using espionage and the state-controlled presses to counter the American propaganda offensive. Compiling the plentiful evidence they had of Western embassies and NGOs working to topple the government, Lukashenko ordered that the state-owned *Sovetskaya Belarus* newspaper print a full account of the Western coup plot against him two days before the election. The 8,700-word article that ran on September 7, 2001, cited "leaks from intelligence and diplomatic circles" and claimed that Western embassies, as well as organizations such as the Soros Foundation and the OSCE, were behind "a thoroughly masterminded organizational and political operation . . . code-named White Stork and aimed at deposing incumbent Belarusian president Alexander Lukashenko in the course of the September presidential election." The goal, the article alleged, was to duplicate what had happened in Belgrade and to install a pro-Western leader in Minsk who would act as a buffer against a newly resurgent Russia and its renewed "imperial policy." The article was bang on.

The article added, correctly, that the opposition was planning mass demonstrations on September 9 and would claim that the election result had been tampered with in Lukashenko's favour.

Demonstrations will be organized [claiming] the opposition candidate's victory in the first round and [claiming] mass-scale falsification of the election results carried out by pro-government election commissions. They do not rule out a possible attack on the presidential residence, which would lead to inevitable clashes with law-enforcement agencies sparking off unrest with casualties.

These casualties and the authorities' brutal treatment of the protesting youth would give a strong reason to the West to declare the election in Belarus invalid and the election results falsified, while re-elected Lukashenko would be called illegitimate. All this will contribute to turning Lukashenko's personality into a demon, to growing instability in Belarus and possible social chaos, while the West possesses a wide range of tools to stabilize the situation.

In other words, it would be Belgrade all over again—only this time, the Kremlin knew what was coming. A cocky Lukashenko went on the attack, warning the opposition that he would do what Milošević had not: he would use force. "There will be no Koštunica in Belarus," Lukashenko said on television. "I will not be sitting in a bunker like Milošević. I am not afraid of anybody. I have not stolen anything from my people." Special troops, he added pointedly, "will be defending the president and will never give him up."

Election day, September 9, 2001, came and went with few surprises. Shortly after polls closed, the Central Election Commission said Lukashenko had won an "elegant victory," taking 76 per cent of the vote, with a record 82 per cent turnout. Goncharik took less than 13 per cent.

That night the revolution machine fell apart. Just two thousand Belarusians, mostly students from the Zubr movement, gathered on October Square, across from the presidential administration building. They blew whistles, waved the red and white flag of Belarusian independence and chanted, "Shame! Long live Belarus!" and "Freedom! Freedom!" in the cold rain amidst a heavy police presence. Though a few shop windows were smashed, the police never felt the need to move in. This was not a coup in the making but a disheartened gathering of the defeated.

Those who demonstrated that night gathered knowing that they could go to jail or lose their jobs just for taking part in the unsanctioned protest. The tiny crowd represented the only Belarusians willing to face prison for the uncharismatic Goncharik, who had proved a flop with Lukashenko's constituency and who had been deserted even by some pro-Westerners because of his Communist past. "He was a functionary, without any political charms, shall we say. Choosing him was a strategic mistake," Ales Antsipenka, former head of the Belarus chapter of the Soros Foundation, told me later. "From the moment when the protests were beginning, Goncharik made it clear he was not a real leader."

After the economic hardships suffered by Belarusians from 1991 to 1994, not even the opposition disputes that much of the population craved Lukashenko's strongman approach. Civil rights may have been knocked back to the Brezhnev era, but Lukashenko delivered things Shushkevich had been unable to, such as salaries and pensions paid on time, employment (80 per cent of it state-subsidized) and low inflation. There's not much selection in the Minsk markets, but the shelves are never bare and critical supplies like bread, milk and oil are much cheaper than in neighbouring Poland or Lithuania, a fact the presidential press service makes an almost daily habit of repeating.

When the regime and the media it controlled repeated other, less credible statements—that Poland and Lithuania were descending into chaos, for example, and that life was much better in Belarus than in neighbouring countries—the rural poor who had grown up on a steady diet of Soviet propaganda didn't doubt them. After seventy-five years of Cold War thinking, they were ready to blame all the country's ills on their perceived enemies in the West.

The West's belief that Belarusians were ready in 2001 to rise up against their president was also misguided, Antsipenka said. "Lukashenko might have destroyed the political space, the independent media and the public sector, but ordinary people were not negatively affected by it to the point that they would protest or take aggressive action against the situation."

The distraction of the 9/11 attacks didn't exactly save Lukashenko—he already looked likely to weather the storm—but he was certainly among the few clear winners that day. The Bush administration had been bloodily reminded that it had bigger problems than who ruled Belarus. Furthermore, Russia had a lot to offer the U.S., particularly on-the-ground intelligence leftover from the Soviet invasion of Afghanistan. As Russia swung behind Bush's "war on terrorism," even lending support as the U.S. established military bases in former Soviet Central Asia, American foreign policy took a decidedly pro-Russian turn. U.S. diplomats stopped mentioning Putin's own "anti-terrorism war" in the breakaway republic of Chechnya, and the push to oust Lukashenko died a quiet death.

Back in Belarus, Kozak eventually moved on and Lukashenko basked in his victory. "The revolution which dark forces have talked about for so long has collapsed," he said in his televised victory address to the nation.

"Or at least it has been postponed."

———

FIVE

LIBERAL IMPERIALISM

Moscow and Kiev

In czarist Moscow, before Communist dictators flattened entire sections of the once-charming city centre and filled it with buildings tall enough to match their egos, nothing stood higher than Ivan the Great's Bell Tower, a white stone spire topped by a gleaming golden dome that still stretches above the Kremlin's red walls. Before the Bolshevik Revolution of 1917, it was illegal to build anything in Moscow that exceeded the eighty-one-metre height of the Bell Tower, which stretches above a trio of magnificent Orthodox cathedrals— Assumption, Archangel and Annunciation—that house the tombs of a long line of czars, czarinas and crown princes. In pre-revolutionary Russia, it would have been hard to get past the impression that God and the czars—perhaps not in that order—were observing everything you did.

But in today's Moscow, the building that stands imperiously over everything else in the city's jumbled skyline is the thirty-five-storey grey concrete and blue glass headquarters of Gazprom OAO, the giant energy company that would become as vital to Vladimir Putin's influence over Russia's neighbours as the horse-borne Cossack armies had been to the czars, or the Comintern to Lenin.

Gazprom was born in 1989 out of the remains of the Soviet Gas Ministry. It didn't share its predecessor's control of the natural reserves and pipeline networks outside of the Russian Federation, but nonetheless Gazprom emerged massive. It enjoys a monopoly of Russia's enormous gas reserves—the largest in the world, at 30 trillion cubic metres—and a vast pipeline network that stretches some 144,000 kilometres. The company's economic importance to Russia is hard to overstate. With 300,000 workers across eleven time zones, Gazprom accounts for 8 per cent of the country's gross domestic product and contributes 25 per cent of its tax base.

In the early 1990s—like many state assets—Gazprom underwent a murky privatization process that left the company intact but under unknown ownership and unpredictable direction. Though the state remained the largest shareholder and Viktor Chernomyrdin, Yeltsin's longest-serving prime minister, was the former chair of the board of directors, the state held a minority stake and it was unclear who had the final say in corporate decisions, or who profited. Billions of dollars disappeared every year into a morass of shell companies that most believed were affiliated with Chernomyrdin and other members of Yeltsin's "Family." Boris Nemtsov, the reformist governor of Nizhny Novgorod who rose under Yeltsin to the position of deputy prime minister, once told a TV interviewer that "to be very frank, no one knows anything about Gazprom."

One of Putin's first acts as president was to end this confusion and re-establish firm state control over the behemoth. By July 2000, he had ousted Chernomyrdin and installed Dmitry Medvedev, the thirty-nine-year-old deputy head of the Presidential Administration and a close ally from Putin's time in St. Petersburg, as the chairman of the company's board of directors. Soon afterward, Putin installed another member of his St. Petersburg cadre, Alexei Miller, as the company's chief executive officer, and the state began gradually building up its stake, from 38 per cent to a controlling 51 per cent by 2005.

The board of directors, which during the Chernomyrdin era had comprised six private business figures and five government representatives, was shrunk to nine members, five of whom were still from the government. From the moment Medvedev arrived as chair of the board of directors, Gazprom was a foreign policy tool of the president of Russia.

The company began a rapid expansion. Domestically, its tentacles reached into the ownership of hotels, schools, airports and yacht clubs.

Its media arm, Gazprom Media, bought control of dozens of news-papers and television and radio stations, including Vladimir Gusinsky's old flagship television station, NTV. If the Kremlin took a dislike to a television station or a renegade oligarch, Gazprom would swoop in and buy up the offending company, usually at a rock-bottom price. The case of NTV was typical: while Vladimir Gusinsky was in prison, facing the prospect of a prolonged stay, he agreed to sell his network to the gas giant. Gusinsky was soon freed and went into exile, while NTV's feisty reporting—which had irked Putin not only during the election campaign, but with its critical coverage of his response to the *Kursk* submarine disaster in 2000—was soon replaced with blander, pro-Kremlin broadcasting.

Abroad, Gazprom had an equally imposing reach. The company that Medvedev and Miller took over controlled 25 per cent of the world's proven natural gas reserves and supplied all, or almost all, the gas consumed by the countries of the old USSR and much of Central Europe. In 2000, 35 per cent of the European Union's natural gas came through Gazprom's pipes. When the EU expanded in 2004 to take on ten new members—Eastern European countries that had relied on Russian gas for decades—that number leapt to 60 per cent. As a hang-over from the Cold War, countries like Poland, Slovakia, Austria, Hungary and the Czech Republic were all almost completely reliant on the Russian delivery of natural gas.

Putin first used Gazprom as a weapon in the wake of the Serbian rev-olution. The company cited a $400 million debt owed to Gazprom by Belgrade. The debt was years old and had never been an issue while Milošević was firmly in power, but with winter approaching and the pro-Western Koštunica sworn in as the new president, Gazprom decided it was time for the Serbs to pay up, and during the upheaval in the fall of 2000, quietly cut off all gas deliveries to Yugoslavia. The desired effect was achieved: less than three weeks after he took office, Koštunica found himself on a plane to Moscow, where he would beg Vladimir Putin to order the gas back on. Putin intervened, but not before reminding Koštunica that he owed the Kremlin a big favour. If the West believed it had managed to wrest Belgrade out of Moscow's sphere of influence, Putin had just reeled it halfway back in. How Putin would make up the $400 million shortfall on Gazprom's books was never explained.

In the wake of Milošević 's fall, Putin realized that the West's tolerance for using tanks and attack helicopters as a way of expanding influence was on the wane. Russia's resurgent economic strength, as well as its abundant supply of natural resources—oil and, in particular, natural gas—could strengthen his hold on the near abroad far better than could any conscript soldier. He didn't need to send in the army to settle a dispute. All he had to do was flip the switch and let the neighbours shiver until they came around to seeing things his way.

Next up for a demonstration of modern *realpolitik* was Georgia, a former Soviet republic in the South Caucasus whose defiant displays of independence had particularly riled the Kremlin. Since he had taken office in 1992, Georgian president Eduard Shevardnadze—the former Soviet foreign minister who was reviled by Russian nationalists as Gorbachev's co-conspirator in breaking up the Soviet Union—had resisted the pull of Moscow's orbit, and now he was making overtures to NATO.

So Putin left Shevardnadze in the cold, literally. With the tiny country almost entirely reliant on Gazprom for natural gas, the Kremlin flipped the switch in the middle of January 2001. Shevardnadze, reminded of the precariousness of his position, began a slow drift back toward deference to Moscow. "It is too early to speak of Georgia's possible accession to NATO. The people will decide. It is possible Georgia will become a neutral country," he told a news conference soon after the supply of gas resumed. No army could have broken a country's independent spirit so quickly.

"You have to create a system of pipelines which will [establish] the Russian role . . . Russia wants to be regarded as the mother interest in post-Soviet countries," Sergei Markov, the Kremlin spin doctor, once explained to me. "It was absolutely clear in the case of Georgia."

Even pro-Moscow leaders could feel a Gazprom-induced chill when they resisted Kremlin dictates. Belarus's unpredictable president, Alexander Lukashenko, had for years negotiated with Yeltsin toward their shared goal of eventually reunifying Belarus and Russia, and aspired to leading the unified country. He was thereby shocked when Putin arrived on the scene and proposed something very different than the grand reunification of two countries: the wholesale absorption of Belarus into the Russian Federation, with Lukashenko immediately demoted to the status of presidential envoy to Russia's new, ninetieth, region. Lukashenko lashed out in public against the new Russian leader, musing that he would have been better off if, like other former Soviet republics, he'd courted the West instead of remaining loyal to Moscow. Putin's response was swift—Gazprom cut its natural gas deliveries to Belarus. And Lukashenko quickly got used to life as the Kremlin's junior partner.

Putin's Russia developed other economic levers for potential use against its neighbours. Encouraged by the Kremlin, Russian companies moved swiftly into the former Soviet territories, snapping up key firms in crucial sectors. Unified Energy Systems, under the leadership of Anatoly Chubais—the privatization czar who was once viewed as one of the country's "young reformers"—led the way, buying up stakes in the electricity distribution networks of Armenia, Kazakhstan and Georgia and shopping for assets in the Baltic states and as far away as Bulgaria and Slovakia. It was Chubais, whom the West had once trusted to overhaul the Russian economy, who coined the term "liberal imperialism" to describe the Kremlin's new strategy.

"Former Soviet states can't afford to ignore Russia's wishes," Chris Weafer, a former adviser to the OPEC cartel, told the *Moscow Times*. "At the end of the day, Russia can just turn the lights off. You can't run an electricity cable from Washington."[1]

Sitting in 2004 on the covered balcony of a café on Moscow's Old Arbat Street—a pedestrian mall where vendors peddled busts of Lenin and other Soviet kitsch outside of gleaming new Mexx and Miss Sixty outlets—another interested observer told me that the West and Russia were again coming to view each other in Cold War with-us-or-against-us terms. "The message is that if they can't be a political or nuclear superpower, then they're going to be an economic superpower," said a veteran Western diplomat, speaking to me under the customary condition that he wouldn't be named in print. "The frightening thing is that they've got the ability to do it. They've got the resources, and they've got the [technical] skills."

No place was dearer to the soul of the neo-imperialists who had taken over the Kremlin than Ukraine. Many, if not most, Russians view Ukrainians as blood kin—backward peasants who are nonetheless relatives and of whom Russians say, both affectionately and derogatorily, that they are from Malorossiya, "Little Russia." Kiev, the elegant Ukrainian capital that stretches across the winding Dnipro River, is seen as the mother city of the Rus, the people from whom Russians, Ukrainians and Belarusians all descend.

The Ukrainian capital is one of Europe's more naturally beautiful cities, green and leafy in the summer, with plentiful park space and beaches tucked neatly into the curving banks of the Dnipro. The skyline is crowned by the gleaming gold domes of St. Sophia's Cathedral and St. Michael's Monastery and by an awkward grey metallic arch meant to celebrate Ukraine's forced unification with Russia in 1654.

When the Soviet Union dissolved in 1991, few in Moscow were surprised to see the Baltic republics of Lithuania, Latvia and Estonia pull away. Fewer still—except for those concerned with finite matters of geopolitics and natural resources—were bothered when the far-flung former Soviet republics of Central Asia and the South Caucasus declared their independence. Despite decades of forced living together and government social planning, a post-racism *Homo sovieticus* had never materialized, and the light-skinned, fair-haired Slavs who inhabited Moscow, St. Petersburg and Irkutsk had never become entirely comfortable with the large number of Azeris, Armenians, Georgians, Uzbeks and other nationalities living in their midst under the banner of communism. As racist sentiments rose during the economic chaos of the 1990s, the darker-skinned peoples from the southern edges of the old empire became collectively and derogatively referred to in Moscow street slang as *chorniy,* or "blacks." So Russians were stunned when the Ukrainians joined the lineup of those looking to escape Moscow's rule. As Lenin himself had once said, "If we lose Ukraine, we lose our head." The Ukrainians themselves were less concerned about such things, voting overwhelmingly for independence in December 1991.

Moscow had little choice at the time but to accept the dissolution of the old union: all the states that broke away did so legally, availing themselves of mechanisms in the Soviet constitution that the authors must have assumed would never be put to use. Almost immediately, however, the Kremlin started working to reel Kiev back in. Over the next few years, the Kremlin ensured that Kravchuk—a barely reformed Communist apparatchik who had cleverly positioned

himself at the head of the Ukrainian nationalist movement, though
he hardly seemed to have it in his blood—never strayed too far
toward the West. Ukraine was nearly 100 per cent reliant on Russian
energy and had already learned the lessons Gazprom had given
Belarus and Georgia, experiencing frequent politically motivated
cuts in service between 1992 and 1994.

The Kremlin also stirred up unrest in the east, Ukraine's coal-
producing economic heartland. The region was predominantly
Russian-speaking, devoutly Orthodox and suspicious of the Ukrainian
nationalism and Catholicism that had taken hold in the centre and
west of the country. While cities in the west of the country—like
Lviv, nestled in the Carpathian Mountains just seventy kilometres
from the Polish border—were Central European in their architecture,
attitude and outlook, eastern cities like Donetsk resembled Anywhere,
Russia, with their broad boulevards and cookie-cutter apartment
blocks. Where people in the west spoke predominantly Ukrainian,
with a liberal sprinkling of German and English, only Russian was
heard on the streets of Donetsk. Given the example Kiev could see to
its west in tiny Moldova—another former Soviet republic, where
Russian-backed separatists had set up their own independent enclave
after a bloody civil war in the early 1990s—there could be no doubt
that Moscow could and would inflame pro-Russian groups if it suited
the Kremlin's interests.

The same threat existed in the Crimean peninsula, where Russia's
rusting Black Sea Fleet still slumbers in the czarist-era deepwater port of
Sevastopol. The Crimea was historically part of Russia until it was given
as a "gift" to Ukraine by Nikita Khrushchev in 1954 (locals swear he
must have been drunk), and, like the east, it remains heavily Russified.

The election of Leonid Kuchma in 1994, a former missile-factory
boss from the Russian-speaking city of Dnipropetrovsk in the east of
the country, led to a slow thaw in relations between Ukraine and its old
colonial master. Initially welcomed as an economic reformer by the
West, Kuchma won the election by sweeping the east, winning 80 per
cent of the vote in Donetsk and its sister coal town of Lugansk but just
4 per cent in the Westernized province of Galicia. Even less of a nationalist than Kravchuk, he could barely speak Ukrainian. Nonetheless,
like Shevardnadze in Georgia, Kuchma saw the benefits of playing the

West and Russia off against each other, and from time to time spoke of Ukraine's future as being in Europe and even NATO.

His efforts to alternately appease Washington then Moscow were perhaps best exhibited by his decision to hire Viktor Yushchenko, the country's successful, Western-friendly central bank chief, as prime minister in 1999. Kuchma fired him less than two years later under heavy pressure from Moscow, which accused Yushchenko of being an anti-Russian "ultra-nationalist" after he blocked a series of attempted takeovers of Ukrainian companies by Russian firms.

Kuchma's flirtation with neutrality came slamming to a halt with the grisly discovery of a headless, decomposed corpse in a shallow grave in the woods seventy kilometres outside Kiev in November 2000. The body belonged to Georgiy Gongadze, a thirty-one-year-old muckraking journalist who had disappeared two months before. *Ukrayinska Pravda* ("Ukrainian Truth"), the feisty Internet newspaper he had founded, had gained prominence—and Kuchma's personal animosity—by publishing a series of articles alleging corruption within the president's inner circle. Gongadze, dark-haired and square-jawed, had also led a campaign to draw domestic and international attention to Kuchma's slow strangulation of press freedoms, and his website had begun to draw the support of Western donors. Three months before his death, Gongadze wrote an open letter to the country's chief prosecutor claiming that he and his family were being followed by the Ukrainian secret service, the SBU. Many immediately saw the killing as a crude attempt to silence an outspoken critic of Kuchma. He was the thirteenth Ukrainian media figure to die unnaturally in the country's first ten years of independence.

Three weeks after the discovery of Gongadze's body, opposition politician Oleksandr Moroz produced a cassette recorded by Mykola Melnychenko, the president's bodyguard, that appeared to catch Kuchma discussing Gongadze with his top aides and suggesting something needed to be done to "get rid of" the pesky journalist. Kuchma later admitted it was indeed his voice on the recording but said the tape had been heavily edited and had to have been the work of foreign intelligence agents. "I've personally never issued any orders to persecute any newspaper, any TV or radio channel, or any journalist. If it happened, and I repeat I was not involved, it would have been a mistake and part of the learning process," he told BBC2 in April 2001. "Melnychenko did not play any role, because I do not know him. I can't even remember what he looked like."

Despite his protests, the scandal caused immense and irreparable damage to Kuchma's reputation. The man the West had greeted as a reformer was now viewed as just another nasty post-Soviet autocrat. The Organization for Security and Co-operation in Europe dubbed Gongadze's death "censorship by killing," and the Council of Europe— citing a deeply flawed investigation that suggested a pair of conveniently already dead gangsters were behind the murder—considered suspending Ukraine's membership. Tens of thousands of Ukrainians took to the streets of Kiev in 2001, calling for Kuchma to be impeached and charged with Gongadze's murder. A youth group called Ukraine Without Kuchma led the protests; with Western financial help, Miloš Milenković and others from Otpor had already begun training the group in the burgeoning overthrowing-a-tyrant trade.

With his regime in crisis and his legitimacy in Western eyes forever tarnished, Kuchma turned back toward Moscow, where Putin was quick to lend him support. The speed with which the Kremlin capitalized on the crisis led to rampant rumours, even within Ukraine's anti-Kuchma opposition, that the entire operation—from the bugging of Kuchma's office to the murder of Gongadze—had in fact been directed from Moscow in order to compromise the Ukrainian president and force him to look east for support.

In January 2001, Ukraine and Russia signed an agreement that effectively ended the former's cooperation with NATO through the Partnership for Peace program. Kuchma, meanwhile, started telling Ukrainians that they could not think of joining the European Union unless Russia, their fraternal neighbour, was set to do the same thing. Months later, Russian prime minister Mikhail Kasyanov and his new Ukrainian counterpart, Anatoliy Kinakh, signed an "energy union." This led to the real price of Russia's support: an agreement, signed in October 2002, that put Ukraine's energy grid under Russian control for thirty-five years and gave Gazprom a 51 per cent share in Ukraine's pipeline network. Kuchma also agreed to reverse the flow of a crucial 674-kilometre pipeline that ran from the Black Sea port of Odessa to a terminal at Brody, near the Polish border, so that instead of taking oil drawn from the Caspian Sea by British and American firms to Central and Western Europe—thereby weakening Russia's growing monopoly on the continent's energy supplies—the pipeline would flow south, carrying Russian oil to markets around the globe.

When Kinakh resigned in objection to the deal, he was replaced by a pro-Russian ex-convict named Viktor Yanukovych, a man who, like Putin and Lukashenko, mourned the fall of the Soviet Union. Yanukovych was immediately dubbed Kuchma's likely successor.

Putin's vision of how to formally restore Russian influence in the post-Soviet space began to take shape in May 2003, when he met with Kuchma for a five-day summit in the Crimean resort of Yalta. It was the nineteenth time the two men had met in person since the Gongadze crisis. Reflecting the new closeness between the two men, they didn't bring their regular entourages of advisers. Two months later, Russia, Ukraine, Belarus and Kazakhstan—the four largest former Soviet republics—signed a draft deal calling for the creation of something innocuously named the Common Economic Space. The four countries pledged to move toward free trade, joint economic and energy policies, a tax and customs union, and coordinated talks with international bodies such as the World Trade Organization that had previously shown more interest in admitting Ukraine or Kazakhstan than Russia's still lawless and unpredictable economy; now one would not join without the others. (The continued obstacles that the U.S. would throw up to block Russia's entry into the WTO—while post-Soviet countries like Kyrgyzstan and Georgia were admitted, not to mention still-Communist China—would remain one of the biggest irritants in relations between Moscow and Washington throughout Putin's time in office.)

Kuchma and Lukashenko rejected a Russian push to make the ruble the sole currency of the new CES, but the organization nonetheless established a new form of Russian hegemony over its member states. Voting on all matters would be weighted according to the size of the countries' economies—meaning that Russia, which dwarfed the other nations in every respect, would effectively be the only one with a say.

Lawmakers in Ukraine—the only country of the four with a broadly based opposition movement—immediately slammed the deal as a violation of their country's constitution and sovereignty. "Ukraine will become a puppet in the hands of a restored imperial power," said Oles Shevchenko, a former parliamentarian who organized a small protest outside the cabinet offices in downtown Kiev after the deal was signed. Only two hundred people turned up at the demonstration, reflecting public apathy about the deal as well as a growing acceptance that Ukraine's future, like its past, was inevitably tied to Russia. And there was another factor at play: though Kuchma was distrusted and widely disliked by ordinary Ukrainians, the same people looked east and admired the way Putin was restoring a sense of order in Moscow, which not long before had seemed as mired in the *bardak* (a term that actually means "brothel" but that Russians and Ukrainians alike use to describe chaos) as Kiev. Some polls suggested that were Putin allowed to stand in Ukraine's next presidential election, he'd win in a landslide.

The West, though, had not given up on the idea of pulling Ukraine out of Moscow's orbit, nor of re-reversing the Odessa-Brody flow. Their hopes, however, were pinned on the uninspiring former central banker Viktor Yushchenko. When I landed in Kiev shortly after the CES deal was signed, I met Yushchenko at the office of his Our Ukraine party in Kiev's bohemian Podil neighbourhood.

The CES, he told me, was a threat to Ukraine's sovereignty, giving Russia the final say in far too many matters. The next presidential elections, he foretold, would be "a good time for Ukraine to choose between East and West." Yushchenko, already by then identified as Ukraine's great democratic hope, had the monotone voice of an economics professor. As he droned on about the relative benefits and drawbacks of free trade with Russia, I started looking around the room, focusing first on the grandfather clock behind his chair, then on the gold telescope pointed out the window, then on an oversized Faberge egg in the corner. I thought to myself that this man couldn't hold the attention of a dinner party, let alone convince a nation of famously laid-back Ukrainians to follow him. Furthering our absent-minded professor impression, he'd left a button undone on his shirt that day, leaving my friend and translator Yuriy Shafarenko and me trying not to look at the exposed white belly of Ukraine's would-be president.

Faced with a slate of options that included a boring ex-banker, a president implicated in murder, a prime minister with a history of violent assault and Yulia Tymoshenko, the beautiful and fiery opposition leader who had allegedly made her fortune by illegally siphoning Russian gas, I could understand why some Ukrainians wanted to see Putin's name on the ballot.

The nightmare of Chechnya, however, continued to haunt Putin's efforts to rebuild both his state and his empire. On the streets of Kiev, opponents of Kuchma's eastward drift reminded Ukrainians of the potential costs of getting too close to the Kremlin. Anti-Kuchma youths slapped stickers featuring gory scenes from the war in Russia's south onto the sides of buildings. The bloodshed ate at Putin's already mixed reputation in the international community, and the war became a bigger symbol in the West of what Putin stood for than the domestic *stabilnost* he'd brought to Russia or his skilful pipeline diplomacy.

Putin knew it, too, though he saw no way out of it. He was notoriously quick to anger when asked about the subject, once seeming to threaten a French reporter with circumcision after the reporter prodded Putin about the war during a 2002 press conference in Paris. "If you are prepared to become the most radical Islamist and prepared to get circumcised, I invite you to Moscow . . . We have specialists that deal with this problem. I suggest that you do such an operation that nothing grows out of you again," Putin snarled at the reporter, who had asked why Russia was using land mines, as well as other tactics that kill and maim civilians, in what is supposed to be a war against "terrorists."

The war, which because of Kremlin-imposed restrictions on journalists travelling to the region often seemed forgotten, burst back into the world's consciousness on Wednesday, October 23, 2002, when a group of masked Chechen gunmen burst onto a Moscow stage during a showing of the hit Russian musical *Nord-Ost* and took the entire audience of eight hundred hostage. The Chechen war, which Putin had declared over several months earlier, had arrived back in the Russian capital, at the Dubrovka Theatre, a former Soviet House of Culture just five kilometres from the Kremlin gates.

At first, Vasselin Nedkov and the rest of the audience assumed the gunmen were part of the second act, which had just begun. *Nord-Ost* was set during the Second World War, and the Chechens in camouflage hardly seemed out of place. Then one of the men on stage let out a burst of gunfire from his Kalashnikov and reality sank in. The Chechens told audience members to remain in their seats with their hands behind their heads; they were now hostages until the Russian army completely withdrew from Chechnya. Nineteen "black widows"—Chechen women who had lost their husbands to the war—set themselves up around the theatre, each wearing a black niqab, or full-face veil, and a suicide-bomb belt.

The leader of the hostage-takers, Movsar Barayev, the twenty-five-year-old nephew of a ruthless Chechen commander named Arbi Barayev, who had been killed by Russian soldiers four months earlier, instructed his men to place land mines and explosives around the building. "I swear by God we are more keen on dying than you are keen on living," Barayev said in a video released to the press soon after the theatre was seized. "Each one of us is willing to sacrifice himself for the sake of God and the independence of Chechnya."

Nedkov, a thin man with short, cropped hair and a goatee, wound up spending much of the next fifty-seven hours staring at a fifty-kilogram bomb. The twenty-eight-year-old resident of Canada began to doubt he'd ever leave the theatre alive. "The women [hostage-takers] were shocking—some were just twenty-two or twenty-three years old," Nedkov said. "Their faces were empty and they were really willing to die. I've never seen anything like this anywhere."

For nearly three days, he and the other hostages subsisted on little but water and soft drinks from the concession stands, and even those ran low. Although the Chechens refused to bring in food from outside, occasionally they threw chocolates from the stage into the crowd. At night, the hostages slept in their seats with the lights burning overhead. Three times a day, they were taken in groups to the washrooms, where they were confronted with the sight of the bullet-riddled body of a young woman killed early in the ordeal. The rest of the time, they had to use the orchestra pit as a makeshift latrine.

Despite the militants' repeated threats to blow up the theatre, Nedkov said they were generally "quite friendly." He said he spoke with Barayev personally ten or fifteen times, acting as a representative of the seventy-one foreign hostages. But by early Saturday morning, he could sense the Chechens getting tense. They began taking up defensive positions around the theatre to prepare for a Russian attack they were increasingly sure was coming. Each held an automatic weapon in one hand and a grenade or detonator in the other.

"That's when we realized for sure that they were planning to kill us," Nedkov told me afterward, as he lay in his Moscow hospital bed. "They were about 1.5 seconds from blowing the whole place up. All they had to do was push the button."

But in those early hours of October 26, the militants' plans began to unravel. A young hostage named Pavel Zakharov suddenly threw a bottle at one of the militants, a move that snapped nerves in the tense atmosphere. Some of the male hostage-takers opened fire, killing two of their captives. From where I was standing outside the theatre in the gently falling snow, I heard the gunshots. I didn't know who had fired them, but I was certain the standoff would come to an end that night, for better or for worse.

Barayev, too, realized immediately that the shootings would give the Russians a reason to attack and perhaps turn international opinion even further against their cause. He started yelling at his men and dialled the International Red Cross, trying to explain that the shootings had been an accident and offering to release some hostages as a conciliatory gesture. He needn't have bothered. Russian special forces troops, who, unbeknownst to the Chechens, had been watching every move with fibre-optic cameras, took advantage of the chaos. A mysterious gas—later identified as being based on an aerosolized version of the anesthetic fentanyl—began pouring from the theatre's ventilation system. Some of the militants staggered to put on masks they had brought for exactly this situation, but most collapsed within seconds. So did almost all the hostages. Nedkov grabbed a handkerchief he had with him, dipped it in water and put it over his mouth and nose. He woke up in a hospital bed.

Not everyone was so lucky. Standing outside the theatre in the hours after the siege, I stared in horror as busloads of unconscious, slack-jawed former hostages were driven to hospital—some hurriedly piled on top of each other, some inexplicably stripped of their clothes. The raid had been carried out in such secrecy that the special forces hadn't notified the hospitals to be on standby; nor were doctors, even after the fact, told what gas had been used to render everyone unconscious. The commandos had accomplished a minor miracle: they'd killed all

41 hostage-takers before any of the explosives in the theatre could be detonated. But the gas also killed 129 hostages.

In the wake of the siege, I did something I had previously been loath to do: I took a Kremlin-organized tour of Chechnya in November 2002. Along with dozens of other Moscow-based foreign correspondents, I decided that a peek at what the war-ravaged republic looked like now, even a Kremlin-authorized peek, was better than leaving it completely in the shadows.

I had previously been to Kabul, where half the city still lies in ruins as a result of the reckless use of heavy weaponry by Afghan warlords who battled for control of the city after the Soviet pullout in 1989. But even that didn't prepare me for my first glimpse of Grozny, the Chechen capital. As we drove through what was once the city's downtown, I could not spot a single building that didn't bear the scars of heavy-weapons fire. Whole apartment blocks had been reduced to piles of smashed concrete and twisted metal. Those that still stood had gaping holes ripped through them, the result of tank rounds and missiles fired at people's domiciles. Several buildings had *zdiece lyudi zhivut!*— "people live here"—spray-painted on the walls, pleading reminders to Russian soldiers and Chechen rebels who had long since stopped worrying about such niceties as they continued their blood feud. Not one of the flats I saw in any of the buildings had an unbroken window, but laundry hung on the balconies and expressionless residents stared out from their destroyed homes at our passing convoy.

Smaller houses fared no better than the big apartment blocks—some had been cut in half as the war quite literally exploded into people's living rooms. Even telephone poles were pockmarked with bullet holes, a testament to the sheer number of rounds fired in the capital during nearly a decade of intermitent warfare. Half a million people once called the city home, but fewer than half that many were believed to remain. It certainly had nothing in common with the pleasant southern city with tree-lined boulevards I once came across in an old Soviet guidebook to the Caucasus region. *Grozny* means "terrible" in Russian, a name given to the city because the fort that originally stood here was meant to intimidate the Muslim rebels who resisted the czar's rule. Centuries on, the name still fit.

In this obliterated place, it was easy to find the hatred that had motivated Movsar Barayev and his band. To some here, the man himself
had become a hero for striking back in the heart of Russia; his name
was spray-painted on several buildings. This was not the Chechnya that
the Russian army wanted us to see, however. Instead of letting us choose
whom we wanted to interview, they gave us a ridiculous tour of the few
sites that, on the surface, fit their argument that the republic, now back
under firm Russian control, was rebuilding.

We met with Russian apparatchiks in the gleaming new administrative offices of the Russian-installed government, the only unscathed
building in all of Grozny until it was destroyed in a truck bombing a
month after we visited. We saw a bakery on the edge of town that had
never closed, even during the worst of the war. And we visited the
computer room of the city's only functioning university, though it had
no Internet access that day. At one point, we even received a press
release that informed us that "the situation is now normal" in
Chechnya. However, despite the presence of 80,000 Russian soldiers
in a republic slightly larger than the state of Maryland, the situation
was anything but.

Even as Major General Anatoly Kriachkov, the senior Russian commander in Grozny, explained to us all the progress made in tracking
down the last bands of rebels, a nearby explosion rattled the windows
of his office, though not Kriachkov's composure. He continued on until
a second, louder blast shook the ground. I instinctively ducked, but the
major general stood tall, obviously accustomed to such occurrences.

"What was that?" I asked him nervously. "I have no idea," he
replied, never letting the calm smile slip from his face. That night, as
the press bunked down in the relative security of the massive
Khankala Russian military base on the outskirts of Grozny—a
sprawling mini-city with billboards of a debonair-looking Vladimir
Putin watching over the soldiers—I sat listening to the sounds of
not-too-distant gunfire interspersed with small explosions. The
Interfax newswire later reported that three soldiers were killed by an
explosion in Grozny's central market. Eight more were killed in a
clash with rebels outside of the capital.

At the base, Colonel Boris Podoprigora, the assistant commander of
the Russian forces in the region, gave us a straighter answer than his

boss had. "When we speak of having all of Chechnya under control, we speak of the quantity of territory under control. But as for the quality of territory, that's another pair of shoes," he told us in flawless English inflected with a British accent.

The soldiers described the situation in rougher terms. When I stepped out of the barracks that night to call my editors on my satellite phone, I noticed a thin young recruit eying it eagerly. When I offered him the chance to call home, the soldier (his name was Sergei) literally leapt at the chance—he hadn't spoken to his parents in the four months he had been in Chechnya. He wasn't sure that his parents, in the far-away Siberian city of Omsk, even knew that he was there.

The phone call was heart-wrenching to listen to. After he told his father with a quivering upper lip that he was doing fine, his mother took over the phone, and tears started rolling down his face. "Don't cry, Mother," he said repeatedly. "It'll be all right." From several metres away, I could hear the sobs on the other end of the line.

Later, as I shared some vodka I'd brought on the trip with me, Sergei confessed that he was absolutely terrified every time he had to leave the base to go into Grozny with his unit. He was unsure of who was friend and who was foe, and unsure of where to put his feet in a place that by 2002 had more uncleared land mines than anyplace else in the world. "None of us wants to be here. It's not our war."

After almost two days of being led around by the nose by Colonel Podoprigora and our other minders, I was increasingly desperate to talk to some ordinary Chechens. Realizing that our Russian military guides were outnumbered by the number of foreign journalists they'd invited on the "Chechnya is fine!" package tour, I decided to take advantage of something that had been the bane of my existence since I first arrived in Moscow: that many Russians thought that my dark features and permanent five-o'clock shadow made me look a little like a Chechen.

During another inane visit, this one to a classroom of medical students who were about to graduate, I spotted my chance. As the other foreign journalists were escorted out of the room, I calmly sat down at an empty desk near the back. Quickly understanding what I was doing, two male students stood up so that it was difficult for the soldiers scanning the room to see the back corner where I was sitting. The ruse worked, and the students eagerly gathered to tell me stories they had been afraid to tell while the Russian officers were present.

Milana, a twenty-year-old medical student with long, dark hair and almond eyes that blazed with anger, told me in hushed English that we journalists were being lied to by our guides. Life in Grozny was not getting better, she told me, it was getting worse. The Russian military maintained a semblance of control during the day, but the night was filled with explosions and gunfire as the rebels conducted hit-and-run attacks on Russian checkpoints and planted fresh land mines. Some of the Chechens who cooperated with the Russians by day—even those who wore Russian-issued police uniforms—turned and fought against them after dusk. Terrified, the Russian conscripts got drunk and shot wildly into the shadows.

Milana said she had been working the night shift at Grozny's Hospital No. 4 just weeks before when a grim parade of dozens of maimed teenagers was whisked into the emergency room. Their school bus had been attacked, she claimed, hit by a shell fired by a Russian tank. "Some of them were missing their legs," Milana said, gritting her teeth at the memory. "The tank driver was just drunk."

"They are the terrorists, not us," she added, using a word that both sides bandy about with such ease that it has long since ceased to have any meaning. At Milana's urging, I headed upstairs into the adjoining hospital, hoping to meet with victims of the school bus attack. Worried that my deception would soon be discovered by our minders, I ducked into the first room full of patients I could find. There, instead of the bus victims, I met Fatima, a forty-eight-year-old woman in a head scarf who looked almost twice her age. Lying in her bed, suffering from dysentery, she was grateful for some surprise company and eager to tell a foreigner about the hell that her beloved Grozny had become.

Like many Chechens, Fatima had been born in exile in Kazakhstan, where Stalin had deported the entire Chechen people in 1944, accusing them en masse of collaborating with the Nazis during the Second World War. Her family moved back to Grozny only in 1956, after Khrushchev denounced Stalin in his closed-door "secret speech" to the 20th Congress of the Communist Party, but she nonetheless came to view the Soviet era as the best that Chechens had ever seen, at least compared to the wars that followed.

"Look at these buildings—our lives are like these buildings. Completely destroyed," she said, waving her hand at the scene out her window, a line of crumpled apartment blocks and fire-scorched stores. Her own home—"it was so beautiful," she told me sadly—had been destroyed twice during the fighting. Only one room now remained, which she shared with her husband, daughter and young grandchild. There was no electricity or running water, and the family had to light fires at night to stay warm.

Her nineteen-year-old son was in hiding, she said. Russian soldiers had won notoriety during the second Chechen war for what became known as *zachistki,* or "cleaning" operations, during which all the fighting-age Chechen males in an area would be rounded up for questioning. Many were never seen again, and Fatima was clearly terrified for her son. "It's a terrible life. There's nothing good about it," she said. Just then my frowning Russian guide finally caught up with me and sharply declared that it was time for me to leave the hospital.

The political chaos in Kiev and the bloodshed in Grozny were very different issues linked by two things. The first and most obvious was Putin's desire to restore Moscow's lost position of dominance over both the Ukrainians and the Chechens. The second was the West's quest for greater energy security, and in particular Washington's desire to ensure access to the oil and gas of the Caspian Sea and Central Asia while reducing the West's growing dependence on Russia's own hydrocarbons.

In Ukraine, the struggle to ensure a supply of energy to the West that didn't depend on Russian goodwill was reflected in the battle over which way the Odessa-Brody pipeline would flow, a battle the West temporarily lost when Kuchma reversed the pipeline's direction. Meanwhile, in the Caucasus, the ceaseless fighting in Chechnya helped convince Western investors to back a pipeline project that would take oil from the Caspian Sea to the Mediterranean via a difficult and expensive route across Azerbaijan, Georgia and Turkey, with the sole benefit of bypassing Russian territory altogether.

The Baku-Tbilisi-Ceyhan pipeline, as it would come to be known because of its route through those three cities, was a clear threat to the viability of Russia's own Caspian pipeline, which ran across Chechnya and southern Russia to the Black Sea port of Novorossiysk.

A month after construction began in September 2002, Foreign Minister Igor Ivanov warned that Russia "would not put up with attempts to crowd Russia out of regions in which we have historic interests." Understanding perfectly well that Western investors would desert the project if the South Caucasus looked likely to slide back into chaos, the Kremlin decided to show what kind of trouble it could cause.

SIX

A CAUCASIAN KNOT

Baku and Tbilisi

Back in November 1999, as Russian soldiers closed in on Grozny in the wake of the apartment bombings, U.S. president Bill Clinton travelled to Istanbul for a meeting with three regional heads of state: Georgian president Eduard Shevardnadze, Turkish president Süleyman Demirel and Azerbaijan's president, Heydar Aliev. The meeting received scant attention outside the business pages at the time, but the four men forged an agreement that was to alter the geopolitical map of the region for decades to come. They would build a pipeline to transport Caspian Sea crude oil across the territories of Azerbaijan, Georgia and Turkey to the Mediterranean Sea port of Ceyhan.

The Baku-Tbilisi-Ceyhan, or BTC, pipeline was to be the world's longest and, by the time it finally came online in 2005, the most expensive ever built. The agreement Clinton presided over was a portentious one. Since the pipeline was intended to cut Russia out of the burgeoning Caspian oil game, the $3.6 billion project put Washington's and Moscow's interests in the Caucasus irrevocably on a collision course.

Though Georgia would receive just 43 cents on every barrel of oil that flowed across its territory (the Turkish government would get $1.50), the Georgian government was thrilled with its end of the deal. Tbilisi had come to see the U.S. as the sole guarantor of its sovereignty against Russia, and the pipeline provided assurance that the Georgia file would never slip entirely off desks at the U.S. State Department.

After an initially halting start—and talk that investors would never back a project that required stability in the notoriously unstable South Caucasus—the project picked up steam as the U.S. scrambled post-9/11 to find alternatives to oil from the Middle East. Vice President Dick Cheney named the Caspian Sea oil a "vital strategic interest" to America, and construction of the BTC pipeline finally began in September 2002.[1]

The project also had the backing of Shevardnadze's old friend James Baker (the pair had developed a close friendship as they negotiated the end of the Cold War). Following his stint as the first President Bush's top diplomat, Baker returned to a lucrative law career that saw him emerge as a key player in the Caspian oil game. He headed an all-star cast of Washington insiders with the political heft to ensure that Baku-Tbilisi-Ceyhan could never fail. Among the other American bigwigs with a toe in the Caspian oil business were Brent Scowcroft, Bush Sr.'s national security adviser; John Sununu, Bush Sr.'s chief of staff; and Zbigniew Brzezinski, Jimmy Carter's national security adviser.

The Kremlin naturally viewed Baku-Tbilisi-Ceyhan as a threat to the viability of the existing Novorossiysk pipeline, which for decades had carried Caspian oil to the Russian port on the Black Sea, and Moscow made its displeasure plain. The Kremlin was even less enthralled when Shevardnadze invited 500 American soldiers into his country to train the Georgian army in counter-terrorism. "Putin perceives that Russian weakness in the post-Soviet space will result in others trying to fill that vacuum," a Moscow-based Western diplomat told me as we drank coffee and watched the passing show on the Arbat. "Russia and the U.S. keep saying that everyone's getting along, but underlying that is a real rivalry."

When Eduard Shevardnadze handed in his resignation as foreign minister of the USSR on December 20, 1990, he thought he was quitting high-level politics for good. He was already sixty-one years old, and he didn't like the direction the Soviet Union was heading as the hardline old guard was assuming more and more power in Gorbachev's Politburo. "Boys in colonels' epaulettes are pushing the country to dictatorship," he said in a nationally televised speech. That same day, after a lifetime of membership, he quit the Communist Party.

Eight months later, history proved him correct: Gorbachev's vice president, along with his defence minister, his interior minister and the head of the KGB, set in motion a putsch that saw tanks on the streets of Moscow. The coup failed when Boris Yeltsin rallied his supporters to defend the Moscow White House, and soon afterward Shevardnadze was back as foreign minister, in November 1991, to oversee the final breakup of the Soviet Union a month later. With that done, Shevardnadze figured he was headed for a quiet, distinguished retirement. But this second break from high-level politics lasted less than a month before he was called on to resolve an emerging crisis in his native Georgia.

During Soviet times, fertile and mountainous Georgia had one of the highest per capita standards of living in the USSR. Thanks to its reputation as both the playground and the vineyard of the union, Soviet citizens flocked there on vacation, basked on its sunny Black Sea coast and drank its famously full-bodied red wines.

Georgians are a fiercely independent people who still treasure the legend of their eleventh-century king, David II, who united the country's regions and raised an army that drove out the combined (and numerically superior) Turkish and Persian forces. Home to just 5.4 million of the Soviet Union's 280 million plus citizens, Georgia produced three of the most prominent figures in the country's history. One was Shevardnadze; the others were Iosif Vissarionovich Dzhugashvili, better known to the world as Joseph Stalin, who was born in the ancient city of Gori in 1888, and his murderous henchman Laventry Beria.

Georgia's famously hospitable people are also notoriously hot-blooded. Excited by the freedoms gained under Gorbachev's glasnost, Georgians were among the first to assert their reborn nationalism, leading to a series of demonstrations in Tbilisi that culminated in April 1989 when the Red Army opened fire on protestors, killing twenty-one people in one of the bloodiest episodes in the Soviet Union's slow-motion implosion.

The fledgling modern state had the messiest of beginnings; a full-blown civil war killed two hundred people before the United Nations even recognized Georgia as an independent state. The country's first elected leader, Zviad Gamsakhurdia, was driven into exile in Armenia after his forces lost the civil war. By early 1992, Georgia had an economy crippled by conflict, a capital in the hands of armed rebels and no functioning government. That's when the appeal for help went out to Shevardnadze, who returned in March of that year—promising that Western aid and investment would follow him—to cheering crowds at the Tbilisi airport.

Though many Georgians harboured bitter memories of Shevardnadze's years as Communist Party boss, they knew he had clout and respect in the West, and they were desperate to believe him. By the end of the month, Shevardnadze had been made interim head of state, a step so reassuring to the United States that President George Bush responded almost immediately by establishing full diplomatic ties between the two countries. Within weeks, the U.S. embassy officially opened in Tbilisi.

A month later, Secretary of State James Baker was in Tbilisi to lend his support as well. "This is a difficult road," Shevardnadze said at Tbilisi airport on Baker's arrival, referring to Georgia's fledgling experiment with democracy. "But we will never turn away from this road because we have such good friends as Mr. Baker and such strong friends as the United States." Soon tiny Georgia was receiving hundreds of millions of dollars in annual aid from the State Department, enough to make it the second largest per capita recipient of U.S. aid in the world, behind only Israel.

Just as quick off the mark was George Soros, who had first met Shevardnadze over cocktails in a Moscow hotel in 1988 to talk about what Soviet society might look like after glasnost and perestroika. At Shevardnadze's invitation to help turn Georgia around, Soros set up a Tbilisi branch of the Open Society Foundation in 1994. Shevardnadze told Georgian radio that Soros had mused that Georgia might be a ripe testing ground for certain "experiments." What Soros had hoped for in Georgia was rapid implementation of the structural reforms called for by the International Monetary Fund. Driven by his belief in the power and effectiveness of free markets, he thought that tiny Georgia, with all its resources—and with Shevardnadze's leadership—could be the economic "tiger" of the former Soviet Union, the model state that lit the path for the others to follow. He poured money into independent media and civil society groups like the Georgian Young Lawyers' Association.[2]

Shevardnadze, at least in the beginning, understood that corruption was the state's greatest problem, and shortly after returning in 1992 he went on a talent hunt that soon attracted a trio of up-and-coming young Georgians to his side: Zurab Zhvania, Nino Burjanadze and Mikhail Saakashvili. Saakashvili, who was only twenty-six at the time and fresh out of Columbia Law School, later recalled being approached by Zhvania at his Manhattan law office and being told that Shevardnadze was looking to surround himself with talented, idealistic young Georgians with no ties to the country's Communist past. Saakashvili, who ten years later still bubbles with boyish enthusiasm about his country, was flattered. By 1995 both he and Zhvania were in Parliament, and three years later Zhvania was parliamentary Speaker and Saakashvili was head of a powerful committee charged with tackling corruption.

But Shevardnadze, back in his native Caucasus, was not the reformer Soros and Saakashvili had believed him to be. The Silver Fox, as he was dubbed by the Western press during the Cold War, saw the region the same way all Soviet leaders had: as a tinderbox of ethnic and religious divisions that had to be cautiously managed. The country was a basket case, battered by years of Soviet decline and post-Soviet conflict and plagued by electricity outages, food shortages and uncontrolled crime. Armed gangs roamed the streets, gunfire was a regular feature of a Tbilisi night and the country was on the verge of splitting along its many ethnic seams. Tribalism, Shevardnadze understood, still played a dominant role in the region, and sometimes deals had to be cut with unsavoury characters—warlords, criminals and corrupt local officials, not to mention whoever held sway in the Kremlin—in order to keep the peace. Naturally, those deals undermined the "civil society" Soros had committed himself to building.

In June 1992, Shevardnadze had negotiated an end to three years of off-and-on fighting in South Ossetia, a province that wanted to join with its ethnic Ossetian kin north of the border in Russia. The cost Shevardnadze paid was to grant South Ossetia de facto independence— something that would come back to haunt him, as it guaranteed a lingering Russian influence over one of Georgia's regions. Shevardnadze would also order troops into the capital of the coastal province of Abkhazia when it, too, declared independence, only to see the Abkhaz leader, Vladislav Ardzinba, granted refuge on a Soviet-era military base that Russia still maintained on Georgian soil.

Georgia's troubles with its old colonial master were just beginning. The Kremlin had quickly grown disenchanted with Shevardnadze's rapid moves to orient his country toward the West. Though Yeltsin's nationalism and desire to see Russia regain its great-power status were later to pale in comparison to Putin's, Yeltsin nonetheless conceived of the Commonwealth of Independent States as a means of maintaining Russia's influence over its old colonies, and Georgia was the only former Soviet republic (except the three Baltic republics, which even the most calcified cold warriors in Moscow were forced to concede were long gone) that had not joined. As Shevardnadze wined and dined Bush and Baker and spoke of Georgia one day joining NATO, the Kremlin decided to remind him of the *realpolitik* of the region.

In September, Ardzinba's forces mounted a fierce counterattack and, within a year, drove the Georgian army, along with the region's entire Georgian population—some 250,000 people—out of Abkhazia. Shevardnadze's new enemies in Moscow sent soldiers to help Ardzinba's cause. Abkhaz troops, with the support of followers of former leader Gamsakhurdia, then marched on Tbilisi. With his own forces disorganized and in disarray, Shevardnadze was forced to call on Russia to act as a peacemaker.

Russian troops switched sides and rapidly put down the insurgency, and Gamsakhurdia was later found dead. But the price was high: Shevardnadze was forced to bring Georgia into the CIS and to allow Russia to maintain two Soviet-era military bases in the country, seemingly locking the country back into Russia's orbit for the foreseeable future.[3]

"Unfortunately, the politics of the Kremlin was always the politics of empire," Shevardnadze told me later. "Who gave them the right to go to Abkhazia and conquer it? But they had lost the Baltics, they had lost their main base in the Crimea at Odessa, so the minister of defence, [Pavel] Grachev, decided that they could not give up Abkhazia or they would lose the Black Sea as well." He sat back in his green leather chair, shaking his head slowly. "Russia put itself to shame."

As the Airzena Boeing 737 crossed over the snow-capped Caucasus Mountains on my first visit to Georgia in September 2002, I could see why the Kremlin was reluctant to let go of the place. In contrast to the long, dull, rolling plains of its giant neighbour to the north, Georgia is a veritable Eden. The inhospitable mountains with their winding traders' trails give way to lush vegetation—vineyards, tea plantations, citrus groves—all of which are scarce across the rest of the former Soviet space. To the west stretches the curvaceous and inviting Black Sea coast. In the centre sits the historic capital city of Tbilisi, with its centuries-old churches and with Mother Georgia—a massive statue of a woman with a bowl in one hand for guests and a sword in the other for invaders—overseeing it all.

The runway at Tbilisi International Airport is cracked and uneven, making landing there an unnerving experience for even the most blasé of fliers. Inevitably, the back wheels touch down only briefly before they're jolted back into the sky. The plane settles more gently on the second touch, and the passengers drown out the sound of the aircraft braking to a halt with loud, grateful applause. It's a habit that people all over the former Soviet Union have in common from their shared history. Locals say it's because they're happy to be home. Foreigners joke that after several hours on an aged Ilyushin or Tupolev, everyone's just happy to be alive.

Even before I cleared customs, touts approached offering me a ride into town, hoping to get agreement on a price before I stepped outside into the waiting mob of taxi drivers and the bidding began in earnest. Then I was stuffed with my luggage into a battered Lada and we headed along the cratered Kakheti Highway toward the city centre.

Downtown Tbilisi was dark at night. Though the grand buildings of the city centre recalled Old Europe, or at least czarist Russia, the lack of working street lights reminded me of the slums of South Africa, where the dark corners everywhere fed the imagination and made harmless alleyways look like threatening hideouts for criminals. As in Africa, Georgia's lack of lighting was a symptom of crushing poverty. To reach the Villa Mtiebi in Tbilisi's Old City, I had to walk under a two-storey building that leaned over the narrow street at a 65-degree angle to the ground, a remnant from the 1988 earthquake that shook neighbouring Armenia. Someone had wedged a ten-metre iron bar under it, and so it somehow stayed, a metaphor for a country on the verge of collapse.

On that first visit, I remember looking out the window and trying to figure out whether I'd landed in the Second World or the Third World. Before I reached a conclusion, the driver interrupted my thoughts.

"Where are you from?" he asked. I told him I was Canadian but was now living in Moscow. "You live in Moscow?" he said in a tone that indicated sympathy for my plight. He asked how life was there. I told him that yes, I liked living in Moscow, and no, I didn't think all Russian people were cold-natured. He was unswayed.

"Tbilisi—better," he said with a nod of his head and a thumbs-up signal he must have learned from watching American television. He went on to name all the ways in which his city exceeded the Russian capital. It was a long list: better food, better weather, nicer people. I laughed. If attitude accounted for anything, Georgia was Second World with a bullet.

But the undampened cheerfulness of its residents—at least when you weren't talking politics—couldn't cover up the dire problems that the country faced. Ten years into Shevardnadze's presidency, Georgia had barely recovered from the traumas of the early 1990s and remained plagued by many of the same problems, inherited from Gamsakhurdia.

Chief among these was corruption. As in most post-Soviet states, the police force was more an extension of the criminal system than an obstacle to it. Baton-wielding policemen pulled cars over at random to extract booty from the passengers. You didn't need to be speeding or committing any other offence to attract the attentions of the *militsia*. You just had to be one of the unlucky ones randomly chosen to top up the officer's salary that day.

The lingering corruption, along with Shevardnadze's apparent unwillingness to deal with it, frustrated Mikhail Saakashvili, now the justice minister, to the point of quitting. He realized that the Silver Fox, his old idol, either would not or could not make the tough decisions that the young reformers believed were necessary to save the country.

Soros, too, eventually went from pouring money into the government's anti-corruption drive to openly criticizing the regime and shifting his money into media and civil society groups opposed to the Shevardnadze regime. Most prominent of these was the Rustavi 2 television station, which broadcast a popular cartoon called *Our Yard* that portrayed President Shevardnadze as a crooked double-dealer. Rustavi 2 would become Soros's new B92, the "independent" anti-regime station that he would unquestioningly back, even as it became more and more partisan toward Mikhail Saakashvili.

As Saakashvili drifted further and further away from Shevardnadze, Rustavi 2 showed the renegade justice minister brandishing photographs of the palatial homes of some of his cabinet colleagues—proof, he said, that they were corrupt. The stunt struck a nerve with the country's struggling lower classes and immediately made Saakashvili the most popular politician in Georgia. By September 2001, he had quit his post and become the face of the opposition.

Zhvania, a round-faced man with dark, Danny DeVito–like features and a receding hairline that made him seem older than his thirty-nine years, had been at the president's side since 1992. Long considered the heir apparent to Shevardnadze, he made a gut-wrenching decision over the corruption that he called "endemic" in the country and quit his post as Speaker of Parliament. "It became clear that our resources to push for progress and democratic development from within government were limited," he told me a year later. "Shevardnadze was constantly trying to balance between the reformers and the retrogrades around him."

In the fall of 2001, Shevardnadze's carefully assembled coalition of young reformers and ex-Communists began to split along predictable ideological lines. The president cast his lot with the old guard. The decision might have been made partly out of fear: while Zhvania and Saakashvili had portfolios like justice minister and parliamentary chairman, the ex-Party types retained what Russians call the "power ministries": defence and the interior. Shevardnadze, the cautious deal-maker, knew that taking on the old guard could have provoked a coup.

In an effort to re-establish top-down authority, Shevardnadze made a second ill-advised decision that autumn and ordered the closure of Rustavi 2. By then, the station had become the most popular and most trusted channel in Tbilisi. Shutting it down struck free-spirited Georgians as a disturbing reminder of the old days, and they came out in the thousands to defend the channel. Shevardnadze eventually relented.

The anger in the streets that fall—not just over Rustavi, but over the general state of affairs in the country—nearly spilled over into an uprising. "We didn't have the forces then to complete the process. We lacked organization," said Levan Ramishvili, a former Rustavi 2 journalist who had co-founded the Liberty Institute, a pro-democracy NGO, after a previous crackdown on the station five years earlier. But the anger and the passion for change were there, he said.

The organizational skills the anti-Shevardnadze opposition lacked soon came to them. The split in Tbilisi forced George Soros and other sponsors to decide between the two rival camps. Realizing that the aging Shevardnadze could not rule forever, they cautiously backed Saakashvili and Zhvania. "I think he gave up [on Shevardnadze] because of Mr. Shevardnadze's failure to address corruption," said Laura Silber, the philanthropist's senior policy adviser, who described Georgia as "ripe" for change in 2003.

"[Soros] came to the realization that Shevardnadze was just not fighting corruption, and that was the single biggest problem dogging Georgia at that point . . . I think he believed that Shevardnadze's time coming to an end would be best for Georgia, and that Saakashvili and Zhvania represented the more democratic, modern alternative."

In February 2002, the National Democratic Institute flew a group of opposition figures, led by Saakashvili, to Washington to meet with White House officials (including Deputy Defence Secretary Paul Wolfowitz) and Soros. Saakashvili returned ebullient, claiming that the U.S. was throwing its support behind the opposition. "It is felt that the USA is disappointed with President Shevardnadze and Georgia on the whole," Saakashvili said on his return. "The Americans frequently term Georgia 'a failed state' and criticize the Georgian authorities for corruption prospering." He claimed to have been told that the U.S. was ready to "assist" Georgia in building civil society and holding elections and in defence matters.[4]

"The U.S. invested a lot of hope and resources into this country," said Alexander Lomaia, the head of Open Society–Georgia at the time. "I think there was a feeling of disillusionment, the same thing that we were feeling too." Balding and with a striking resemblance to Kelsey Grammer of *Frasier* fame, Lomaia was one of the first to embrace the idea of replicating Serbia's revolution in Georgia. "It became very clear that [the 2003 election] was probably the last chance for us to prove to ourselves and to the outside world that we believed in democracy and that we deserved democracy."

With the Baku-Tbilisi-Ceyhan pipeline in its sights, the U.S. moved quickly to consolidate its influence in Georgia, the most unstable of the countries the "energy corridor" would pass through. In May 2002, the Pentagon sent five hundred soldiers to Georgia to train the Georgian army (something Russia was theoretically supposed to be doing) and poured $64 million into new uniforms and equipment for the ragtag force. Shevardnadze hailed the U.S. boots on the ground as "a very important factor for strengthening and developing Georgian statehood."

While Putin said the arrival of U.S. troops in Georgia was "no tragedy" for Russia, Deputy Defence Minister Alexander Kosovan said the deployment "should worry every Russian soldier," revealing how the country's establishment really viewed the move. Many in Moscow believed that the Americans were there not so much to give the Georgian army "anti-terrorist training" as to protect Baku-Tbilisi-Ceyhan.

The Kremlin soon made its displeasure clear. Shortly after the five hundred American soldiers arrived in Georgia, a shepherd named Guram Otiashvili was killed in a Russian bombing raid on Georgian soil.

Zaza and Guram Otiashvili, along with six other men, had set out in a convoy of cars before sunrise that August morning, looking for firewood to bring back to their village in the wooded hills of the Pankisi Gorge. Zaza, a thirty-two-year-old craftsman, remembers seeing a bright flash that lit the still-dull morning sky, followed by a succession of explosions that convinced the drivers to pull their cars over to the side of the road. As the bomb blasts got closer, the men deserted their cars and ran for the nearby forest.

Zaza remembers nothing about the next ten minutes, only that when he came to, his car was nothing more than a pile of super-heated scrap metal and that sixty-seven-year-old Guram, whom Zaza knew as "Grandfather" despite their being more distantly related, was dead. Zaza himself was bleeding from shrapnel wounds that covered everything but his face and chest. With the other survivors, wounded and dazed, he hid in the forest until daybreak before making his way back to Pankisi.

None of the injured men had any doubt that their convoy had been the unlucky target of a Russian air raid, an occasional occurrence in Pankisi. The Kremlin had long claimed Chechen rebels were using the gorge as a rear base to recuperate and rearm before crossing the mountains back into Chechnya to continue the fight. But Otiashvili wasn't convinced that this was just about the few militants he acknowledged were hiding among the Chechen refugees in the Gorge.[5]

"They say the reason is the Chechens, but when they are gone, Russia will find another reason to attack Georgia," he said as we lunched on Turkish coffee and *khachapuri,* a traditional Georgian cheese-bread, at a café in Akhmeta, a town on the lip of Pankisi. He had trouble hearing me, an after-effect of the bombing. "Russia just wants to control Georgia. This war will continue even when there are no more Chechens."

As the fall of 2002 progressed, the U.S. laid out its wobbly case for invading Iraq—and Russia did the same with Georgia. Largely unnoticed by the Western media, the Kremlin mirrored the U.S. strategy, complaining to the UN Security Council that Georgia was a hotbed of terrorism, at one point equating Shevardnadze's government with the forcibly deposed Taliban regime in Afghanistan. Step by step, a case for war—or at least for an invasion of Pankisi—was prepared, with Putin going so far as to write a letter to Kofi Annan on September 12, 2002, arguing that Russian military action against Georgia would be a matter of self-defence. The Georgian government, he wrote, had committed a "grievous failure" by not complying with UN resolutions to combat terrorism; unless Georgia moved against the Chechens hiding in Pankisi, Russia could invoke its right to self-defence under Article 51 of the UN Charter. Acting "strictly under international law," he wrote, "Russia would take adequate measures to oppose the terrorist threat."

Shevardnadze, who was in Moscow when the Soviet Union used the cover of the first Gulf war to carry out a bloody crackdown on dissent in Lithuania in 1991, knew the foreign media would be distracted by the sight of American bombers flattening Baghdad. He saw the danger he was facing and hastened to make peace with Putin a few weeks later, at a CIS summit in Moldova. When he returned to Tbilisi, he spoke of a "breakthrough" in Georgian–Russian relations: "We have again been convinced, probably once and for all, that relations between Georgia and Russia are a very important factor for Georgia's independence. As you can imagine, if this meeting had not taken place or if our obligations were not fulfilled, Georgia would be without gas, oil and electricity. It would be a bitter winter, accompanied by many unpleasant things. [Putin] said clearly that there would be no talk of economic sanctions if we honoured our obligations to each other."[6]

It's unclear to what Shevardnadze, the man with the gun to his head, and Putin, the man holding it, agreed at that meeting, but a deal was clearly struck, and Georgia's attitude to Russia changed markedly in the following months. Instead of denying that there were Chechen fighters holed up in the Pankisi Gorge, as he had for years, Shevardnadze bowed to the Kremlin and sent crack Interior Ministry troops in to sweep the area. And in the months that followed, he seemed to turn his back on his friends in Washington who had done so much for him.

Shevardnadze, once wary of any Russian investment in Georgia's "strategic" industries—specifically electricity, oil and communications—was suddenly rolling out the red carpet for Russian firms. He allowed Gazprom to buy up Georgia's internal pipeline network. Then he presided over the signing of a twenty-five-year deal to make Gazprom the country's sole supplier of natural gas. It was a difficult move—handing over the keys to the country's energy supplies to a country that had less than a year earlier been threatening to invade it. It also meant that Gazprom could now supply the Turkish market with gas, weakening the demand for Caspian supplies and threatening the economic viability of a separate U.S.-backed gas pipeline that was in the works to take gas from Azerbaijan's Shah Deniz gas field across the South Caucasus to market.

While the Gazprom deal on its own made analysts in Washington anxious, it was likely Shevardnadze's next step that convinced many at the State Department that their old friend had defected to the Kremlin camp. In July, under murky circumstances, the American firm AES-Telasi sold Tbilisi's energy grid, at rock-bottom price, to the Russian electricity monopoly, RAO-UES. The sale took place shortly after AES's chief financial officer, Nika Lominadze, was found dead in his parents'

Tbilisi home with his hands and feet bound, killed by a single execution-style bullet to the head. AES said they thought the murder was related to the company's activities, and their sale of the grid to RAO-UES followed within a year.

News of the murder and the subsequent sale touched off nationalist protests in Tbilisi, and the White House quickly fired off a statement expressing its displeasure. RAO-UES was headed by ex-Yeltsin confidant and self-described "liberal-imperialist" Anatoly Chubais, but that wasn't what concerned Washington most. The White House had backed AES's investment as part of its strategy to guarantee the security of Baku-Tbilisi-Ceyhan. Now that was in jeopardy.

Soon after the deal, Gazprom CEO Alexei Miller asked the Georgian government to divert gas from Shah Deniz to a planned Russian pipeline that would run under the Black Sea to Turkey. Washington was up in arms at the very idea. President Bush dispatched his senior adviser for Caspian energy issues, Steven Mann, to Tbilisi with a warning for Shevardnadze: "Georgia should not do anything that undercuts the powerful promise of an East-West energy corridor."

Shevardnadze replied that Georgia's energy integration with Russia "will not stop. It will develop and deepen." He told Mann that he thought a north-south energy corridor could coexist with an east-west one. Momentously, Shevardnadze would later name Vazha Lordkipanidze, a former ambassador to Moscow, to lead his For a New Georgia bloc into the 2003 parliamentary elections.

It was not what the White House wanted to hear.

The appointment of Richard Miles as U.S. ambassador to Georgia in early 2002 should have been enough to warn Shevardnadze that the ground was shifting beneath his feet. Miles, already known for his role in the toppling of Milošević, made his intentions clear even before he arrived in Tbilisi. At his Senate confirmation hearings, Miles noted that Georgia was entering a "crucial period" of preparing for life after Shevardnadze, and in early 2003 he went to work making sure that life after Shevardnadze would look the way Washington, not Moscow, desired. First, he pronounced the United States deeply interested in Georgia's parliamentary elections, scheduled for that fall, and made a public display of meeting with Zhvania and other opposition leaders.

In an interview with Rustavi 2, Miles said the U.S. was worried the coming vote might not be "free and fair," exhibiting a concern for local democracy he had shown in Belgrade but never while serving in Azerbaijan during the early 1990s, where he watched as Heydar Aliev built his quasi-dictatorship. Miles said "the entire international community" was concerned that Georgia become a full-fledged democracy, and he made it clear he was already knee-deep in the process of getting it there.[7] "I am in touch with representatives of almost all political parties and factions. Hardly a day goes by without my having some kind of a meeting with some political figure in Georgia, because my government is interested in this process," Miles said. "If these elections are not conducted in an open and honest and transparent manner, that would be very bad for Georgia. Frankly, that would also be bad for the American-Georgian relationship and we do not want to see that happen."

Soros's activities in Georgia were also escalating. The initial attack was spearheaded by the Liberty Institute, a prominent Soros-backed NGO, which began a campaign in the Western press to undermine Shevardnadze's image as a hero of democracy and to instead portray his government, with substantial evidence, as a regime that was corrupt and backsliding on human rights. Coming as it did from the Liberty Institute, this was seen as a personal attack by the billionaire financier.

In 2002, days after the Liberty Institute's Levan Ramishvili told the *Christian Science Monitor* that Shevardnadze's pretences of reform had "fooled" Europe, thugs trashed the NGO's Tbilisi offices, beating several employees in the process. Soros responded by suggesting during a news conference in Moscow that Shevardnadze's government could not be trusted to hold a proper parliamentary election in 2003: "It is necessary to mobilize civil society in order to assure free and fair elections because there are many forces that are determined to falsify or to prevent the elections being free and fair. This is what we did in Slovakia at the time of Mečiar, in Croatia at the time of Tudjman and in Yugoslavia at the time of Milošević."

A few months later, Soros provocatively named Saakashvili and Zhvania, by now both in loud opposition to Shevardnadze, the joint winners of his international Open Society Prize, which he personally awarded them at a ceremony in June 2002 at the Central European University he had founded (and funded) in Budapest. Members of the

Liberty Institute would later run for parliament as candidates for Saakashvili's newly formed National Movement.

Contacts between Georgia's aspiring revolutionaries and those who had defeated Milošević had begun shortly after the Serbian strongman's ouster; the head of Open Society–Serbia, doing a favour for a colleague in Tbilisi, put in a call to Mike Staresinic, Freedom House's man in Belgrade. Staresinic put the Georgians in contact with Otpor. "The people from Soros here [Belgrade] came to us and said, 'We would like you to go to Tbilisi, there are kids there who want to learn about your experience,'" recalled Otpor veteran Ivan Marovic. "We thought, 'Where the hell is Tbilisi?'"

In November, Marko Blagojevic, the head of the Serbian election-monitoring group Citizens for Free Elections and Democracy (CeSID), which had used parallel vote tabulations to such great effect in exposing Milošević's attempts at fraud, travelled to the Georgian capital to meet with a similar fledgling organization called the International Society for Fair Elections and Democracy. It, too, was getting help from NDI and Soros, and, like CeSID, it had a mandate: find the fraud and expose it.

Like Milošević's, Shevardnadze's crumbling regime was sure to deliver the goods if anyone went looking. Trained by experience, the ex-Communist officials would fix the election figures without being told. It was a common phenomenon across the entire former Soviet Union, one Gleb Pavlovsky and his fellow spin doctors had encouraged and helped spread. In the face of Western pressure, you could hold a vote without offering real choice, and you could allow private companies to own televisions and newspapers, so long as they knew what red lines not to cross.

As the old man himself was always careful to note, Georgians enjoyed a more dynamic democracy than did Putin's Russia or the neighbouring regimes of Robert Kocharian's Armenia and the Aliev dynasty in Azerbaijan. As evidenced by Rustavi 2 and a host of anti-government newspapers, the press was freer, too. Freedom House rated Georgia as "partly free," putting it ahead of all the other former Soviet republics except the Baltic states. Ironically, if Georgia had been led by Putin, Kocharian or Aliev instead of Shevardnadze, the young reformers would never have had such freedom to operate.

Two of Otpor's travelling revolutionaries, Slobodan Djinovic and Alexander Maric, accompanied the Serbian election-monitoring specialist Blagojevic on the four-day trip to Tbilisi. Open Society paid their way. The intense, bespectacled Blagojevic said that when he arrived in Georgia, he immediately understood that the Serbs had something to offer their hosts. "Their spirit was great. I've been in other big towns in different countries . . . I met with many people from the civil sector, but Georgia was the first time I saw something similar to what we had in Serbia prior to the 2000 elections."

Blagojevic, Djinovic and Maric returned repeatedly to Georgia over the next twelve months, meeting with Levan Ramishvili and others in the high-ceilinged converted loft that was the Tbilisi headquarters of the Liberty Institute. There they created Kmara (Georgian for "enough"), a youth movement modelled on Otpor and just as dedicated to regime change. By this point, just as in Serbia, NDI was deeply involved in trying to unite the opposition around a single figure. The favourite of Tbilisi's Westernized intelligentsia was Zhvania, who was seen as more mature and less egotistical than the brash Saakashvili. But Zhvania had two big strikes against him, at least in the eyes of Georgia's conservative, nationalistic electorate: he was Armenian-born and he was rumoured to be gay. Burjanadze was seen as too close to Shevardnadze, so it had to be Saakashvili.

Georgia's opposition now had a charismatic leader to rally around, as well as their B92 equivalent in Rustavi 2 (staff at both stations had received training from Internews, a regular grantee of the Open Society Institute). With the election-monitoring NGO receiving cash from NDI, Soros and the Eurasia Foundation, and with Kmara now up and going thanks to a $350,000 start-up grant from Soros, the revolution-makers were fully geared up for a rerun of Belgrade.

Throughout the lead-up to the election, Open Society tried to keep Kmara at arm's length, but this was a farce. Kmara and the Liberty Institute shared an office and were, as Ramishvili told me later, virtually indistinguishable from each other. "Georgia is an example of where we established contact [with Kmara] through a very dynamic international NGO that was the only one that cared about Georgia," said Otpor's Marovic "Georgia was lucky it had Soros."[8]

Tinatin Khidasheli, who as the head of the Georgian Young Lawyers' Association was on the receiving end of Soros's largesse and who later would see the inner workings of Open Society as the head of its Georgia office, said the groundwork for the uprising was laid with the billionaire's knowledge. "George knows, of course he knows," she told me a few years later. "Generally speaking he knows everything that the foundation is doing. The foundation here is a Georgian NGO but it is . . . almost 100 per cent funded by the New York office. They approve our strategies and our action plan, so of course George knew basically everything what we were doing. We don't tell them, 'Today I do this, tomorrow I do that,' but yeah, he knew."

Soros waffled on his foundation's role in what was happening across Eastern Europe, sometimes denying that it played any part and other times brashly taking credit. "My foundations contributed to democratic regime change in Slovakia in 1998, Croatia in 1999, and Yugoslavia in 2000, mobilizing civil society to get rid of Vladimir Meciar, Franjo Tudjman, and Slobodan Milosevic, respectively," he wrote in his 2004 book, *The Bubble of American Supremacy.* He went on to describe the precise role he saw his foundations and the NGOs they supported as playing: "Working with the government may be more productive, but working in countries whose government is hostile may be even more rewarding . . . In such countries, it is important to support civil society to keep the flame of freedom alive. By resisting government interference, the foundation may be able to alert the population that the government is abusing its authority."[9]

Laura Silber, a former *Financial Times* journalist in the Balkans who in 2000 became a senior policy adviser to Soros, told me that the billionaire took a special interest in those countries that were trying to stand up to the Kremlin's aggression. "I think that came from growing up and having the childhood that he did and surviving on his wits and his father's wits," she said at the Soros Foundation's New York headquarters. "He likes the little countries . . . he likes the plucky countries like Georgia and Ukraine, which is not a tiny country, except vis-à-vis Russia. I think he likes the underdog."

In May 2003, three weeks before he stood alongside Shevardnadze at a ceremony marking the beginning of work on the Baku-Tbilisi-Ceyhan pipeline on Georgian soil, Richard Miles joined British ambassador Deborah Barnes-Jones in a press conference to express their displeasure with preparations for that fall's vote. They placed the responsibility for the success or failure of the polls on Shevardnadze—even though two years remained in his presidential term and he wasn't a direct participant in the parliamentary race. Shevardnadze's old friend Baker added a final warning. Though he spoke all along of his affection for his old Cold War dance partner, Baker's first meeting upon landing in Tbilisi that July was not with Shevardnadze but with the leaders of the opposition, primarily Saakashvili. The young reformer came away from the encounter triumphant, again convinced that he had the world's only superpower behind him. Baker, Saakashvili said, had come to Tbilisi "to convince Shevardnadze that should his regime hold unfair elections, Georgia will be completely isolated from the international community."

When Baker finally did meet with Shevardnadze, the two men emerged looking like something less than the close chums they had always claimed to be. Asked by a Georgian reporter afterward whether he had come to Tbilisi to suggest that Shevardnadze step aside, Baker acted as if he was stunned by the very suggestion. "President Shevardnadze has been a good friend of the United States," he told the news conference. Many in Georgia's opposition camp noted Baker's use of the past tense with glee.

"That was very powerful. For us it was important to know the U.S. was behind us," Khidasheli recalled later, referring to Baker's visit and to a subsequent trip by key U.S. senator John McCain, who headed the International Republican Institute. "We were not even afraid of being arrested because we knew that there was an American embassy in Georgia which would have made a big thing of it. And it was morally very, very important, much more important than money. Because, I mean, you could have millions and get harassed but we had this support."

In February 2003, Open Society—through a knowledge-sharing program called East East—paid for a team of NGO leaders, including Liberty Institute co-founder Giga Bokeria, Open Society–Georgia chair Alexander Lomaia and Khidasheli to fly to Belgrade and Bratislava for three days to meet again with those who had led the overthrow of Milošević three years earlier—CeSID's Blagojevic, Saša Mirkovic of B-92 and Srđa Popović of Otpor—as well as with veterans of OK'98.

The Georgians came away impressed with the intensive how-to-run-a-revolution course, and particularly with Popović. "Popović was the most impressive guy we met in Belgrade," said Khidasheli, who has short black hair and a round face. A Yale law graduate, she leaves the impression that she isn't easily impressed. "He was very provocative and he was talking about techniques, which was the most important for us. He taught us how, if you have five hundred people [taking part in a demonstration], you can make it seem like you're five thousand. That sort of thing."

Popović also explained to the Georgians how Otpor had managed to mobilize so many of the country's youth, how they made Otpor "cool to join," as Khidasheli put it. Popović, along with Ivan Marovic, was also a star of the PBS-produced documentary *Bringing Down a Dictator,* a film—gravely narrated by Martin Sheen—which portrays Otpor as democracy's spunky new heroes. The Georgians brought the film back to Tbilisi with them to show to their own would-be revolutionaries.

"It was very motivational to see someone who is similar to you and has accomplished what they accomplished," the Liberty Institute's Ramishvili told me. "They're like missionaries." However, Soros, whom Ramishvili knows personally, had different motivations. "He was a great friend of Shevardnadze, he helped a lot with the anti-corruption drive," Ramishvili said, "but finally he was disappointed. He was disappointed in Shevardnadze, not in Georgia. And he saw that the democratization experience could go on without Shevardnadze."

As the revolution machine kicked into gear, the Serbs—Maric and Djinovic—along with veterans of Slovakia's OK'98 campaign, ran three-day training courses outside Tbilisi for over a thousand Kmara recruits who would later form the vanguard of the anti-Shevardnadze uprising. The recruits watched *Bringing Down a Dictator,* and they studied how to grab domestic attention with graffiti campaigns and catchy slogans and how to put on a show for the international audience when CNN and the BBC were watching. They also learned tactics for countering police: when to stand and lock arms, when to plant a kiss on the officer's cheek and hand him a rose. Unabashed about their roots, they even adopted Otpor's trademark symbol, the black and white clenched fist.

The Kmara kids got the message that Soros had apparently intended them to receive. "We told ourselves, if the Slovak society did all that, and if the Serbian society did all that in a non-violent way, why couldn't we?" said Giorgi Kandelaki, a founding member of Kmara.

Mark Mullen, the head of the Tbilisi office of NDI, took part in the same training sessions, which were held at an abandoned Communist Young Pioneers camp outside of Tbilisi. He spoke to the youths about the importance of non-violent protest—and thereby of clinging to the moral high ground—in the coming street demonstrations. Mullen helped train Kmara despite overt disapproval from his own bosses in Washington. USAID, which funded NDI, was concerned about maintaining the appearance of neutrality, even though there was little question by this point that most of the "democracy-building" money that poured into the country was aiding Saakashvili and his allies at Shevardnadze's expense.

Mullen, a tall, good-natured Texan with receding red hair and the imposing stature of an ex-bouncer, says the officials carrying out the USAID projects on the ground believed their Washington employers had little idea what was really happening in Georgia. "Our goal was to spend as little time and effort as possible on [the targets set out by USAID], just feeding the beast, while at the same time acting as political actors and doing what needed to be done." After having lived seven years in Georgia, marrying a Georgian and raising his kids in Tbilisi, Mullen was as fed up as the locals with the corruption he saw, and he believed it was time to oust Shevardnadze. And while Mullen's side projects were met with official disapproval, he says they were watched "with a wink" by the U.S. embassy, headed by Ambassador Miles. In all, the U.S., through NED, USAID and their various grantees (mostly NDI and IRI), would spend $2.4 million on Georgia's election.

On a USAID- and NDI-approved level, Mullen worked with Blagojevic to train the locals in the parallel vote tabulation that had proved so devastating to Milošević in 2000. On a less official level, he helped to find and hire Global Strategy Group, the American firm that would carry out the Soros-funded exit poll and broadcast the results to the country on Rustavi 2. On a very personal level—knowing that if they were going to prod the regime with a stick, they needed to be wielding a hammer—he helped train Kmara.

"NDI couldn't be a part of it, couldn't be anywhere near it because of political sensitivities . . . but I said, look—we need civil disobedience training. So I just did it," Mullen reflected. "[Kmara] was a threat. Either the elections are fair, or we're going to know exactly how unfair they are and people are going to take to the streets."

As they'd done for Otpor, the international NGOs didn't fund Kmara directly but instead paid for its poster campaigns, spray paint and T-shirts. Giorgi Meladze, a student who was a member of both the Liberty Institute and Kmara, was among those who travelled to Belgrade to learn at Otpor's knee how to stage non-violent regime change. He acknowledged that, from the beginning, the plan was to take over the streets in order to force Shevardnadze into a corner. "From the very beginning we never expected to have free elections," he told me, slumping into one of the green couches of the Liberty Institute's dingy Tbilisi headquarters, which with its mixture of buzzing activists and amicable slackers had the feel of a student newspaper office. "The idea was how to defend our votes."

Kmara made its first appearance on April 22, 2003, when about three hundred students burned a picture of Shevardnadze and his inner circle in front of the State Chancellery building on a hilltop in central Tbilisi. Notable amidst the graffiti they left behind was the phrase *Gotov je!*, or "He's finished"—written not in Georgian, but in Serbian.

SEVEN

THE ROSE REVOLUTION

Tbilisi

The morning of Sunday, November 2, 2003, broke sunny and clear in Tbilisi. It was cool enough that old men wore sweater vests over their button-down shirts but still warm enough that women lined up outside the polling stations across the country in short-sleeved tops. The enthusiastic Kmara youths paraded in headbands reading "Enough!" and in white T-shirts featuring the clenched fist.

Election day was going exactly as Marko Blagojevic had expected, exactly as it had gone three years before when people had gone to the polls in Serbia. The Georgian election observation team—five hundred monitors trained by the National Democratic Institute—assigned its members to every polling station. An exit poll, carried out by the U.S.-based Global Strategy Group and sponsored by Soros, NDI, the Eurasia Foundation and the British Council, was in the works. Its results would be broadcast live on Rustavi 2.

Eduard Shevardnadze's For a New Georgia party was a main contender in this parliamentary election; however, the presidency itself would not be disputed for another two years. But, Blagojevic says, the revolution-makers' real goal was always to oust the president. "Shevardnadze was the true problem, not the parliament," he said later. "Doing good work prior to parliamentary elections, and perhaps even winning parliamentary elections, would be an excellent exercise for overthrowing Shevardnadze. I knew this at that time, and I was communicating this with our counterparts in Georgia: that if they . . . won the parliamentary elections, Shevardnadze [would] soon be history himself. They didn't believe it."

As predicted, gathering evidence against Shevardnadze was easier than it had been against Milošević. Where Milošević's regime obstructed and harassed the Western monitors, Shevardnadze treasured the good-guy aura he still had from the end of the Cold War and ordered that the monitors be allowed to do their work. "I call upon you all to come to the polling stations and cast your vote," he said as he cast his own ballot. "The elections should be democratic and fair." Those doing the parallel vote tabulation simply had to keep their own records of who people voted for and contrast it with the final result, which the unreformed apparatchiks could be counted on to inflate.

The early official results showed For a New Georgia with a slim lead, collecting just over 25 per cent of the vote—less than the combined vote for Saakashvili's National Movement and the Burjanadze-Democrats, a coalition jointly led by Zurab Zhvania and Nino Burjanadze. It was hardly a resounding victory for the Silver Fox, or an endorsement of his rule. And though the results were not yet final, Shevardnadze wasn't gloating. "I'm ready to cooperate with any political force in a new parliament. I don't expect any confrontation between me and a new parliament in which the opposition will be dominant," he told a news conference on November 3, effectively conceding that he had lost control of Parliament. Even Alexander Lomaia, the head of Open Society–Georgia, initially seemed satisfied. "I regard that result as a victory of the opposition," he told a reporter.[1]

The OSCE, as it had for previous elections, noted irregularities, especially with the lists of registered voters, but it also lauded the government for improved transparency. The vote, while riddled with minor problems, was seen as a positive step toward democracy. A small crowd of Kmara activists—estimated by those who took part to be about a thousand people—demonstrated. Most of the public looked on with curious disinterest.

Then came the Global Strategy Group's exit poll, with its provocative figures. Saakashvili's National Movement had finished first with 26 per cent of the vote, the data showed, while For a New Georgia had taken just 19 per cent. While similar exit polls have proven wildly wrong in other circumstances, these were treated as gospel by Rustavi 2, which quickly broadcast its message to the electorate: you have been deceived, and Shevardnadze is to blame. Kmara led the planned charge into the streets.

On Tuesday, November 4, Mikhail Saakashvili—who had campaigned on the slogan "Georgia without Shevardnadze"—led a crowd of ten thousand onto Rustavelis Avenue, where they marched through the downtown to Freedom Square, a traffic circle once dominated by a statue of Lenin that had long since been replaced by an occasionally functioning fountain. Riot police stood guard but did not intervene, a decision that was to mark Shevardnadze's response to the growing election crisis. "Shevardnadze should admit the victory of the democratic opposition," Saakashvili told his patrons, even though the president had already done as much. "If he does not before tomorrow, we will go to the state chancellery and force him to step down." Zhvania, who had taken U.S. advice and reluctantly agreed to play second fiddle to the more charismatic Saakashvili, declared that Georgians should be ready to "fight to the end" to protect their votes.

It was compelling, rabble-rousing stuff. Shevardnadze quickly said he would step down "if people demand," but cautioned that passions shouldn't be needlessly inflamed. The hot-blooded Saakashvili took the opposite tack. "If he wants a revolution, he will get it," he predicted.

The next day, Ambassador Miles added fuel to the crackling fire. "The mismanagement and fraud of Georgia's November 2 parliamentary election denied many Georgian citizens their constitutional right to vote," the embassy said in a statement just two days after the State Department had followed the OSCE's line and taken care to note both the good and the bad about the elections.

Tinatin Khidasheli, the Georgian lawyer, said the split message was a reflection of the divide she herself had seen when NDI had brought her to the United States. While the neo-conservatives in the Bush administration were willing to ditch Shevardnadze and move on, the liberals who still ran matters at State clung to the old notion that Shevardnadze was a friend of the West and the only person they could trust to lead Georgia. Now the U.S. embassy's statement made it clear that the new guard had won out.

Mark Mullen, the director for NDI in Georgia at the time, acknowledged later that the U.S. administration and his own bosses had an obsession with bringing democracy to Georgia that was out of step with their willingness to tolerate semi-dictatorship in, for example, neighbouring oil-rich Azerbaijan. There's no question in his mind that much of it had to do with securing the Baku-Tbilisi-Ceyhan pipeline route. "There was an overarching understanding that Russia having a lock on the movement of hydrocarbons to Europe is a problem," he says. "Threading the needle between Russia and Iran [with the BTC pipeline route] stuck it to them pretty good."

The fuss over the elections, including American support for the opposition, was stunning to anyone who had paid attention to Azerbaijan's presidential race, which had taken place in October 2003, just two weeks before Georgians went to the polls. There, Heydar Aliev, the strongman who had run the Muslim state since it was a Soviet republic, suffered a heart attack just thirteen days before the vote, creating a sudden power vacuum. Into the gap stepped Aliev's son, Ilham, with little political experience.

But to the West—and to Western oil firms in particular—Ilham's succeeding Heydar meant continued stability and a predictable business environment. Transparency International ranked Azerbaijan as one of the most corrupt countries on the planet year after year (124th out of 133 countries in 2002), but the elder Aliev was the one who had negotiated the $7.4 billion "deal of the century" that gave BP, Exxon Mobil, Total and other Western oil majors access to the Caspian Sea reserves.

So, though opinion polls ahead of the election favoured opposition leader Isa Gambar, the official result gave Ilham Aliev almost 80 per cent of the vote. When the opposition took to the streets two days later— some of them carrying iron bars and smashing shop windows—they were met by truncheon-wielding police, who also used dogs, tear gas and rubber bullets. Two protestors were killed. The repercussions from the West for the crackdown were nil. The Alievs were seen as pro-American and therefore tolerated as a "force for stability" (as Milošević had once been termed by the CIA). Shevardnadze, however, was seen as increasingly unpredictable, weak and beholden to Russia. In September of 2003, the U.S. administration made it plain that it was finished with him.

Shevardnadze's government received a total of $778 million in American aid between 1992 and 2000. But on September 24, barely five weeks before the parliamentary elections, Thomas Adams, a State Department official responsible for aid-related issues in the former Soviet Union, announced that the taps were being turned off, citing corruption and a lack of commitment to reforms. One key detail he provided said much about the motivation for the sudden reversal of policy: a $34 million package to refurbish hydroelectric stations and other energy-related projects would be immediately cut. The U.S. government wasn't forgiving Shevardnadze for ousting AES and welcoming Gazprom.[2]

A decade of U.S. aid had effectively turned Georgia into a ward of the American government, something people in Washington felt Shevardnadze had forgotten. The drop in aid sent a ripple of fear through the Georgian bureaucracy and security services. There was frightened talk that without U.S. aid, the government would have to slash salaries or even stop paying civil servants altogether. If, as some in the local media were now forecasting, Shevardnadze was about to meet Milošević's fate, such measures would cost him the loyalty of institutions essential to his surviving a revolution.

After the U.S. embassy statement, the election crisis quickly escalated, with Saakashvili calling for Shevardnadze to be put on trial and Shevardnadze alleging on television that it was George Soros who was now calling the shots in the Georgian opposition. He accused foreign NGOs of going "as far as interfering in the internal affairs of Georgia," naming Open Society–Georgia in particular. "George Soros is set against the president of Georgia," Shevardnadze told a press conference during which he threatened to close down Open Society's Tbilisi office.

Soros had already spoken to Shevardnadze before the crisis. "I explained to him that we are not supporting political parties, we are supporting free and fair elections," Soros told a press conference in Moscow, describing a phone conversation he had with Shevardnadze. But, he suggested, Shevardnadze's time was coming to an end. "I believe that the fund's activities will be successful because the people of Georgia very much want to see a regime change."

On Friday, November 7, the peaceful nature of the standoff, which both sides claimed to hold dear, was briefly broken as masked gunmen broke up an opposition rally in the town of Zugdidi, west of Tbilisi. Witnesses said most of the shots were fired into the air, but a woman was shot in the leg and a young man took a bullet in the arm. While Saakashvili and Zhvania would later call their revolution "bloodless," it actually came very close to deteriorating into civil war, something Shevardnadze warned of repeatedly. The president called for dialogue with the opposition leaders, promising that everything— including his resignation—was negotiable. He was rebuffed, and the next day Saakashvili led a crowd of fifteen thousand, the largest to date, into the streets of Tbilisi. He promised to oust the "scumbags and rogues" who were running Georgia. It was a hint of things to come, with Saakashvili brazenly leading to the front, ignoring the advice of some of the cooler heads around him.

As the demonstrations carried on, Kmara set up camp on the square in front of the arched stone main entrance of the parliament, a Soviet-era building finished in 1953 by German prisoners of war. The all-night protest was small in comparison to the tent cities that would later fill the streets of downtown Kiev, but it was crucial to maintaining the opposition's momentum. Several times, Kmara leader Giorgi Kandelaki later recalled, rumours spread that Shevardnadze had ordered the police to come during the night and put a forceful end to the all-night protests. But the crackdown never came.

"Shevardnadze thought we would just shout and then go home. He was increasingly out of touch with reality," said Kandelaki, an intense young man with thick, connected eyebrows. Though the rumours of imminent police intervention made for some sleepless nights, the Kmara kids kept the mood light and passed the time holding impromptu folk concerts. And instead of petering out, the protestors grew in number and became more and more determined with each passing night. "We understood that we had passed the point of irreversibility. We knew that if we stopped, we would have lost, and nothing would change," Kandelaki said.

By this point, Rustavi 2 and the hip, new, Soros-financed newspaper *24 Hours* had thrown their full weight behind the demonstrators and their demand that Shevardnadze resign over the election irregularities.

Rustavi, in particular, was a clarion, going live to the square in front of Parliament every time Saakashvili, Zhvania or Burjanadze spoke, and repeatedly broadcasting *Bringing Down a Dictator.* Money provided by foreign donors, meanwhile, allowed the opposition to set up a stage and a giant-screen television in front of Parliament to broadcast Rustavi 2 to the crowd.

"They were a tribune," said Giga Bokeria of the Liberty Institute, one of the Georgians who had been flown to Belgrade to study the Serbian uprising. "People knew where to get real information. They were informed about the details of the election, when to go into the streets, where and how." He compared Rustavi 2's role to that of Serbia's B92 radio.

As the protests dragged on, the government delayed, again and again, the release of the final results. A full week after the vote, only 80 per cent of the results were known. Saakashvili and his supporters interpreted the wait as a signal that the government was planning to further manipulate the final 20 per cent to weaken opposition representation in the next parliament. The uncounted 20 per cent was the vote from Adjara, an autonomous region where election monitors had faced more harassment than in any other part of the country.

On November 14, Saakashvili put on another display of his increasing sway with the unhappy masses. A crowd of twenty thousand National Movement supporters linked hands in a human chain that stretched all around Shevardnadze's heavily guarded offices. At least five armoured vehicles, as well as buses full of soldiers wearing body armour, massed a few kilometres from the demonstration. Shevardnadze again warned of the possibility of civil war, but the moment passed peacefully.[3]

That day, Shevardnadze finally called Vladimir Putin to ask for help. Until that moment, the Kremlin, which had little affection for Shevardnadze, had watched the events in Tbilisi with bemusement, not fully realizing the threat to its own interests. Who ruled in Georgia, Russia's Caucasus experts felt, mattered little so long as the Kremlin maintained control over the supply of gas and electricity to its former colony, not to mention over the military bases and allies it had in the renegade regions of Abkhazia, Adjara and South Ossetia.

After the phone call from Shevardnadze, and another one the next day, the Kremlin decided to come to the aid of its erstwhile ally. Aslan Abashidze, the pro-Russian leader of the autonomous Muslim region of Adjara and a long-time thorn in Shevardnadze's side, was summoned to Moscow—after stops in neighbouring Armenia and Azerbaijan—for talks with Foreign Minister Igor Ivanov, and returned to Georgia with a call for his supporters to back Shevardnadze. Rumours spread among the opposition that Abashidze—a tyrant in the truest sense, who had carefully nurtured a cult of personality in his tiny Black Sea empire—had been promised the prime ministership. On November 18, Abashidze, who proved far less popular than he, Shevardnadze or the Kremlin had understood, played his weak hand. He bussed in some three thousand members of his Revival party, few of whom had any choice about attending, to stage a pro-Shevardnadze rally in front of Parliament.

Two days later. the government, confident it now had the backing of Moscow, went ahead and finally published the official election results. For a New Georgia came in first, with 21.3 per cent of the vote. Abashidze's Revival movement, brazenly, was given the second spot with 18.8 per cent, while Saakashvili's National Movement was a close third with 18 per cent. The new parliament would convene on November 22, Shevardnadze said, with or without the opposition members present. It was the final straw.

U.S. State Department spokesman Adam Ereli said that the results reflected "massive vote fraud" in some regions (Revival had only received 8 per cent of the vote, according to the Global Strategy exit poll) and did not "accurately reflect the will of the Georgian people." The next day, Saakashvili called his supporters once more onto Rustavelis Avenue, saying the time had come to stage a "bloodless, velvet revolution." "Shevardnadze's regime ends tonight," he told his followers. "It is better for him to flee, otherwise tomorrow we will trample his regime."[4]

The day after the official figures were released, tens of thousands stood outside the parliament building and chanted "Resign! Resign!"—and Shevardnadze's regime began to crumble from within. Tedo Japaridze, the head of Shevardnadze's Security Council and a former ambassador to Washington, broke ranks and declared that the elections had been marred by "falsifications during both the ballot and the vote count." The same morning, Abashidze's supporters acknowledged that, in exchange for his support of Shevardnadze, their man expected to be appointed either prime minister (a post that didn't exist at the time) or parliamentary Speaker.

Faced with what he saw as a U.S.-backed coup, the Silver Fox seemed ready to sell his country to Moscow. In exchange for Moscow's support and the backing of Abashidze, Shevardnadze cut a devil's bargain that would have seen the Adjarian strongman first become prime minister and then get Shevardnadze's backing in a 2005 presidential bid. "Abashidze told me later that if he agreed to make reuniting the country a serious goal, he would become prime minister and later president," said Hamlet Chipashvili, a Revival MP who also served as Abashidze's representative in Tbilisi. Abashidze's frantic travels to Moscow, Armenia and Azerbaijan were aimed at sealing the deal and gaining support for bringing Abkhazia and South Ossetia back into Georgia.

On the afternoon of Saturday, November 22, the exact details of the Shevardnadze-Abashidze pact were still being worked out (they were haggling over who would serve as parliamentary Speaker) when Shevardnadze convened the new parliament, with opposition MPs absent from their desks. The president hoped this would deflate the enthusiasm of Saakashvili's supporters and defuse the protests. Instead it inflamed them.

With Kmara and Saakashvili in the forefront, Saakashvili clutching a red rose that was to become the uprising's symbol, hundreds of protesters charged into the parliament building and burst through the locked door of the chamber. Panicked by the sight of the angry crowd charging at the president, Shevardnadze's bodyguards cut him off in mid-speech and hustled him out a side door. He was packed into a waiting car, which sped off to the presidential residence in the hills above the capital.

The bodyguards were Shevardnadze's last supporters. When the opposition rushed into Parliament to interrupt his speech, not one of Georgia's six separate security forces did anything to stop them. In the preceding hours, one army unit after another had proclaimed its loyalty to the opposition and said it would ignore any orders to fire on demonstrators.

Nonetheless, the storming of Parliament was very much an impromptu move. "Nothing was planned," said Giorgi Meladze of Kmara. "I was close to the gates and we could see the politicians coming and going, and someone just said, 'Let's go in.' The guards didn't expect it, and they just moved out of the way. Once we started, there was this big push that just carried us all the way in. Nobody was thinking about what we were doing. It was like, 'Whoa, what just happened?' Then people started jumping on the tables and chairs and hugging and kissing and saying it was a different Georgia."

Carried down the narrow corridor between the rows of parliamentary deputies' seats, Saakashvili grabbed a microphone and—red in the face from exertion and occasionally taking a swig from a bottle of Coca-Cola—claimed his victory. "We are those chosen by the people, and we are against violence," he told the chamber. He was mainly preaching to the converted; after some brief scuffles, most of the pro-government legislators had followed Shevardnadze's lead and fled. Outside, the largest crowd to date—somewhere between 50,000 and 100,000 people—chanted their rose-bearing hero's nickname: "Misha! Misha!"

Nobody but Saakashvili seems to know where his rose came from. It seems to have been a genuinely impromptu gesture by a politician with a knack for stylish gestures. He said later that he carried it to make clear to those guarding the building that no one was going to pull a weapon.[5] If it really was a spontaneous gesture, it was one of the few in the Rose Revolution that was. "For months people were planning for it," Khidasheli told me. "Psychologically it was easy and less painful because people were ready for it. People were prepared to go. People knew where to go, where to stand and in which square."

I returned to Tbilisi in the middle of this scene, greeted at the airport by a grinning taxi driver named Nodar who told me on the long sun-drenched drive to the Villa Mtiebi—long because his aging Volga sedan stalled four times on the way into town—that the revolution was all but complete. "The police are saying, 'We don't want Shevardnadze.' The army guys are saying, 'We don't want Shevardnadze.' In the West you think he's a hero, I know, but now the whole world is watching him run away from the people." On the third stall, Nodar got out to look under the hood while I paced anxiously, worried that the only thing I'd have to offer my editors from the scene of the Georgian revolution would be an exclusive interview with Nodar the cabbie. The car grumbled to life, and Nodar picked up where he left off. "He's an old thief. People want jobs, they need money."

As we entered the city centre, crowds of cheering protestors sur-rounded the car, waving the red and white banners of the National Movement, as well as numerous American, British and German flags. Whatever tension had been in the air hours earlier was gone. I could see soldiers in green combat fatigues—their helmets and weapons nowhere to be seen—mixing with the protestors, smoking cigarettes and joining in the revelry. Occasionally, one would turn to face the Georgian Orthodox Kashveti Church of St. George, which stands opposite Parliament, solemnly crossing himself as if to thank God that they were never forced to fire on their fellow Georgians.

By now, the whole scene was live on CNN, adding to the pressure on Shevardnadze to step aside peacefully in favour of Saakashvili, who was being portrayed as a cuddly pro-Western reformer. Shevardnadze's halo was gone, and reporters now spoke only of the corruption and poverty he had wrought upon the country. "We were lucky enough that there was nothing else going on in the world then, so it was kind of front-page news," Saakashvili told me later, breaking into his boyish giggle. "We had the first televised revolution in history. We were live on CNN for four and a half hours without a commercial." CNN's unin-terrupted attention, he said, meant that the authorities could not use force, something Shevardnadze says he never would have allowed. Saakashvili, however, remains convinced the president gave orders for a bloody crackdown that were ignored by the rank and file.

Somehow, in the mass of people, I found Lika Peradze, my friend, translator and guide to all things Georgian. First we headed to the State Chancellery—the presidential offices—where we dashed inside to find empty room after empty room. The only living soul, except for the few nervous security guards who hadn't deserted their posts, was Peter Mamradze, Shevardnadze's long-time chief of staff. Happy for the conversation on a day when he had little to do but wait and see what happened next, he said his boss had long since stopped listening to his advice, relying instead on a corrupt inner circle. As a result, Shevardnadze never understood how unpopular he had become, or believed Saakashvili's street protest could be a serious threat. Rather than realizing there was a genuine anger that was bringing people into the streets day after day, Shevardnadze saw it all as theatre staged by Soros and Rustavi 2. "I tried to tell him [the threat was real], but I was in the minority. Sometimes he would become angry if you informed him about something bad," Mamradze said. "Any time a politician is cut from reality, it's always the end of their career. President Shevardnadze himself taught us this."

As temperatures dipped toward freezing, Lika and I headed back down the muddy hill that linked the deserted chancellery to the opposition-occupied parliament. A long-time employee of the legislature, Lika grabbed my arm and led me inside the stone building, which by then had become a zoo of activity, with protestors picking through the thoroughly trashed assembly chamber, hooting with celebration and looking for souvenirs. Upstairs, we saw and spoke briefly with first Zhvania, then Burjanadze, who both looked a little bewildered, as if unsure just where the hot-headed Saakashvili was leading them. Both were sweaty and in an obvious hurry. They were rushing to a crisis meeting at Shevardnadze's residence, where the Silver Fox had agreed to see the three young reformers and Igor Ivanov, who had flown in from Moscow.

Shevardnadze had called a state of emergency after the seizure of Parliament, but he told me later that he rejected the use of force. "When I came home, when I was sent home, I said, 'What does this state of emergency mean? In my power I have the whole army . . . all those tanks, all those weapons. These people are, in comparison, youngsters. They are a huge number, but they couldn't resist the army. On the way home I made a decision that there shouldn't be bloodshed." His son, Paata, called from Paris to urge him not to use the army. "He called me and asked me, 'No bloodshed please, or whatever you've done—all the good things in your whole life—you will spoil it." Shevardnadze spoke at length to his son but refused to take calls from James Baker. The Silver Fox may have decided that it was time to exit the stage, but he had one last trick up his sleeve.

Ivanov arrived at the meeting believing he had already negotiated a pact that would keep everyone happy: Shevardnadze would declare the elections null and void, conceding the opposition's main point and paving the way for a fresh vote that all anticipated would secure Saakashvili's hold on Parliament; the president, meanwhile, would remain in office for another six months, and then he would step aside for early presidential elections. Ivanov left the meeting early and flew to

Batumi to inform Abashidze—the man the Kremlin planned to back in that vote—of the new arrangement, which the opposition had also agreed to.

By the time Ivanov reached the Black Sea port, the ground had shifted under his feet. Shevardnadze had resigned. He had no desire to see Abashidze succeed him, and after more than a decade of quarrelling off and on with the Kremlin—a relationship that had worsened after Putin had succeeded Yeltsin—he felt he owed Moscow no favours. It's likely that he also hoped that the inexperienced and divided team of Saakashvili, Zhvania and Burjanadze would crumble when faced with the heavy burden of ruling, and ask him to resume his post. It had happened before, a decade earlier, when he had resigned the presidency during a dispute with Parliament only to be begged to stay.

"I see that all this cannot simply go on. If I was forced tomorrow to use my authority, it would lead to a lot of bloodshed. I have never betrayed my country, and so it is better that the president resigns," Shevardnadze said in remarks that were broadcast to the crowd on the giant-screen television in front of Parliament. "I had seven months left as president. I had to choose someone [to succeed me]," he told me later, his chin lost in his jowls as he reminisced about the last days of his rule. "I chose the youngsters."

The snap resignation on November 23—Shevardnadze signed the papers in his green-walled study, surrounded by photographs of himself in his past glory—caught Ivanov and Abashidze flat-footed. The former quickly returned to Moscow, leaving the impression that it was he who had convinced Shevardnadze to peacefully resign. The latter hunkered down in Adjara for a conflict with Saakashvili that he believed he could no longer avoid. He began buying weapons.

The opposition, however, was ebullient. Burjanadze declared herself acting head of state, and Saakashvili headed out to address the crowd. As news broke of Shevardnadze's resignation, I stepped out the main door of Parliament and fireworks exploded overhead. While I stood there, beneath one of the high arches that decorate the front of the building, taking in the scene of tens of thousands of people dancing madly and waving flags, the young woman standing next to me with her young son recognized me as a foreigner in their midst. She walked up to me and asked me in Russian where I was from.

"Canada," I answered, shouting to be heard over the joyous din. "I'm a reporter." She responded by grabbing the back of my head and planting a forceful kiss on my lips. "Thank you for being here," she said before turning back to watch the fireworks.

A man named Koba Kurtanidze was next in line to thank me for attending. "The happiness we felt in 1991, we have twice that today," he explained after administering a rib-cracking bear hug. "Georgia can breathe freely now."

In time it hardly looked like a victory for democracy. The results of the January 4, 2004, elections that completed Saakashvili's rise to power had more in common with the landslides Saddam Hussein used to win in Iraq than with the outcome of a fairly contested election. Western-funded exit polls gave Saakashvili 86 per cent of the vote. The official results, released ten days later, said he'd received 96 per cent.

When I met him later, Saakashvili seemed almost embarrassed by the figure. "I would have been luckier if I got 51 per cent," he said, only half joking. Though by now he was thirty-six years old, with permanent five-o'clock shadow and with flecks of grey intruding on his full head of jet-black hair, his baby face still made him appear too young to be president of anything but a university students' association.

Despite the improbable result, no one in the West raised a peep of concern about the election process that had seen Zhvania and Burjanadze step aside to allow Saakashvili to run effectively unopposed. Three days after the election—and well before the results were official—Bush phoned Saakashvili to congratulate him and invite him to Washington. "America is pinning great hopes on the new Georgia and will render it all-round assistance in international affairs," Saakashvili's press secretary, Georgy Arveladze, said when asked by reporters what message Bush had communicated during the phone call.

Saakashvili was quick to reward those who had helped him. Burjanadze got her old job back as Speaker, while Zhvania was given the newly created post of prime minister. In true revolutionary style, Alexander Lomaia, the head of Open Society–Georgia, was brought into the cabinet as education minister. Giga Bokeria, the Liberty Institute co-founder, would eventually become the National Movement's leader in Parliament. None left the Soros payroll. Under a plan to help end corruption by raising official salaries, all cabinet ministers and deputy ministers, including Saakashvili himself, would have their pay subsidized by Soros.

"Soros definitely plays too big a role here. Let's start from the fact that he's paying the salaries of our top officials; as the saying goes, he who pays the musicians calls the tune," Zaza Gachechiladze, the gregarious editor-in-chief of Tbilisi's English-language daily newspaper, the *Messenger,* complained to me. Gachechiladze, a bellwether of public opinion and a rare beast in the world of Georgian media in that he had no obvious love for either Shevardnadze or Saakashvili, was the first person I visited whenever I was in Tbilisi. "It's generally accepted public opinion here [in Tbilisi] that Mr. Soros is the person who planned Shevardnadze's overthrow," he told me. "It's wrong, absolutely wrong."

For Russia, the outcome was a disaster. Not only did it lose Tbilisi to the Americans, but a May 2004 copycat revolution in the breakaway region of Adjara cost the Kremlin a valuable means of pressuring Saakashvili. As Kmara youths surged through the streets of Batumi, Igor Ivanov flew in once more, this time to take a panicked Aslan Abashidze back to Moscow with him.

Immediately after coming to power, Saakashvili stepped up pressure for Russia to close the military bases it had maintained on Georgian soil after the collapse of the Soviet Union. The Bush administration coyly offered to help pay for the move. Ambassador Miles, meanwhile, said the two hundred U.S. soldiers deployed in Georgia in 2002 to train the Georgian army would stay past the end of their two-year mandate, perhaps indefinitely. There was excited chatter about Georgia eventually joining NATO. "The Cold War is over, and we will not give up our independence. Russia cannot treat us as their former colony," Saakashvili said. "We are friends with the Americans because they helped us."[6]

Eighteen months after the Rose Revolution—following a ceremony that was attended by U.S. secretary of energy Samuel Bodman, by Saakashvili, the democrat, and by Azerbaijan's Aliev, the anointed son of the autocrat—oil started to flow west through the Baku-Tbilisi-Ceyhan pipeline.

EIGHT

THE END OF POLITICS

Moscow

ikhail Khodorkovsky was fast asleep on his private jet when the FSB agents arrived. The billionaire's plane was making a refuelling stop at Tolmachevo Airport, outside the central Siberian city of Novosibirsk, when it was directed to an isolated parking spot and surrounded by a battery of trucks that trained their high beams on the plane. The FSB SWAT team, wearing masks and flak jackets and carrying automatic weapons, charged aboard, waving their guns around the plane. "Guns down! Guns down!" they yelled at Khodorkovsky's bodyguards, who weren't carrying any.[1]

Though he was jolted awake, the billionaire was probably unsurprised by the turn of events. Russia's richest man, who controlled a company that accounted for 2 per cent of the world's oil supply, had by this day, October 26, 2003, known for months that arrest was possible, even probable, as long as he remained in Russia. His growing wealth and clout, combined with his barely disguised political ambitions, made him a threat in the Kremlin's nervous eyes. He knew well, from watching the falls of Boris Berezovsky and Vladimir Gusinsky, what happened to billionaires the Kremlin didn't like. Three months earlier, police had dragged his own partner at the giant Yukos oil firm, Platon Lebedev, out of the Moscow hospital where he was being treated for heart trouble and charged him with fraud in relation to the privatization of a fertilizer company a decade earlier.

Khodorkovsky had the time and resources to flee the country, as Berezovsky and Gusinsky had done. Instead he poured money into opposition political parties and went on a provocative campaign-style tour of Russia in which he repeatedly warned audiences of the dangers of the country's authoritarian slide under Putin. For deciding to stay, the billionaire was thrown in a four-person cell in Moscow's notorious Matrosskaya Tishina prison and fed a diet dominated by brown bread, fish soup and buttered porridge. Like Lebedev, he was charged with massive fraud and tax evasion related to the privatization processes of the early 1990s. Though it's indisputable that some of Khodorkovsky's estimated $8 billion wealth came through methods that wouldn't get the approval of the U.S. Securities and Exchange Commission, most Russians would quickly add that everybody probably broke a rule or three in the scramble to get ahead in the early 1990s. Few saw his prosecution as anything but political—punishment for daring to butt heads with the Kremlin.[2]

Khodorkovsky's new political activism quickly crossed the line that Putin had famously drawn for the oligarchs immediately after his election in 2000. Stay out of politics, he told them, and they could keep their companies and their fortunes; challenge the Kremlin, and you would go the way of Gusinsky. Khodorkovsky started pouring money into Boris Nemtsov's Union of Right Forces and funded the liberal Yabloko party, headed by perennial presidential candidate Grigory Yavlinsky, to such an extent that he effectively privatized it. He also gave money to less likely candidates—the Communist Party and Putin's own United Russia movement—in what Kremlin officials told me they saw as a brazen effort to buy enough loyalty in the Duma to effectively control it.

Khodorkovsky's emergence as one of Russia's most prominent democrats was an unlikely one. A former Young Communist leader who grew up living with his parents in a two-room apartment in Moscow, he dreamed in his youth of growing up to be a factory director. Had it not been for glasnost and perestroika, he might have achieved that ambition. He graduated from university with a chemistry degree, was already well connected within the Party and seemed on track to become an upper-echelon Soviet apparatchik. But Mikhail Gorbachev's reforms opened up possibilities that Khodorkovsky had never considered. After getting his second degree, this one in economics, he founded one of the country's first quasi-private enterprises, a co-op that later grew into the Menatep bank. Even before the collapse of the Soviet Union, he was earning millions of dollars a year. When Yeltsin, desperate to get cash for the state's empty coffers, began the haphazard privatization of Russia's key assets, Khodorkovsky was one of the few Russians with the money to capitalize on the process. Through Menatep, he snapped up companies and factories at a fraction of their real value. Along with the other oligarchs, he made billions of dollars and gained nearly unlimited access to Yeltsin's Kremlin, though, unlike his flamboyant peers, who threw their money around at outlandish parties at their villas in the south of France, Khodorkovsky never flaunted his fortune. Instead he went on speaking tours, lecturing audiences about the importance of education and the possibilities of the Internet. Asked once why he didn't have property in Nice like the other oligarchs, the forty-year-old quipped, "I don't like the seaside very much." He often showed up at the office in a T-shirt, and rarely wore a tie.

In 1995, Khodorkovsky set his sights on his real target: Yukos. As the date for the company's privatization neared, he set about befriending its directors, all holdovers from the Communist era. The oil giant was classified as a "strategic" firm, meaning that foreigners were forbidden from purchasing it; Khodorkovsky used his Kremlin connections to ensure no serious domestic competitors made a bid either. Through the controversial loans-for-shares auction process, he acquired a 78 per cent stake for a measly $159 million. Eight years later, the company was worth $45 billion.

Khodorkovsky's machinations originally turned off Western investors, but Russia's crippling 1998 financial crisis, which saw foreign capital flee the country as the banking system collapsed, sparked what appeared to be a genuine change of heart. Khodorkovsky told those around him that he'd learned that foreign investors would put their money only where they thought it was safe and where they understood the rules of the game. He set out to make Yukos the most Westernized and transparent firm in Russia, and succeeded.

He also began to get involved in politics, borrowing heavily from the model of his friend George Soros. In 2001, he founded Open Russia, a charity modelled directly on Soros's Open Society Institute.

He started giving out $100 million a year—some believed it to be far more—funding Internet education programs for children and projects like the Tatarstan Human Rights Centre, as well as a summer camp called New Civilization that taught young people about the "rule of law and open markets." He recruited some of Russia's leading lights— including Yakovlev, the one-time Politburo member who was the brains behind glasnost and perestroika—to sit on the supervisory board, along with international dignitaries like Henry Kissinger. Many saw it as an effort by a repentant oligarch to legitimize his wealth and become the "Russian Soros." The startling thing about that comparison was that by 2003 Khodorkovsky, with an estimated wealth of $7 billion, was in fact wealthier than the American philanthropist. *Forbes* magazine ranked the Russian tycoon as the twenty-sixth wealthiest person in the world that year; Soros, for all his notoriety, was thirty-eighth.

The nature of some of his grantees made Khodorkovsky's politics clear: he donated $1 million to the Eurasia Foundation (a USAID-backed democracy-promotion group), $500,000 to the Carnegie Endowment and even $1 million to the U.S. Library of Congress. He later purchased the *Moscow News,* a liberal newspaper that had been one of the standard-bearers of reform during the Gorbachev era. "Khodorkovsky deeply believes that Russia deserves something beyond authoritarian rule," said Bob Amsterdam, a boisterous Canadian lawyer who was part of Khodorkovsky's defence team. "He believes Russia deserves a free and open democratic society." And Khodorkovsky believed that Putin was an authoritarian defined by his KGB roots.

"I think it's very important to remember that he chose to go to jail," Amsterdam said after his client had been arrested. "That's very potent stuff in terms of [countering] the efforts of the Russian government to blacken his name." Each time we met in the lobby of Moscow's gleaming new Ararat Park Hyatt hotel, a short walk from the elegance of the Bolshoi Theatre, Amsterdam was edgy, believing he was being followed by the FSB and that our conversations were being listened to. I thought he'd read one too many Tom Clancy novels—until the fall of 2005, when he was evicted from his hotel room in the middle of the night by FSB agents informing him that his visa had been revoked.

As if meddling in politics wasn't enough to earn Putin's wrath, Khodorkovsky went further and did the unthinkable: he publicly lectured the president. At a February 2003 meeting between Putin and the oligarchs, Khodorkovsky complained about a recent deal that saw the state-owned oil company, Rosneft, gobble up a smaller firm called Severnaya Neft that Yukos had also been eying. In remarks that were caught on television, Khodorkovksy implied that the deal was cooked and that there was corruption within the president's inner circle. "The population is skeptical about the government's readiness to combat corruption," the soft-voiced billionaire said. Without naming names, he urged Putin to fire "some of the most odious" officials in his government.

Putin seethed. For a long moment, he fixed Khodorkovsky with his trademark steely gaze. Then he responded by wondering aloud about the legality of the process by which the state's assets had been sold off in the 1990s. Clearly, he meant Yukos. "I, too, can criticize," Putin said icily. The war between Russia's richest man and its most powerful was on.

Sixteen months after their televised quarrel—when I watched Khodorkovsky ordered to stand with Lebedev inside a two-metre-high steel cage and read out his name, age, registration and employment history to a Moscow courtroom—it was clear Putin had won. A similarly blunt order to sit down followed minutes later. On May 31, 2005, the head of Open Russia and former CEO of Yukos, once the wealthiest person in Russia, was sentenced to nine years in prison. Six months earlier, the key production unit of the company Khodorkovsky had helped build had been effectively repossessed by the state in a brazenly rigged auction that saw Yuganskneftegaz, the biggest chunk of Yukos, bought by a previously unheard-of company called Baikal Finance. The charade didn't take long to play out. Baikal was bought by the state-owned Rosneft oil company. Like Gazprom, Rosneft wasn't just close to the Kremlin, it *was* the Kremlin. The company's chairman was Igor Sechin, Putin's deputy chief of staff.

By the time Khodorkovsky's sentence was read out to the packed Moscow courthouse, the message was clear to all potential opponents of the president: in Putin's Russia, as in Soviet times, as in the czarist era, you don't win against the Kremlin.

The takedown of Mikhail Khodorkovsky, who besides his money had high-powered connections (he was a frequent guest at the Moscow residence of U.S. ambassador Alexander Vershbow), created a storm of protest led by his expensive lawyers and high-placed friends in the West. Many other anti-Kremlin dissidents, however, were silenced without nearly as much media coverage.

A foreigner is a rare sight in the tiny Chechen village of Ben-Yurt. Abu Bakar Guchiyev saw me and saw a chance to tell someone about the grim reality of life in this corner of a war zone. "We're ruled by bandits. Whoever has a gun, has power," the thirty-eight-year-old told me. His fine features were hardened by a layer of black stubble on his chin. It was an incautious statement, and a bold place to make it. Guchiyev was just emerging from a polling station set up at Ben-Yurt's school for the occasion of Chechnya's October 2003 Kremlin-sponsored presidential elections. Fearing that rebels would target the election, the school's lobby was filled with nervous men fingering their Kalashnikovs. Several narrowed their eyes at Guchiyev.

"I voted against all the candidates," Guchiyev continued, waving his hand dismissively in the direction of the voting booths. "I'm for Malik Saidullayev," he said proudly. The declaration that Guchiyev was a supporter of a disqualified opposition candidate rather than Putin's hand-picked viceroy, Akhmad Kadyrov, was apparently a step too far. Two of the gun-toting thugs guarding the polling booth interrupted our conversation. Each man took one of Guchiyev's struggling arms, and they dragged him away down a hallway and into an empty classroom. When I protested and tried to follow, a Russian officer stepped in my way. You could tell from Guchiyev's statements that the man was drunk, the soldier said in a voice loud enough to warn other voters against repeating the mistake of speaking their minds. The officer said he had instructed his men to intervene "for my protection." I was taken by the arm and roughly escorted out of the school by the FSB minders who were accompanying us on the trip. I never saw or heard what happened to Guchiyev.

Saidullayev's aborted bid for the Chechen presidency was equally instructive about the nature of the "democracy" Russia was building in its troubled south. A millionaire businessman popular among Chechens as a local boy who had made good, Sadiullayev entered the presidential race—offering himself up for a post few others wanted— and quickly shot to the lead in opinion polls. Soon afterward, he received a summons to the Kremlin from Vladislav Surkov, Putin's powerful deputy chief of staff.[3] Surkov's message, though coded, was simple: this wasn't a real election. The Kremlin wasn't interested in a fair fight between candidates with broad appeal to ordinary Chechens. Putin was just looking to give a stamp of legitimacy to Kadyrov. Surkov told Saidullayev to withdraw from the race.

Saidullayev refused, and four days later he was disqualified when another candidate—who was actually an aide to Kadyrov—charged that he had falsified some of the signatures on his nomination papers. One by one, the other serious challengers to Kadyrov also disappeared from the race. One, businessman Khusein Dzhabrailov, dropped out voluntarily after his own meeting with Surkov. Another, Aslanbek Aslakhanov, an anti-war politician who was Chechnya's sole representative in the State Duma, bowed out to take a job as an adviser to Putin.

On October 5, 2003, Akhmad Kadyrov, a religious mufti and one-time rebel whose son terrorized the republic with a vicious score-settling militia, was elected president of the Republic of Chechnya. Despite widespread loathing of Kadyrov and his psychopathic son Ramzan (one independent poll found 61 per cent of Chechens objected to Kadyrov becoming president), official figures showed that the Kremlin's man in Grozny had won more than 80 per cent of the vote.

Even more telling was the official turnout, which the state-run ITAR-TASS news agency said was 64 per cent, a rousing democratic performance that would put many peaceful Western democracies to shame. But at a polling station in the town of Tolstoy-Yurt—a relatively calm town north of Grozny that was under firm Russian control—an official allowed me to flip through her records of who had and hadn't voted. By my math, the turnout was closer to 11 per cent. At another polling station in the centre of Grozny, I waited nearly an hour for a single voter to arrive.

Nearby, at a grocery store she ran in a muddy market surrounded by the skeletal remains of bombed-out apartment blocks, a forty-seven-year-old woman named Anna Saslambekova sneered at the idea of casting a ballot in an election rigged to deliver an easy win for Kadyrov. "There's nothing good I can say about this man," she said, her head covered by a brightly coloured scarf. "Stalin would be better than him."

It didn't matter. With breathtaking cynicism, the Kremlin declared that Kadyrov was the people's choice. Managed democracy had come to Chechnya.

The Chechen elections were something of a dry run for what Marat Gelman, the Kremlin spin doctor, would later call Russia's "Master and Margarita" elections: a parliamentary vote in December 2003 and the re-election of Vladimir Putin four months later.

Referencing Mikhail Bulgakov's classic anti-Soviet novel was telling. The Russia inhabited by the Master and Margarita is absurd and surreal, a place where a giant fast-talking cat and the devil himself walk the streets of Moscow and wreak havoc on an unsuspecting city. The back-to-back election campaigns, which began in earnest with a police raid on the Moscow offices of George Soros's Open Society Institute and which later featured the mysterious disappearance and reappearance of an opposition presidential candidate and the rise of a Kremlin-backed neo-nationalist movement, would end in sweeping victories for both United Russia and Putin.

That it was Gelman who made a comment so disparaging of the elections was even more revealing, since he was one of the masterminds of all that transpired. The Kremlin hired him, as one of Project Putin's original spin doctors, at the beginning of the 2003–2004 election season to shape Putin's message on the state-run Channel One. It was Gelman who was ultimately responsible for ignoring and belittling those who ran against Putin and his United Russia party, and Gelman who filled the national newscasts with fawning coverage of Putin, the president who was managing to hold Russia together with his bare hands and making life better for ordinary citizens in the process.

Gelman, along with his colleague Gleb Pavlovsky and the presidential deputy chief of staff Surkov, had been one of the inventors of the *temnyki,* or "themes," that were distributed to all the state-controlled media. These were printed sheets outlining what could and couldn't be said on the air that week, a tactic Gelman acknowledges was used to promote the president and attack the Kremlin's enemies. The *temnyki,* he says, were one of the most important tools of managed democracy. They contained "recommendations" that editors should take care to praise United Russia or to cover Putin's trip to the Far East. And there would be recommendations that editors should ignore other issues, such as Chechnya. "A *temnyk* is just the policy of the channel," Gelman explained to me. In the West, he argued, media owners can control what does and doesn't go on the air. In Russia, it's the government that sets a few simple ground rules. "All journalists know that Chechen *boeviks* ["warriors"] can't be called rebels," he said. "Everyone knows that you can't refer to the *vlast* ["the power," a colloquial Russian way of referring to the Kremlin]; you have to say the government or the president. The rules apply until a new rule replaces them."

Even those who didn't work for the state-controlled media got the message and knew they could stray only so far from the party line. "All the people who work for the Russian media know that the easiest way to create problems for your publication or your TV channel is to attack Mr. Putin in a personal way," said Yevgeny Kiselyov, the popular, walrus-faced anchorman on NTV before Gusinsky's ouster and the takeover by Gazprom. Kiselyov later went on to become editor-in-chief of the *Moscow News* after Khodorkovsky bought it. But even though the paper remained one of the most fiercely independent voices in the Russian media, even after Khodorkovsky's arrest, Kiselyov told me that there were two things he and his colleagues were still leery of doing: criticizing Putin personally and devoting big space to developments in Chechnya.

It wasn't just the media who were whipped into line for election season. In early November, at the same time that Shevardnadze was going public with allegations that George Soros was behind the ongoing demonstrations on the streets of Tbilisi, masked gunmen burst into the Moscow offices of the Open Society Institute and carried away computers and documents related to the foundation's Russian democracy-building efforts—though the official reason for the raid was a dispute between the foundation and a landlord who wanted to raise the rent.

Earlier in 2003, Soros had announced that after spending fifteen years and $1 billion helping the country make the transition from communism, he was withdrawing from Russia. Ironically, he fingered Khodorkovsky and Open Russia as those who would pick up the slack once he left. However, on the day that his offices in Moscow were raided, Soros spoke on National Public Radio in the United States, sounding uncharacteristically defeatist about the direction Russia was now heading. Democracy, he said, is "under attack now. Everyone has to recognize that. Now, it's not a lost battle by a long shot. There are a lot of other people working towards an open society. There are economic reformers in the government. So it's not a lost battle, but it is moving in the wrong direction."[4]

With Khodorkovsky in jail, Soros fuming from the sidelines and other U.S.-backed democracy-promotion groups largely idling as President Bush continued to describe Putin as a friend and ally in the "war on terror," Pavlovsky, Gelman and their colleagues had the stage to themselves and could write the script as they saw fit. Khodorkovsky's arrest had been the biggest blow, debilitating the liberal Yabloko party and robbing even the Communists of one of their main sponsors. With little opposition left, the Kremlin team set about building United Russia into such a formidable political juggernaut that seasoned observers such as Alexander Yakovlev dubbed it "the Communist Party, Part Two."[5]

United Russia, in many ways, epitomized Putin's dream of the "power vertical." The party—which didn't even exist until 2001, when Putin's Unity party joined forces with Moscow mayor Yuri Luzhkov's Fatherland–All Russia movement—soon became known among Russians as the "party of power." As with the old Communist Party, membership in United Russia came to be seen as key to getting ahead in business or politics. Twenty-nine regional governors, people once renowned for their independence and their willingness to butt heads with Boris Yeltsin's Kremlin, joined United Russia in the run-up to the elections. They did so in rapid succession after Putin dropped the non-partisan facade of his early days in office and openly expressed admiration for United Russia.

Demonstrating loyalty to United Russia evolved into an obsequious art form during the election campaign. Staff at the Sedmoi Kontinent chain of grocery stores were forced to wear buttons reading "I'm for United Russia!" during working hours as the owner tried to impress the Kremlin. Teachers at a high school in the Volga River city of Saratov assigned their students to write essays about the benefits of a "united Russia" and encouraged their parents to help. My wife, Carolynne, and I watched in shock one evening as Anastasia Volochkova—the former lead ballerina at the Bolshoi Theatre who was fired from the troupe for being too heavy—thanked "God and United Russia" at the end of a solo performance at the Kremlin Palace of Congresses.

However, unlike the Communist Party of old, United Russia espoused no particular ideology. It didn't even have an election platform beyond supporting the president. Campaign advertisements that appeared in the Moscow metro system featured dozens of photographs of Russian historical figures, ranging from Joseph Stalin and secret police founder Felix Dzerzhinsky to Nobel Peace Prize–winning dissidents Alexander Solzhenitsyn and Andrei Sakharov, provoking the rage of Sakharov's widow, Yelena Bonner, who called the ads "a travesty" that would never have been allowed to happen in "a state where the rule of law existed." The billboards left you wondering whether the party supported or was vehemently against genocide. Above the mosaic of photos floated Putin's words: "Together we must make Russia united, strong . . ."[6]

"Putin's approval rating is more than 70 per cent. United Russia is the party of Putin, so maybe all their votes are because of Putin," Vyacheslav Nikonov, a Kremlin spin doctor, told me in the middle of the campaign as United Russia continued to rise in the polls. Putin was so popular, Nikonov said, that the party didn't need to further define what it stood for. It just had to associate itself as closely as possible with the president.

Though the Organization for Security and Co-operation in Europe, in a post-election report, complained of media manipulation, the misuse of administrative resources and the overall regression of democracy, the results of the December 8, 2003, parliamentary elections seemed to bear Nikonov out. United Russia won 37 per cent of the vote, well ahead of the diminished Communists, who saw their share of the vote sliced in half to 13 per cent. The other big gainers were Vladimir Zhirinovsky's ultranationalist Liberal Democratic Party of Russia, which saw its once flaccid support rise to 12 per cent, and a new party called Rodina, which blended the LDPR's xenophobia with socialist economics. A Kremlin creation designed to draw votes from the Communists, and led by Dmitri Rogozin—a forty-year-old politician who camouflaged his angry xenophobia with cool charisma—Rodina picked up 9 per cent.

The two main liberal and pro-Western parties, Yabloko and the Union of Right Forces, were obliterated, missing the 5 per cent barrier required to win seats in Parliament. Under the Duma's seat allocation system, the results left United Russia with a controlling two-thirds share of the parliament. The party could do virtually anything, including what Russia's liberals feared most: amend the constitution to allow Putin to run for a third consecutive term. Surkov was ebullient. "We are living in a new Russia now," he said after the results were announced. "A new political era is coming, and the parties that have not gotten into Parliament should be calm about it and realize that their historical mission has been completed.[7]

But if Putin had become an outright authoritarian, it must be said that he ruled with the people's consent. Opinion polls, even those done by Yuri Lavada's independent firm, showed that his popularity remained unwaveringly high, usually in the 70 per cent range, the kind of figures a Western politician could only dream about. People told pollsters that while they mistrusted big business, the media and even the Putin-appointed cabinet, they had unbroken faith in the president himself.

Perplexed at why Putin's popularity was undented by the thousands of deaths that could be laid at his doorstep—four years of carnage in Chechnya, plus his egregious mishandling of first the *Kursk* submarine disaster and later the *Nord-Ost* hostage taking—I drove to the factory town of Ivanovo, some three hundred kilometres northeast of Moscow. There, I found my answer: the upside of Putin's *stabilnost*.

Known during the Soviet era as the City of Brides because of the number of young women drawn to the city by its relatively high-paying textile-mill jobs and immortalized in the song "Honest, Intelligent, Unmarried," Ivanovo had been one of the places worst hit by the economic collapse of the 1990s. Once, its forty-four textile mills had accounted for two-thirds of all cotton produced in the Soviet Union. By the late 1990s, most of the mills had fallen into disuse.

While there may not have been an economic miracle in Ivanovo during Putin's first term in office, the bleeding was staunched, if not stopped. The textile mills that once employed 70 per cent of the city's workforce were no longer in danger of shutting down, and people were no longer in danger of losing their jobs. The factories that had survived the tumult of the 1990s were even beginning to thrive again. They were selling out their stocks, expanding their lines, buying new machines and, most crucially of all, hiring extra staff.

As I toured the Noviy Ivanovskiy textile mill, a giant red-brick monument to better days gone by, the story that the factory manager told me explained Putin's astonishing popularity. In 1998 and 1999, the factory had been on the verge of shutting down for good. Then, on the eve of the 2000 presidential election, Putin visited the factory, on one of the few campaign-style stops he made. He quickly breezed through, saying little other than promising to prove his worth by "concrete deeds, not advertising," but his election was seen by workers here as the moment things started to get better for them.[8]

When I asked her who she planned to vote for, Irina Korobleva, a machine operator at the textile factory, looked at me as if I had just stepped off the moon. "Of course I'm voting for Putin," the lithe, auburn-haired twenty-two-year-old said, pausing in the midst of a long shift of folding bed linens. "We live normal lives now. If it were not for him, things would be much worse."

Korobleva said her family and friends felt the same way, and that all were planning to vote for Putin. Ideas like press freedom were ephemeral to her; the war in Chechnya was far away and, to her understanding, nearly over. She didn't even blame the president for the way the *Kursk* or *Nord-Ost* had been handled. All she knew for sure was that her job was safe and her parents' pensions were getting paid on time and in full, something that was never certain under Yeltsin. If another "democrat" got elected, she said, the country would be ruined.

I heard the same argument all around the country during my pre-election tour. While the West looked at Putin's Russia with growing concern about its political direction, ordinary Russians looked at the same period with relief. Their lives had gotten a little bit better and a lot more predictable under the leadership of the "authoritarian" Kremlin. In the old imperial capital of St. Petersburg, the former gulag town of Vorkuta, the Siberian centre of Irkutsk or the Ural mountain industrial city of Chelyabinsk, I was told the same thing: voters looked at the small but tangible economic progress in their lives and decided they wanted more of the same.

During Putin's first term, the GDP grew by 29.9 per cent, a stunning number even if most of the new wealth was concentrated in

Moscow and, to a lesser extent, St. Petersburg. Unemployment fell by one-third and the minimum wage quadrupled. Even the ruble was stabilized. Although much of that economic success could be attributed to the rise in world oil prices, voters didn't care. They weren't so much voting for Putin as they were voting against the possibility of another Yeltsin.

Some of the things the West worried about, such as the fate of Mikhail Khodorkovsky and the other oligarchs who had fallen from favour, were seen by most ordinary Russians as a feather in their president's cap. Russians saw Khodorkovsky, Gusinsky and Berezovsky as thieves who had become wealthy snapping up the country's resources at fire-sale prices just as Russia was plunging into poverty. They saw Khodorkovsky's jailing as his just deserts and cheered Putin for taking action. Many openly applauded him specifically for doing what many in the West were accusing him of: taking Russia back to Soviet times.[9]

"We are not afraid of the old times, because then we had free hospitals, free schools, free summer camps for children. We lived well, better than this," said Tatiana Sablina, a forty-year-old woman who ran a stall on Moscow's cobblestoned Arbat Street, where she sold her nephew's artwork. Her careworn face made her look at least twenty years older than she was. Sablina told me that in a good week, she might make 1,500 rubles (about $50) selling watercolour paintings and handcrafted wooden cats, an amount that she said was barely enough to live on. Though the economy had gotten better in recent years, she still lived a hard life, and she resented Khodorkovsky and the other oligarchs for getting rich at what she saw as the people's expense. She was happy to see Khodorkovsky behind bars and hoped that four more years of Putin's rule would restore more of the *stabilnost* she treasured. "Step by step, I hope, we are coming to a situation where there's law and order in the country," she told me. I didn't need to ask Sablina who she planned to vote for. Her vision of Russia fitted perfectly with Putin's: a strong country where things like stability and order are prized and concepts like freedom and openness are viewed with suspicion. The words she used could have been drafted by Surkov himself.

With Putin's popularity still sky-high, he could have won re-election without resorting to manipulation. But Putin and his team didn't want just a re-election, especially not one that saw the president take less than 50 per cent of the vote in the first round and thereby have to endure the indignity of a second-round runoff election that would turn the second-place finisher into the face of the opposition for the next four years. They wanted a convincing first-round victory—big, but not too big—with enough debate to demonstrate that Russia was still a democracy and a wide enough margin to show that Putin was the only person the people could imagine leading the country. Sixty per cent was not a convincing enough win. Eighty per cent, a figure some polls suggested Putin was actually approaching, looked a little too improbable to appear legitimate. Seventy per cent—actually 72 per cent—was the target.

The first step was to convince the main contenders to drop out of the race. Days after the parliamentary vote, Gennady Zyuganov, the leader of the Communist Party who had finished second to Putin in the 2000 presidential vote, stepped aside in favour of an unknown lieutenant, Nikolai Kharitonov, who was named the Communist candidate for the elections. Next Vladimir Zhirinovsky withdrew, just days after announcing that he would run, and announced that his former bodyguard, Oleg Malyshkin, would stand for president in his place. Without explanation, the parties that had finished second and third in the Duma elections had effectively conceded the presidency to Putin.

The Kremlin quickly torpedoed most other serious candidates. Sergei Glazyev, an economist from the Rodina faction, threw his hat in despite repeated warnings from Surkov not to run. When he defiantly went ahead and submitted his nomination papers, Dmitri Rogozin, the party's co-founder, quickly abandoned him, leaving Glazyev to twist in the wind without the support of his own party. A more bizarre fate befell Ivan Rybkin, a candidate with ties to the exiled Boris Berezovsky. Rybkin disappeared in the middle of the campaign, days after publishing a letter in the Berezovsky-owned *Kommersant* newspaper charging that Putin "has no right to power in Russia. And we have no right to be silent about it." Five days later, Rybkin—previously a respected politician who under Yeltsin had been secretary of the National Security Council and Speaker of the Duma—reappeared in Kiev, telling a strange story of having fled there for his own safety, not having told even his wife what he was doing or why. Then he flew to Berezovsky's side in London and changed his story again. He had been drugged and kidnapped, he said, by FSB agents. The Kremlin, meanwhile, spread a story that involved binge drinking and Ukrainian mistresses. Another candidate in the race, Sergei Mironov, barely campaigned, and said he personally intended to vote for Putin.

That left Irina Khakamada as the sole serious anti-Putin candidate. Khakamada, a forty-eight-year-old Muscovite of mixed Japanese-Russian descent, never had any illusions about winning. Though she had been elected Russia's woman of the year in a magazine poll in 2003 (Putin, of course, was man of the year), the veteran opposition politician knew Russian voters were not ready to elect a woman, much less one who looked like a foreigner. She joined the race out of despair, after the usual standard-bearers of Russia's democrats all declined to run, some calling for a boycott of what was sure to be an unfair election, others citing the hopelessness of running against the Kremlin machine and hoping prospects would be better in 2008, when Putin was constitutionally expected to step aside. Even her own party—the Union of Right Forces (SPS)—refused to give formal backing to her candidacy, in large part because her co-leaders, Boris Nemtsov and Anatoly Chubais, wanted either to completely boycott the election or to field a single democratic candidate supported by both SPS and the rival Yabloko movement. The latter idea failed largely because Yabloko's egotistical leader, Grigory Yavlinsky, insisted that the unified candidate had to be him.

Khakamada rejected the idea of boycotting, arguing that if no liberal candidate ran against Putin, the message would be that the only opposition to the Kremlin was the Communists and the ultranationalists. Given such choices, the West could hardly be blamed for accepting the Kremlin's current occupants as the least bad option. With a nod to her father's heritage, she dubbed her campaign a "kamikaze" campaign, her sole intent to throw a wrench into the works of managed democracy.

She partially succeeded. By accepting the help of Khodorkovsky's Open Russia foundation as well as direct funding from the jailed tycoon's long-time business partner, Leonid Nevzlin (who himself was facing murder charges and had fled to Israel), Khakamada put to rest rumours that she had joined the race to please the Kremlin and to give the election credibility in the eyes of the international community. She launched a public broadside against Putin, charging that he was leading the country back to authoritarianism and, more personally, that he had bungled the *Nord-Ost* hostage situation.

"We have a society based on lies, a society in which democracy is used only as a formal procedure, a society based on a completely closed nature and, most importantly, a society based on fear," she told me mid-campaign, her dark eyes flashing behind trendy oval eyeglasses. "Name me a single democratic country—even one that has only the trappings of democracy—where the opposition party does not take part in the elections. Some people are just scared to speak out against Putin. I am not."

Her words caused a firestorm among the Moscow and St. Petersburg intelligentsia, many of whom were now firmly set against the president, and made front-page news in both cities. But they were never heard by the tens of millions of Russian voters who lived outside those cities, where newspapers like *Kommersant* and *Novaya Gazeta* were almost impossible to find and where people relied primarily on state-run television for their news. A study by the think tank Russian Axis found that during the campaign, Putin received 61.4 hours of coverage from the major television networks, almost all of it slavishly positive. That was nearly five times the coverage Khakamada got, and almost six times what Rodina's Glazyev received. Most Russian voters knew nothing about the two main opposition candidates, except that even their own parties wouldn't back them.

The 2004 presidential elections were the first ones in which Alexander Yakovlev did not cast a vote. In a gesture full of portent, the man many considered the grandfather of Russian democracy forsook the right to vote that he had once been so insistent on, and went instead to a conference in Prague. "It was useless to vote. It was known beforehand who would win," he said shortly before his death in 2005, his thick eyebrows knitting together in disgust over eyes that locked you in place with an intelligent, alert stare. "This was not an election. This is what we had for seventy years before."

Despite Khakamada's noble effort, the only drama of Russia's third post-Soviet presidential election campaign was the firing of Putin's long-serving prime minister, Mikhail Kasyanov.

After the revolving-door governments of the Yeltsin years, Putin had made a point of sticking with Kasyanov and the deep-voiced economist's cabinet for his entire first term in office. He had even tolerated occasional bursts of dissent from his prime minister, who was viewed as one of the last powerful holdovers from Yeltsin's "Family." Kasyanov had spoken out against the arrest of Khodorkovsky, warning that it would scare off foreign investors if it looked as if the law was a tool of the state. He had battled Putin in private over the storming of the theatre during the *Nord-Ost* hostage siege and over the cutoff of gas supplies to Belarus.

The *siloviki*, as the ex-KGB types who dominated Putin's inner circle became known (the word translates roughly into "men of power"), had long agitated for Kasyanov's dismissal. Surkov, Dmitry Medvedev and the influential defence minister Sergei Ivanov resented the residual influence of Yeltsin holdovers like Kasyanov and Putin's chief of staff, Alexander Voloshin. When Voloshin—who had approved Khodorkovsky's financing of opposition political parties—quit after the tycoon's arrest, it left Kasyanov as the last key Kremlin figure with ties to the old regime.

Kasyanov eventually gave the *siloviki* the excuse to push him aside that they were looking for. Above all else, Putin demanded loyalty from his inner circle, and Kasyanov, in the run-up to the election, had entertained a pitch from Boris Nemtsov, who wanted him to run as the joint "democratic" presidential candidate against Putin. Confronted with evidence that Kasyanov might be conspiring against him, Putin summoned him to his office on February 24 and fired him and his entire cabinet, eventually replacing him with an unknown, unambitious technocrat named Mikhail Fradkov.[10]

Other than Kasyanov's firing, the election campaign created little drama. Putin boycotted the televised debates, so few people watched and there was little for the candidates who did show up to argue about. What campaigning Putin's opponents did manage did nothing to dent the president's massive lead in the opinion polls.

On election day, March 14, 2004, I visited polling station after polling station—most of them set up in schools and libraries—and watched as voters unenthusiastically cast their ballots and then enthusiastically shopped for bargains in the mini-markets set up outside to draw voters. Desperate for something interesting to photograph after a dreary morning of talking to pro-Putin voters, the photographer I was working with, Heidi Hollinger, called up an old friend who was Russia's first-ever *Playboy* centrefold, Maria Tarasevich, and got her to look pouty while lounging sexily around a polling station on Kutuzovsky Prospekt.

That evening, Heidi and I went to Santa Fe, an expensive Mexican restaurant in the centre of Moscow, to watch the televised results with Irina Khakamada and her supporters. What had been billed as a party quickly turned into a wake. The state-run Channel One showed results that surprised no one. Vladimir Putin had won in a landslide, with 71.3 per cent of the vote, more than five times the 13.7 per cent won by his nearest rival, the stand-in Communist candidate Nikolai Kharitonov, and almost precisely the 72 per cent Gelman and the others had set as their target. Sergei Glazyev had finished third with a paltry 4.1 per cent, just ahead of Khakamada, who finished with an embarrassing 3.9 per cent.

Leaning against a wall with a glass of French white wine, Lev Ponomarev, a veteran activist who had helped create Memorial, the group dedicated to exposing the human rights crimes of the Soviet regime, tried to be philosophical about what was happening to his country. All revolutions, he told me in slow, carefully measured words, come unstuck at some point, and it was predictable that Russia's peaceful overthrow of communism thirteen years earlier and its hesitant embrace of democracy would be challenged one day.

Ponomarev, a man with a thin, careworn face and gradually greying hair, was nonetheless bitter. He had been involved in the creation of Democratic Russia, the first formal opposition to the Communist Party when it was founded in 1990, and had been among those elected to the Supreme Soviet in Mikhail Gorbachev's initial experiment with multi-party elections. There's a classic photograph of him standing on Lubyanka Square, in front of the KGB headquarters, as a crowd vents its anger on the iconic statue of Felix Dzerzhinsky that would soon afterward be violently yanked from its plinth. Scratching his head in the photographs, he looks as though he's the half-mad director of the chaos around him.

Now Ponomarev could see it all coming undone as a cadre of ex-KGB agents solidified its hold on power. "We had a peaceful revolution, and now we have a restoration of the old. We didn't think it could happen so fast," he said, pausing to acknowledge Alla Gerber, a Duma deputy from the early Yeltsin years, as she stopped by and squeezed his shoulders in a sad, gentle hug. "This may be the lowest point yet, and there's a real danger it could get worse."

As Ponomarev went in search of Khakamada, I sidled up to the bar for a drink of my own. The man next to me was drunk and nostalgic for the optimism of 1991. "We were so romantic back then, and believed in such good things," said Vitaly Tretyakov, a white-haired journalist who had helped turn the *Moscow News* into a reformist bugle during the Gorbachev era and then had jumped ship in 1990 to establish *Nezavisimaya Gazeta,* which lived up to its name ("Independent Newspaper") and became the first above-ground newspaper published since 1917 that was completely free of the influence of the Communist Party.

Like Yakovlev, he blamed Yeltsin and the reformers more than he did Putin. He couldn't believe that the country had fallen so far so fast from the heady days of August 1991, when Yeltsin had climbed on top of the tank in front of the White House to denounce the coup attempt by Soviet hard-liners. "The last thirteen years were dedicated to making all possible mistakes that could have been made," Tretyakov said, staring into his drink. "'Democracy' now means the same thing as 'corruption.' 'Liberal' means 'thief,' and 'friendly toward the West' means 'robber of the country.'"

He was interrupted when a band took the stage and started playing in a vain attempt to coax the party-goers onto the dimly lit restaurant's empty dance floor. Trying desperately to lighten the mood, the master of ceremonies offered to take bets on what the final vote breakdown would be. He had few takers. "I'll put 100 rubles on Putin," someone yelled out from the back. No one around me even smiled.

It wasn't Western-style democracy, Sergei Markov acknowledges, but in his version of events, the 2004 elections represented a step forward. Putin's success showed that stability had been restored. Now the economy would continue to grow, and at some point in the future (Markov didn't say when), Russia would be ready for more political openness.

In the 1990s Russia had moved too fast from totalitarianism to total freedom, resulting in political and economic chaos. Now Russia had a system somewhere in between, one that Markov argued suits it best for the time being. "It's a bureaucratic authoritarian regime," he said proudly. "Russia is on the path from the hell of the 1990s toward a normal country. We are in a transition period."

Not everyone was as enamoured with what Putinism had grown into. Though Marat Gelman, like Markov, been involved with the Putin Project and with establishing managed democracy from day one, there are times when he doesn't sound much happier with the outcome than Yakovlev, Ponomarev or Tretyakov. The 2004 presidential elections, he told me later, marked "the end of politics" for Russia. "After the elections, our politicians stopped being able to influence anything. There remained only one politician in the country—Putin. All the other politicians in the country were separated from the sphere of actions and were relegated to the sphere of words and gestures only. The main political scientist in the country in these circumstances is Vladimir Surkov, because he knows who visits Putin. Even though there are still elements of political struggle, it's not the opposition versus the authorities, it's a struggle within the authorities."

In other words, it was the victory of the managed democracy that Gelman had spent years working toward. But as he spoke, I realized he wasn't happy with what he had created—which made sense. His father, playwright Aleksandr Gelman, had earned fame by standing up at a 1988 meeting of the Soviet Filmmakers' Union and complaining that the apparatchiks of the Communist Party were not interested in real reform—they wanted only a mild tinkering, dictatorship under a different name. The father was warning against what the son would build. I asked Gelman if he was proud of what had become of Russia, and of his role in it.

"No," he answered me straight out. He avoided my gaze and stared out the window instead. "I have this other project that I work on from time to time. I call it Russia 2."

He wouldn't tell me what that Russia looked like.

NINE

———

A CHESTNUT OF AN IDEA

Kiev and Moscow

Watching on television as Georgians took to the street to overthrow Shevardnadze, Yulia Tymoshenko was struck by a single, overwhelming thought: why couldn't the same thing happen in Ukraine? She immediately fired off a letter of congratulations to the interim president, Nino Burjanadze. "The experience of Georgia, [of] a peaceful, democratic revolution," Tymoshenko wrote, "must be borrowed by the democratic forces of Ukraine."

Others soon came to see what Tymoshenko—a fiery and charismatic millionaire with braided golden hair who had become one of the key figures in Ukraine's opposition—was talking about. The Ukrainian regime's hold on power was as weak as Shevardnadze's had been. In his efforts to maintain his image as a reformer, even as he moved Kiev more and more back into Moscow's orbit, Leonid Kuchma had allowed a free press to exist and a vibrant opposition to flourish and had given Western NGOs plenty of space to operate. With a presidential election set for November 2004, and with a regime that history showed could be counted on to tinker with the results, there seemed to be all the necessary ingredients for a rerun of Belgrade and Tbilisi.

The West, and specifically America, had several reasons for wanting to see a friendly regime in Kiev: reversing the Odessa-Brody pipeline so it could carry Caspian crude to market in Europe and seeing the back of a corrupt regime that had squandered hundreds of millions of dollars in aid and had sold weapons to Iraq. The U.S. and Poland genuinely desired to see Ukraine, the largest country in Europe, join the European Union, so as to shift the union's centre farther east, away from Paris and Berlin. And then there was Russia.

The Kremlin's lingering dreams of empire had suffered a near-mortal blow in early 2004 when NATO expanded its membership from nineteen to twenty-six countries by adding seven new members that had all once been part of the Soviet-dominated Warsaw Pact. Watching Romania, Bulgaria, Slovakia and Slovenia join an alliance still perceived in Russia as anti-Moscow was a bitter pill to swallow. Striking much closer to the heart was the "loss" (as it was viewed in the Kremlin) of Estonia, Latvia and Lithuania, the three Baltic states that had once been member republics of the USSR. Their decision to join NATO put them seemingly forever out of Russia's grasp, and put NATO warplanes a short flight from Moscow.

The Kremlin's powerlessness to block the NATO expansion was a harsh reminder of its diminished status in the world, and redoubled Putin's desire to tighten his grip on the remaining "near abroad." The NATO enlargement, combined with the Rose Revolution and the presence of American troops in Georgia and Central Asia, smacked of U.S. encirclement of Russia, and gave ammunition to the hawks inside the Kremlin who had long been urging Putin to again treat the West as hostile. Defense Minister Sergei Ivanov, a leading anti-Western hawk, warned of a "cold peace" and backed it up with naked saber-rattling.

Within a week of Estonia, Latvia and Lithuania's formally joining NATO, Russia's Baltic Sea Fleet practised amphibious landings near their coasts, while Russian warplanes mocked the air defences of the tiny countries by repeatedly violating their airspace. It was a warning aimed as much at Ukraine as at the Baltics.

"Without Ukraine, Russia ceases to be a Eurasian empire," former U.S. national security adviser Zbigniew Brzezinski wrote in his book *The Grand Chessboard.* "However, if Moscow regains control over Ukraine, with its 52 million people and major resources, as well as access to the Black Sea, Russia automatically again regains the wherewithal to become a powerful imperial state spanning Europe and Asia." In May 2004, he gave a speech at Kiev University in which he made it clear that Ukraine should be the centre of NATO's next expansion.[1]

I took a trip in early 2004 to Belarus and Ukraine, looking for signs that—as Mikhail Saakashvili had predicted to me—the "democratic wave" was spreading to other post-Soviet states. In Minsk I found only despair. In Kiev I saw a machine that was already in motion. "If the authorities try to falsify the presidential election . . . I would hope to see the Georgian example repeated here in Ukraine. I personally will be calling people to go into the streets," Tymoshenko told me, locking my eyes with her fierce brown gaze to make sure I understood she was serious.

The former deputy prime minister even had a name ready for the uprising she dreamt of. It would be called the "Chestnut Revolution," she told me and the *Times*'s Jeremy Page in an interview at her office, after the fruit of the giant trees that line Khreshchatyk Street, Kiev's broad and curvaceous main boulevard. What Tymoshenko didn't tell us that day—but unquestionably must have known—was that the building blocks for staging a Serbian- or Georgian-style uprising were already being put in place.

With the Ukrainian opposition—jointly led by Tymoshenko and Viktor Yushchenko, the former central banker—signalling clearly at the end of 2003 that it wanted Western help overthrowing Kuchma, George Soros and the various groups funded by the National Endowment for Democracy went to work making it happen. Days after the Rose Revolution, David Dettman, director of the National Democratic Institute's Kiev office, flew to Tbilisi, anxious to see at first hand how the revolution had come about and whether the model would work in Ukraine. After a month on the ground and after meeting with Mark Mullen, NDI's man in Tbilisi, Dettman determined that yes, it could.

"I went to Georgia because Georgia was an important example of a democratic flowering, a sudden democratic flowering, and it had a similar political situation to Ukraine at the time: an unpopular government, stolen elections, etc. And a popular opposition with a reasonable chance, which is not the case in a lot of places. Georgia was very important for Ukraine," Dettman told me in NDI's Kiev offices, six months after what would become known—despite Tymoshenko's attempts to brand it otherwise—as the Orange Revolution.

The stage was set. Shortly after Dettman's trip to Tbilisi, Otpor's Alexander Maric and some of the other travelling Serbian revolutionaries began showing up in Ukraine to teach and train Pora, a new Ukrainian youth group that would lead the street protests already being planned for the day after the election. With Western money materializing (donor conferences were organized by the Canadian embassy in Kiev) to support their trips, the Otpor veterans were joined this time by members of Kmara, who were anxious to do for the Ukrainians what the Serbians had done for them. NDI, meanwhile, set about "butting heads" to make sure that the on-again, off-again alliance between Tymoshenko and Yushchenko would hold through the trials ahead.

Ask Ukrainians when they think the Soviet Union started falling apart and it's unlikely that they'll cite Yeltsin's climbing on top of a tank in 1991. It's far more likely that they'll mention Friday, April 26, 1986, when Reactor No. 4 at the Lenin Memorial Chernobyl nuclear power plant exploded, sending a flash of fire into the sky and spewing a radioactive cloud that would settle over a large chunk of northern Ukraine and southern Belarus.

The explosion and the way it was handled by Soviet authorities highlighted everything that was rotten inside the Communist system. The reactor blew not because of technological failure, but because scientists at the plant decided to test how long the reactor could operate if all external power was cut. The cloud of radiation produced by the nuclear explosion that followed was one hundred times larger than that produced by the bomb dropped on Hiroshima.

For days, the Soviet authorities dithered, keeping quiet about the tragedy even as families in the neighbouring town of Pripyat, where most of the nuclear plant's workers lived, spent the first day after the disaster attending sixteen outdoor weddings scheduled by the Communist Youth League. Though everyone in town could see thick smoke pouring skyward from the burning remains of the reactor, schools in the town sponsored outdoor gymnastics, while youths played soccer in the park. The following day, Pripyat was evacuated. Its 47,000 residents were told they would soon return, and so took few of their belongings with them. They had no idea they were abandoning their homes forever.

Almost two decades on, blocks of apartments in Pripyat's main square still stood eerily silent. Furniture and household goods still filled the homes. Envelopes dated April 1986 sat unopened in mailboxes. In a nearby fairground, a Ferris wheel, rusted from disuse, towered over a lot filled with scattered bumper cars, forever frozen in mid-bump. Posters celebrating the glories of the Soviet Union, prepared for a May Day parade that was never held, lay unused in the town hall.

When I visited Chernobyl on a Red Cross–organized trip almost eighteen years to the day after the explosion, the wound still seemed fresh. The last of Chernobyl's four reactors had been shut down four years earlier, but the decommissioning work was expected to continue for decades. Meanwhile, thousands of people still lived and worked in the hot zone, suffering and dying from the effects of the explosion. Though the International Atomic Energy Agency would announce that far fewer deaths could be directly attributed to Chernobyl than previously thought, it seemed to me that the dead and the dying were everywhere. "I'm convinced that people have to leave here," said Olga Davidenko, a visibly shaken sixteen-year-old I met in the nearby village of Laski. Minutes before, she had learned during a visit to a Red Cross mobile clinic that she had a goitre, an inflammation of the thyroid gland that can develop into lymphoma. Of her six friends who had taken the free tests together, two had been told they had thyroid conditions. "I plan to go to university in Kiev and never come back," she told me.[2] Portable radiation meters we brought with us showed that radiation remained extremely high—200 micro-roentgens an hour in Prypyat, compared with a more normal 12 in central Kiev, about 100 kilometres to the south.

Though it took more than two years to develop into street protests, anger over Chernobyl, combined with the events sweeping Eastern Europe, helped fuel the birth of the Ukrainian Popular Movement for Perestroika, which was known simply as Rukh, or "Movement." It was Ukraine's first modern, openly nationalist organization. Rukh held its first anti-Communist demonstrations in the summer of 1988 in Lviv, a western Ukrainian city with almost no Russian population that, even in Soviet times, retained the feel of Austria and Central Europe. By the end of the year they had moved to Kiev, where protestors occupied Khreshchatyk Street, the same place that would become famous in 2004.

Many contend that Ukraine's lingering confusion about its Soviet past (many still openly pine for the "good old days") stems from the fact that it didn't have a Lech Wałęsa or Václav Havel leading the masses against the authorities, or even a Boris Yeltsin defending the White House. Ukraine's independence from the Soviet Union was given freely, not widely demanded or popularly won. In the March 1991 referendum in which Mikhail Gorbachev asked Soviet citizens if they wanted to maintain the USSR, 70.5 per cent of Ukrainians said yes, and many Ukrainian leaders originally supported the hard-line coup against Gorbachev in August of that year. Only in December 1991, after events in other Soviet republics had made the USSR's dissolution inevitable, did Ukrainians belatedly vote in favour of independence.

Though the Communist Party itself was initially banned (only to return a few years later as the most popular political party in the country), the old rulers never let go of their grip on power. Leonid Kravchuk, the parliamentary Speaker during the last years of the USSR, took advantage of the ambivalent attitude many Ukrainians had toward independence and cleverly portrayed himself as a cautious revolutionary, one who would establish an independent Ukraine but without entirely deserting the socialist system or close ties to Moscow. He easily defeated Vyacheslav Chornovil, an anti-Soviet dissident who had spent nearly fourteen years in jail. Chornovil, who was revered in Galicia and Transcarpathia but distrusted in the Russified south and east of the country, won just 23.3 per cent of the vote, while 61.6 per cent chose Kravchuk.

When Kravchuk himself was defeated in 1994—after three years of dramatic economic mismanagement and soaring inflation and unemployment—it was in favour of Leonid Kuchma, a former missile-factory director from the eastern city of Dnipropetrovsk who also favoured close ties to Moscow and who spoke almost no Ukrainian. By the end of the tumultuous 1990s, Ukrainians had a flag and a national anthem, but little definable sense of a binding national identity. Still, despite the efforts of Kravchuk and Kuchma, something had begun to stir.

Leonid Kuchma's decade in power in Ukraine could often be defined by a single word: corruption. While the country occasionally posted years of impressive economic growth under Kuchma's leadership, little of that seemed to ever trickle down to ordinary Ukrainians. As the privatizations of state assets went ahead in the 1990s, a handful of key

Kuchma associates became stratospherically rich while villages barely an hour's drive from Kiev still had mud roads and donkey carts.

Where Putin's inner circle was made up of ex-KGB men, Kuchma's was a collection of billionaires who had gotten rich off running the state. By the end of Kuchma's ten years in office, his son-in law, Viktor Pinchuk, a gregarious steel magnate and member of Parliament, controlled four of the country's biggest television channels and had an estimated wealth of $2.2 billion. Kuchma's chief of staff, Viktor Medvedchuk, was worth an estimated $800 million. Another influential insider was Rinat Akhmetov, one of the richest men in Europe, with a fortune of $3.5 billion, who headed the influential Donetsk clan that controlled business and politics in eastern Ukraine. In the most famous example of how Kuchma took care of those around him, his government allowed a consortium headed by Pinchuk and Akhmetov to purchase the state-owned Kryvorizhstal steel mill in 2004 for a paltry $800 million, less than 20 per cent of its actual worth.[3]

For a while, Ukraine's exclusive group of oligarchs included Yulia Tymoshenko's husband, Oleksandr, as well as her business partner, Pavlo Lazarenko, who briefly served as prime minister under Kuchma before fleeing prosecution in Ukraine, only to be tried and convicted of corruption by a U.S. court. Tymoshenko herself briefly became a billionaire while at the head of Unified Energy Systems of Ukraine, a gas-trading company that Russian authorities allege profited by illegally siphoning off gas that was transiting Ukraine. Though her name was briefly put on the Interpol watch list at Russia's request, the charges have never been substantiated and most observers put her in the same category as Mikhail Khodorkovsky—someone who is resented for making a lot of money during the fast and loose days after the Soviet Union's fall.

During the 1990s many Ukrainians viewed Tymoshenko with disdain as the billionaire "gas princess," even after she entered politics in 1998. She quickly scaled to the position of deputy prime minister in 1999 after Kuchma unexpectedly named a cabinet of pro-Western reformers headed by Yushchenko. Together, they managed to spare Ukraine the worst of the 1998 currency crisis that bloodied neighbouring Russia.

But even as Kuchma's pals lined up at the trough, Kuchma, unlike Lukashenko and, to a lesser extent, Putin, never succeeded in privatizing the country's politics. A vibrant opposition remained in place, and the president's projects were often blocked by a parliament that he could never fully bring under his control. As had happened to Shevardnadze, it's arguable—from the Kremlin's point of view—that Kuchma planted the seeds of his own demise by pursuing a split policy of inviting Western money and ideas into the country while allowing Russia to retain its political and economic dominance: semi-authoritarianism would prove unsustainable when people could read about the crimes and corruption of the regime in independent media and then support a credible opposition candidate.

The Chernobyl-era protests left Ukrainians with a spirit of defiance that emerged several times before the events of November 2004, including the "Ukraine Without Kuchma" campaign launched in the wake of the 2001 Gongadze tapes scandal.

The Gongadze protests brought Maric and other Otpor veterans to Lviv and Kiev, where they began working with a fledgling coalition of anti-Kuchma NGOs called Freedom of Choice, backed by the International Renaissance Foundation (the Ukrainian branch of the Soros Foundation). An Otpor-inspired youth organization dubbed Za Pravdu ("For Truth") led protests that included a tent city set up in the centre of Kiev. Initially, the opposition seemed leaderless, until January 19, 2001, when Kuchma fired Tymoshenko from government and she immediately set about trying to depose her former ally. Tymoshenko was arrested and briefly jailed in February on charges stemming from her time at UES. It blunted her impact on the 2001 protests but endeared her to many of those camped on the streets and began her rapid public conversion from reviled gas princess to beloved Joan of Arc.

Although the initial push to oust Kuchma eventually fizzled—in large part because Yushchenko, who was still prime minister, sided with his boss and signed a declaration comparing the protestors to "fascists"—anti-Kuchma demonstrations continued throughout the next three years.

The anti-Kuchma movement gained fresh momentum in 2001 when Yushchenko lost a Communist-inspired non-confidence vote in the Rada, Ukraine's parliament. The pro-Western prime minister had made many enemies with his attempts to combat corruption and to reform the country's outdated industries, but he had also impressed many others. His dismissal sparked a ten-thousand-strong demonstration in Kiev and gained the opposition a second popular leader, though the opposition was split between Yushchenko's Our Ukraine movement and Tymoshenko's own party, the Yulia Tymoshenko Bloc.

The protests and the evidence contained in the Gongadze tapes left Kuchma, whose rise to power had once been viewed with some optimism in the West, a persona non grata in Europe and the United States. Along with sections in which Kuchma appeared to order his interior minister, Yuriy Kravchenko, to "give [Gongadze] to the Chechens," he was apparently also caught authorizing the sale of four advanced Kolchuga radar systems to Saddam Hussein's Iraq. Kuchma's standing sunk to an all-time low in Washington and London, leading to a decision to "uninvite" the Ukrainian leader from a 2002 NATO summit in Prague. Kuchma went anyway, but was studiously ignored.

The country's burgeoning opposition made a breakthrough during the 2002 parliamentary elections. With a new election-monitoring NGO called For Fair Elections monitoring the voting process and an exit poll funded by Western embassies making mass fraud by the authorities difficult, the regime was forced to concede that Yushchenko's new pro-Western bloc, Our Ukraine, had won a plurality of the popular vote, capturing 23.6 per cent of the vote. The Communists finished second with 20 per cent, ahead of the pro-Kuchma For a United Ukraine party and the Yulia Tymoshenko Bloc, which captured 11.8 per cent and 7.3 per cent respectively. Tymoshenko's result was bolstered by public suspicion that a car crash she survived during the campaign was in fact an organized attempt on her life.[4]

Kuchma was eventually able—using bribes and coercion—to carve a pro-government coalition out of Parliament anyway. But observers, especially in the West, saw the vote as evidence that Yushchenko was on course to win the presidency in 2004.

In February 2003, almost precisely a year after Saakashvili and his cohorts visited Washington, D.C., the International Republican Institute invited Yushchenko for a similar tour. He was given incredible access for a former prime minister from faraway Ukraine: he not only met with IRI head Senator John McCain, he had private meetings with Vice President Dick Cheney and Deputy Secretary of State Richard

Armitage, as well as former national security adviser Zbigniew Brzezinski, a hawkish opponent of what he saw as Putin's new imperialism. Speaking to reporters afterward, Yushchenko said his message to the Bush administration was simple: Don't give up on the opposition.

"We need to work together to make sure that elections in Ukraine are fair and democratic. It's the only thing that democratic forces in Ukraine really need," Yushchenko said. "Political forces in Ukraine need free radio, independent newspapers and independent news agencies as well as independent people who can monitor that legislation has been followed." U.S. analysts were amorous in their assessments of the opposition leader. "Yushchenko is the only hope for Ukraine," Anders Aslund of the Carnegie Endowment for International Peace told the *Washington Times*. "It's not even a matter of U.S. policy; it's pretty obvious."[5]

After the success of Georgia, the revolution-makers knew an inviting target when they saw one. Otpor and Kmara were already shuttling in and out of the country. Pavol Demeš of OK'98 made a series of trips dating back to 1999, meeting with protest leader Vladislav Kaskiv (himself a former program coordinator at Soros's Renaissance Foundation) and "assessing the evolution" of Ukrainian civil society. On later visits, Demeš acknowledges, he had a secondary purpose: he and Kaskiv were planning to establish a new Otpor-based youth group to succeed Za Pravdu. Kaskiv would lead it, and the German Marshall Fund of the United States—which Demeš was director of—would be one of its financial backers.

A new NGO called Znayu ("I Know"), funded by the U.S.-Ukraine Foundation and headed by Serbian revolutionary Marko Markovic, was created to supplement Freedom of Choice's campaign. In 5th Channel, an anti-Kuchma television station owned by key opposition backer Petro Poroshenko, the opposition already had a media outlet to play the role of B92 and Rustavi 2 by making sure the revolution, when it came, would be televised. When NDI convinced Tymoshenko to (briefly) tie her political fortunes to Yushchenko, all the pieces were neatly in place.

"Of course, any politician has ambitions," Tymoshenko told me when I met her in late 2002, while her aides made sure I didn't take my own photographs of Yulia, a strikingly attractive woman who knew the power of her sexuality and didn't want it tarnished by a bad photograph. "But I'm willing to subject my ambitions to the higher interest of getting rid of this political cancer," she said, grabbing hold of my arm to emphasize the point.

With the failures of Serbia and Georgia before it, as well as Lukashenko's successful repression of the opposition in Belarus, Russia knew well what to expect of the presidential elections in the fall of 2004. As Moscow saw it, the West was gearing up to make another push into the "near abroad," this time striking closer than ever before. The 2004 presidential elections would be a no-holds-barred fight, and this time Russia would be ready. In July 2004, the Kremlin dispatched its top political advisers—Gleb Pavlovsky, Sergei Markov and Marat Gelman among them—to Kiev, where they set up what became known as the Russia Club in the city's finest hotel, the Premier Palace. Their task was to counter the West's efforts and to deliver managed democracy, meaning a victory for Viktor Yanukovych, Kuchma's hand-picked successor, to Ukraine.

Yanukovych was hardly an ideal candidate to work with. He lacked Putin's forceful personality and, with two criminal convictions in his past, could hardly have had a worse background to sell to the public. But he was a representative of the powerful Donetsk clan that dominated eastern Ukraine, and vociferously pro-Moscow. One of his key campaign pledges would be to make Russian Ukraine's second official language, an idea that, unsurprisingly, pleased the Kremlin. He did, however, have a decent economic track record during the two years he served as Kuchma's prime minister.

The Kremlin feared that if pro-Western democrats swept to power in Ukraine only a year after Georgia's Rose Revolution, other post-Soviet states would quickly follow. Pavlovsky, in an interview with the mass-circulation Russian daily *Komsomolskaya Pravda,* put it in stark terms that made it clear that the Kremlin would do almost anything to retain its influence in Kiev and that he considered Russia's future intertwined with whatever happened in Ukraine: "If Russia allows Ukraine to be done away with, not a year will pass without us seeing something even worse in our own land. We have to defend ourselves in serious fashion."

"Of course, the Kremlin is working to support Yanukovych," Vyacheslav Nikonov, a sometime adviser to the Kremlin, told me when I called him up on the eve of the first round of Ukraine's presidential elections. "It's in Russia's interest not to have anti-Russian presidents in neighbouring countries."

I asked him how the Kremlin would react if Yushchenko won the election. "He won't win," he replied abruptly, cutting me off in mid-question. I tried again, pointing out that most opinion polls had Yushchenko ahead of Yanukovych by a slim margin with just a few weeks to go in the campaign. "It won't happen," he assured me before hanging up the phone.

——————

TEN

SPIKED ORANGES AND FELT BOOTS

Kiev

Miloš Milenković has a big red stamp in his passport. "Forbidden," it reads. Underneath it, a Ukrainian border guard has marked in bold lettering that the bearer is not allowed to enter Ukraine until January 1, 3000. The genial Serb received the 996-year ban in November 2004 after being forced off a train that was travelling into Ukraine. The Kuchma government had finally grasped the size and scope of the effort being mounted to ensure Viktor Yushchenko would be the country's next president and was moving to counter it.

Milenković laughs about it now—the ban has since been lifted, and it came far too late to stop what he and the other Otpor veterans had been helping to build. He estimates that by the time the border guards caught on, he had already been to Ukraine some twenty-two times to teach non-violent resistance tactics to youth groups looking to form the militant backbone of an uprising. Chief among these was Pora. Throughout early 2004, Britain's Westminster Foundation for Democracy was paying for Milenković, as well as fellow Otpor veterans Alexander Maric and Marko Markovic, to travel around Ukraine, where they met with and held training sessions for local activists. Maric, in fact, arrived almost directly from taking active part in the Rose Revolution in Georgia.

The veterans of the Za Pravdu and Ukraine Without Kuchma movements were being remoulded and rebranded into a group modelled after Kmara and Otpor. After a lot of wrangling, the group chose the name Pora (Ukrainian for "It's Time") and the soon-to-be ubiquitous logo of a ticking clock positioned just seconds before midnight. "We were sitting in these shitty hotel rooms—I don't even remember the city—discussing the name, the logo, everything," recalls Markovic, referring to a meeting in the Transcarpathian city of Uzhgorod. "I like to say that Alexander, Stanko and I are the spiritual witnesses of Pora being born."

While the Kuchma regime, after watching the events in Georgia, certainly smelled the brewing revolt in their country—as well as the outside hand in it—they reacted very slowly to the Pora training camps that Milenković and others were running around the country. As David Dettman, the NDI officer who was intimately involved in the planning of the training sessions, told me, no effort was made to conceal what was going on. The organizers wanted Kuchma and his cronies to know they were coming for them. They wanted to rattle the regime and perhaps frighten some in that inner circle into switching sides when the time came.

Bringing the Serbs in, Dettman told me, "scared the bejeezus out of the authorities, which is unbelievably important, because when you scare the bejeezus out of the authorities, all of a sudden some of the outlying members of the regime start to negotiate with the opposition. The security services start to get a little less aggressive when opposition gets together and there's a rally or something like that. And then all these business people who are kind of supportive of the regime but sitting on the fence start to say, 'Shit, they got Serbians in here! I saw what happened in Serbia, I saw what happened in Georgia. It's time to hedge my bets.' . . . The other thing is that you give those who are going to participate some hope. And [the Serbs] say, look, we did it. And then sometimes what they say is more credible than what Americans or Canadians or Brits are saying."

Stunned by the rapid fall of Shevardnadze, and as conscious of the parallels between Georgia and Ukraine as the opposition was, the Kuchma administration lashed about, knowing it was under threat but unsure how to deal with it. Like its effective masters in Moscow, the presidential administration in Kiev fundamentally misunderstood what had happened in Tbilisi. While it understood the work that American NGOs, particularly those affiliated with George Soros, had done to foment that uprising, it failed to grasp that the revolution-makers had succeded because the uprising tapped into and grew out of a genuine, popular frustration with the regime. And because when push came to shove, the Georgian regime's pillars were weak.

The same could be said for Ukraine, but Kuchma and his powerful chief of staff, Viktor Medvedchuk, believed that if they harassed the local Soros organization, the Renaissance Foundation, and others like it enough, they could prevent a repeat of what they called the "Georgian variant" in Ukraine. Meanwhile, they set out to make sure that if they had to cheat to make sure Viktor Yanukovych won, the fraud would go undetected by the Western-trained election monitors who had been so crucial to mobilizing the masses in Slovakia, Serbia and Georgia.

Kuchma made no secret of his disdain for his former prime minister, and Yushchenko made a popular campaign promise that, if elected, he would reopen the Gongadze murder investigation. But Kuchma, unlike Lukashenko in Belarus, had always cared what the West thought of him. He had been deeply stung when he (along with Lukashenko) had been explicitly uninvited from the NATO summit in Prague. He wanted to be liked.

So while Kuchma had grave suspicions about the preparatory work being done to unseat him by the Renaissance Foundation, Freedom House, NDI and IRI, he didn't expel them outright as the Belarusian strongman had done. Instead he sent his tax police and fire inspectors to make their lives miserable. Thugs sacked the Kiev apartment of Juhani Grossman, director of Freedom House's citizen participation campaign for the elections, but otherwise let him continue to do his job. They tailed Dettman but never detained or expelled him, despite activities that clearly could have been considered foreign interference in Ukraine's domestic affairs. They even called in Canadian ambassador Andrew Robinson to the Foreign Ministry to complain about his public criticism of the heavy pro-Yanukovych bias in the state-controlled media, but they never revoked his diplomatic credentials.[1]

If Kuchma's intention was to hang on to power at all costs, that laxity was a tactical error. By tolerating the activities of the big American NGOs, he essentially signed his own dismissal papers. "If they managed to arrest our leaders, it would have been a catastrophe," Pora's leader, Vladislav Kaskiv, told me later. "But they never did, because there was too much pressure on them. That made me confident in victory."

While Kuchma held back, concerned about the damage that a wide crackdown would make to his already blackened international reputation, Pora was gathering strength. Originally split into clashing factions dubbed "Black Pora" and "Yellow Pora"—the former more stridently apolitical, in the Otpor mould, the latter more overtly pro-Yushchenko—the two sides were brought together at a tense five-day training session in the Serbian city of Novi Sad in May 2004, paid for by Britain's Westminster Foundation for Democracy. Otpor's most seasoned trainers—Ivan Marovic, Siniša Šikman, Milenković and Maric (by now a Freedom House "consultant" for Ukraine)—ran the session.[2]

While Maric and Milenković drilled Pora on the standard revolutionary playbook, Šikman worked on what he calls a "secret mission" given him by Maric. "He told me, they're having problems uniting themselves," Šikman said. "So do the regular training, but your secret mission is to persuade them to take one line. To unite around one goal."

Šikman sat the two groups down for what he calls his "wedding" assignment (the only undertaking the married man believes to be as complicated as organizing a revolution). They were to plan a campaign to mobilize voters ahead of the looming election, with activities—meetings, protests, graffiti and sticker campaigns—scheduled for every day between then and the first round of voting, October 31. He gave them just forty-five minutes to do it, and the Ukrainians passed with flying colours.

"They were so excited when they were finished. They said, 'Wow, why couldn't we do this before?' They needed the time pressure to stop their bickering," Šikman recalls. "I told them to go home, meet with your activists, and start putting this plan you've drawn up into action."

Pora formed in March 2004, just before George Soros arrived for a five-day visit to Ukraine. It was the billionaire's first trip to the country since writing a *Financial Times* article three years earlier, during the height of the Gongadze protests, in which he controversially called for Kuchma to cede power to Yushchenko. Moscow and Kiev still identified Soros with that agenda, and his arrival was heavily criticized by Russia's ambassador, Viktor Chernomyrdin.[3]

Like Chernomyrdin, Kuchma's regime saw the billionaire's trip to the Crimea and Kiev as a provocation. Five days before his arrival, the *Ukrayinska Pravda* website (the same one Giorgiy Gongadze had worked for) obtained a copy of a *temnyk* issued by Viktor Medvedchuk that instructed the local media on how to cover the financier's visit. "Soros acquired his riches in a dubious way," the instructions read. "He uses his money to obtain confidential information . . . and encourage 'brain drain,' especially from the former Soviet states . . . He actively interferes in other countries' internal affairs, which leads to tragic consequences (hundreds of casualties in Yugoslavia in 2000 and the violent overthrow of the government in Georgia, which has put the country on the brink of economic collapse and civil war)."[4]

The government was prepared to go beyond *temnyki* to block Soros's efforts. His first stop, a conference on human rights and the role of NGOs in Yalta, was briefly cancelled after the Livadia Palace, where the conference was to be held, suddenly closed to the public, only to be opened again when Kuchma himself intervened. When Soros arrived in Kiev a few days later for a series of meetings related to the elections—including one with Kuchma—he was pelted with yogurt-filled condoms by members of Bratsvo, or "Brotherhood," a skinhead organization believed to take orders from Medvedchuk.

But the attack only motivated the billionaire. Leonard Bernardo, the regional director of the Open Society Institute, who accompanied Soros on the trip, said his boss came away with a crystallized understanding of what was wrong with Kuchma's regime. "For Soros, despite a few frightening incidents, I think he likes to know who his enemies are, and the people who committed this were quite open about it . . . The clarity about Medvedchuk and Bratsvo and what they were trying to do with respect to democratic institutions became quite apparent."

Soros left convinced that Kuchma and Medvedchuk's rule in Ukraine could and should be brought to an end. "It was so stark because on one hand you had these so-called *temnykis*, these secret decrees issued by the presidential administration dictating how the press should report on specific events, and at the same time you had the civil sector in that country that was very much beginning to engage in a much more profound way," Bernardo continued. "There was political pluralism in the parliament, so the necessary prerequisites for some social change existed, and I think Soros realized that and wanted to, where possible, see if his foundation could help."

But after having considerable public attention drawn to Soros's foundation's role in what happened in Tbilisi, his International Renaissance Foundation decided to remain more in the background in Kiev and to let other NGOs carry more of the load. As it had done to the other NGOs, Kuchma's regime harassed the IRF, targeting its Ukraine offices for tax inspections and almost closing them in early 2004 over a bogus fire-code violation.

"We knew we could not give money directly to, for instance, activists like Pora, because it would be seen as a sign, a strong argument for the political regime [to crack down]," the IRF's director, Yevgeny Bistretsky, told me. So the IRF focused instead on funding what Bernardo called its election "toolkit"—television debates, exit polls and aggressive monitoring on voting day itself—to create the right "context" for revolution. "We mobilized democratic forces, like human rights activists and mass media. We organized independent training of journalists, which became a basis for resistance, for raising the wave of resistance to censorship and falsification during the revolution."

Soros was just one in a long line of American dignitaries to travel to Kiev in early 2004. His visit followed that of NDI chair Madeleine Albright, who had complained that Kuchma was stifling opposition and free media and who in a *New York Times* article called for the Bush administration and Europe to unite behind the cause of "saving democracy in Ukraine." She predicted neatly what would happen next. "This election could well be decided by unfair tactics long before the balloting begins," she wrote. The West, she said, "must increase support for independent news media and civil society. This will require a considerable financial commitment as well as the help of Ukraine's democratic neighbors, which can provide unbiased media and training sites for voter mobilization and monitoring efforts."[5]

Next up was U.S. deputy secretary of state Richard Armitage, who spoke of the need for free elections and made clear that he thought the

Odessa-Brody pipeline should flow from south to north, carrying 180,000 barrels a day of non-Russian crude to the European market. John McCain visited later, as did former president George Bush. Each told Kuchma that the United States was going to watch the presidential elections very closely, and that future ties between Ukraine and the West—as well as Kuchma's own reputation—hinged on how fairly authorities managed the vote. Former national security adviser Zbigniew Brzezinski and former secretary of state Henry Kissinger joined the parade.

"President Kuchma was upset that so many people from outside were talking to him about democratic processes and not other bilateral issues," NDI president Ken Wollack recalled. He said Albright made it clear to Kuchma that, after visiting Ukraine several times as secretary of state, she was disappointed in the lack of democratic development in the country. From that point on, Wollack said, the meeting was "somewhat tense."

If the diplomatic offensive was meant to rattle Kuchma, it seems to have worked. But it also fed his sense that the West had already decided against him and Yanukovych, and he began relying more and more on Pavlovsky and the other Russian Club spin doctors to save the regime. "We could see what was going to happen. Suddenly, we were seeing many guests from abroad—Brzezinski, Kissinger—and all of them told Yanukovych that the elections must be 'free and fair.' We knew they were preparing for the Serbian variant, for non-free elections," Yanukovych's press secretary Anna German told me later. (Brzezinski was a particularly controversial figure for Russophile Ukrainians, having long argued that democratizing Ukraine was the key to keeping Russia from restoring its lost empire.) "Kuchma brought in Pavlovsky and these dirty technologies," German told me in a hushed voice over coffee much later, leaning in as if to make sure her words were not heard by those at the neighbouring tables. "We didn't need these things."

Unlike Kmara and Otpor, Pora claims to have received only "minimal" financial support from foreign donors. It puts its overall budget at 1.2 million euros, plus 5 million euros in "in-kind" donations from the local business community, including "free production of publications, communications, transportation, etc." That allowed Pora to produce and distribute some 40 million leaflets between March and December 2004.

But this was only a small part of the funding. Western governments and NGOs funded both the Freedom of Choice coalition and the Committee of Ukrainian Voters (known by its Ukrainian acronym KVU). Kaskiv was, until 2004, the head of Freedom of Choice, while Pora coordinator Iryna Chupryna was its deputy head throughout the election campaign, highlighting the fact that both the aims and the members of these other organizations were more often than not inter-changeable with Pora's. As Juhani Grossman of Freedom House put it, the Western NGOs were dancing a fine line, just as they had in Serbia with Otpor. "We never financially supported Pora, but we did in fact support the training of activists who later became members of Pora," he told me. But unlike impoverished Georgia or war-ravaged Serbia, Ukraine had its own money men. You don't need so much help from Soros and NED when you have home-grown millionaires like Petro Poroshenko, David Zhvania and Yulia Tymoshenko willing to put their money where their political careers are.[6]

While Tymoshenko's fortune had been whittled down by her years of battling the Kuchma regime and its persecution of her and her busi-nesses (it was commonly said that she was no longer a billionaire, though she comfortably remained a millionaire), Zhvania and Poroshenko remained two of the wealthiest businessmen in Ukraine, despite drifting into opposition along with Yushchenko in 2001. Poroshenko was known as the country's "chocolate king" after making his billions primarily through the confectionary business. Crucially, he was also part owner of 5th Channel, which would soon be nicknamed "Orange TV" for its blatant support of Yushchenko, whose campaign colour was orange.

Zhvania, the Georgian-born cousin of the Rose Revolution leader Zurab Zhvania (who was by now that country's prime minister), was more actively involved, and for longer. Shortly after the failure of the Ukraine Without Kuchma movement, he started fundraising for the next effort to oust the regime, tapping friends in the business world who were fed up, as he was, with the ubiquitous corruption and bribe-taking. He became known as "Yushchenko's treasurer," raising a stag-gering $150 million, including from his own money. He did it at least in part to save his own business. Soon after he followed Yushchenko into opposition, the Brinkford business group he headed (which dab-bled in everything from nuclear waste to banking and shipbuilding) started running into trouble with the authorities. In the summer of 2004, prosecutors raided the Brinkford offices and made it clear that they were investigating how Zhvania came by his fortune and were building a Khodorkovsky-style case against him.[7] But, unlike previous power struggles between Ukraine's pro- and anti-government oligarchs, this one drew unprecedented foreign help and direction.

With the money falling into place, official harassment of Pora, in particular of their Serbian and Georgian advisers, had already become *de rigueur.* Hotel rooms in Uzhgorod became unsurprisingly unavailable for their initial meeting in March of that year, forcing the activists to meet instead in an empty theatre. Having seen this trick before, Pora and their allies camped on the beach in Yevpatoria in August 2004. But this was no typical Ukrainian summer camp-out, which can be a boozy affair. The Pora youths were consumed with their mission and conscious of the fact that the authorities would pounce on the chance to portray them as drunken extremists.

"From the start, they were extremely well disciplined, no alcohol at all. It was organized according to Scout rules," said Pavol Demeš, who took part in the four-day training session focused on teaching the Ukrainians how to win the coming propaganda war and how to wage non-violent warfare against the regime. As with the early Kmara camps in Georgia, organizers distributed Gene Sharp's works and showed *Bringing Down a Dictator.* A ceremonial and solemn raising of the blue and yellow Ukrainian flag alongside the starker yellow banner of Pora opened the session. "Through this camp, we saw the emergence of a new kind of nationalism," Demeš said.

Freedom House paid for Otpor's Alexander Maric to take part, while several key figures from the Georgian uprising joined him. Kmara's Giorgi Kandelaki said he made four trips to Ukraine before and during the election period, but claimed that his and other Kmara members' trips were not paid for by the usual suspects—Freedom House or Soros—but by "American money," refusing to be more specific. What was clear, he claimed, was that the Ukrainians had far more money, from both foreign and domestic sources, than the revolutionaries in Tbilisi had a year earlier.

"Our role was to sort of charge them, to get the inspiration, make them emotional, because being emotional is very key, not so much to draw charts and all that—that also [happens]—we didn't have time to become academic about it," Kandelaki told me later about the training camps. "It was very fascinating. I mean, yeah, we were having fun, but we did a damn serious thing, you know. Damn serious. It's really history in the making."

There were rebel diplomats in Kiev, too. In early 2004, an ad hoc group of more than two dozen Western ambassadors interested in seeing change in Ukraine started having monthly meetings, hosted by Canadian ambassador Andrew Robinson, to coordinate their efforts. The Canadian embassy and others would eventually use special "democracy-promotion" money—money that in Canada's case could be rapidly dispersed, without the normal parliamentary oversight—to fund both election observers and groups like Pora. Though everything, including Pora, was theoretically non-partisan, the ambassadors had no illusions about what result they were working toward. "There wasn't one of these twenty-eight countries that didn't see the advantage of free and fair elections in Ukraine for the security and stability of Europe," Robinson told me. "And one couldn't deny that if there were free and fair elections, it would be to the benefit of one candidate."

Pora's revolutionary headquarters were eventually set up in a cramped basement down an alley off Mikhailovsky Square in central Kiev. Every time I visited, it was abuzz with activity. Young men and women, sporting yellow shirts featuring Che Guevara in Ukrainian national dress, were heading out to or returning from postering and graffiti missions. Most were university students or recent graduates, and many were able to speak English and other foreign languages. In a side room, a team of Pora members worked a bank of computers, keeping the group's website up to date with news about coming protests and the latest reports of electoral hanky-panky. Others scanned the foreign and domestic press, devouring every word written or spoken about Ukraine. Over their heads hung a banner that read "We're not afraid." By the end of October, they claimed to have ten thousand members across the country.

Foreign money helped set up another organization intended to discredit Kuchma and Yanukovych: Znayu (Ukrainian for "I Know"), modelled directly on Otpor's 2000 "Vremia" get-out-the-vote campaign. Otpor veteran Marko Markovic, a fluent Ukrainian speaker, became

Znayu's Kiev coordinator, working from an office on Chervonoarmiyska Street, where Otpor's Alexander Maric and political analyst Marko Serbinsky of the U.S.-Ukraine Foundation—the main financial backer of Znayu—also kept offices. The U.S.-Ukraine Foundation, though supposedly non-partisan and not-for-profit, hardly played a neutral role. Katherine Chumachenko, a former State Department employee, had founded the organization in 1991, with support from USAID; seven years later she had become the second Mrs. Viktor Yushchenko.[8]

Though Znayu was supposedly non-partisan, Yushchenko campaign paraphernalia decorated its office walls. "The regime is scared," Markovic told me with a wide smile in October 2004 as he took me on a tour of some of the apparatus—the offices of Znayu, Pora and 5th Channel—arrayed against Kuchma. "That means we're winning."

Znayu received $1 million from the U.S.-Ukraine Foundation, plus $50,000 from Freedom House, for a leaflet and sticker campaign that was launched in March 2004 with a series of stickers that appeared around seventeen cities asking, "What is Kuchmism?" A few weeks later, activists slapped responses to the question on trains, trees, electricity poles and the staircases of apartment blocks. "Kuchmism is corruption," read one that I spotted on the slow-moving funicular that carries pedestrians uphill through Kiev's forested Volodymyrska Hirka park. Others were equally blunt and accusatory: "Kuchmism is banditry," or, more simply, "Kuchmism is poverty." The campaign branded Kuchma as a quasi-autocrat who had led Ukraine into a morass of corruption and who was keeping the country from joining Europe. And it tainted Yanukovych by association, since few Ukrainians west of Donetsk saw him as anything but Kuchma's proxy in the race.

"Znayu was one of our larger projects in terms of visibility, but it was really just a small part of our whole work," said Grossman, project director for CPEU at the Kiev office of Freedom House and a former NDI officer in Moscow. "The variety of projects we funded was huge, from handing out pamphlets on the beach to rock concerts to door-to-door projects. All of them were crucial in teaching voters about their rights in this election."

Grossman said it's "insulting" to suggest that foreign NGOs manipulated Ukrainians into an uprising they didn't believe in. But, he said, there's no question that supposedly non-partisan projects like his did more to help Yushchenko and Tymoshenko than they did Yanukovych and Kuchma. "If one of the candidates is trying to rig the election, your actions are helping the other candidate. Saying we had no influence is silly. Our projects don't exist in a vacuum.

"Without the voter education programs, would there still have been a revolution? I don't know."

Meanwhile, Pavlovsky's Russian Club was working hard to head off the revolution before it happened. Pavlovsky, as well as Markov and Gelman, would later complain that they had little real chance of winning with a candidate like Yanukovych, who was tainted by his murky history. His 1968 and 1970 convictions for robbery and assault causing bodily harm—and the convictions' mysterious disappearance from official records—were a tough sell in much of Ukraine. Born in 1950, Yanukovych was orphaned as a teenager but nonetheless rose through the rough-and-tumble Donetsk business world to become regional governor, though observers considered oligarch Rinat Akhmetov, the head of the Donetsk clan, to be the real power.

Yanukovych's wife, Ludmila, later become an object of scorn herself. During a speech she gave to a crowd in Donetsk, she seemed to complain about excessive American influence on the election: "Dear friends, I'm fresh from Kiev, I can tell you what's going on there. It's simply an orange orgy there!" she said, referring to Yushchenko supporters who had covered the capital with his campaign colour. "There are rows and rows of felt boots—all of them American made! See! And mountains of oranges, oranges . . . It's a nightmare! And look here, guys: those oranges aren't just any oranges—they're loaded. People take an orange, eat it—and take another one. See! And the hand keeps reaching, keeps reaching for it. I was on my way here, there was news. They said—people in the square are getting poisoned, on a mass scale. Frequent hospitalizations. They bring people in with meningitis! What have we come to! And they keep standing, keep standing! Eyes simply glazed over! Just like that!" Wild-eyed and nonsense-talking, Ludmila Yanukovych looked as though she'd consumed something loaded, but the episode clearly illustrated that neither Yanukovych belonged at the centre of such an important and internationally scrutinized political battle.

Nonetheless, Pavlovsky and his spin doctors managed to briefly push Yanukovych into the lead in most opinion polls by getting him to sharply increase pensions on the eve of the October 31 first-round vote. They sold Yanukovych as a tried and tested economic manager who they told the public was the person most responsible for the country's impressive 11 per cent GDP growth in 2003. In case that didn't work, they were preparing their own exit polls to release on election day, to muddy the waters and confuse the public should Western-funded exit polls, as expected, show a Yushchenko victory.

There are no clear numbers representing how much Russia spent to stop Yushchenko, but the most-repeated estimate is that about half of Yanukovych's $600 million war chest came from Russian sources. The overall figure is a staggering amount (in comparison, George W. Bush's 2004 re-election campaign cost $345 million, and the United States has a population six times that of Ukraine) and, clearly, not all of it got where it was intended to go. While Yushchenko's supporters were treated nightly to a parade of pop stars and impressive laser shows during rallies in Kiev, Yanukovych's counter-demonstrations in Donetsk were uninspired, dimly lit affairs that made onlookers wonder why part of the $600 million couldn't have been used to buy a few spotlights. The West got far more bang for far fewer dollars by targeting its spending on key groups such as Pora, Freedom of Choice, the Committee of Ukrainian Voters and Znayu. By contrast to the Russian financing, the U.S. government acknowledged spending $65 million on "democracy promotion" in Ukraine in 2004.[9]

A sign of just how high the stakes were came in April 2004 in Mukachevo, a provincial city of 100,000. In a city viewed as a stronghold of Yushchenko's Our Ukraine party, the April 18 mayoral election should have been a straightforward affair. But on election day, gangs of local thugs attacked polling stations, stealing voting papers and throwing pre-marked ballots into boxes. According to a parallel vote tabulation conducted by the opposition, the Our Ukraine candidate, Viktor Baloh, won the election by a margin of 5,000 votes. But official results would show the exact opposite.

As stunning as the Mukachevo affair was—and there's little doubt it was the work of the Russian Club, which did much the same with impunity in far-flung areas of Russia to boost Putin's vote count in

2000 and 2004—the reactions of the United States and the European Union were just as revealing. Within days, the Parliamentary Assembly of the Council of Europe held a special debate on Mukachevo. U.S. assistant secretary of state Elizabeth Jones held a video news conference to express her country's "severe disappointment with the abuses" in this previously anonymous corner of Ukraine. By the end of the week, deputy assistant secretary of state Steven Pifer was in Kiev to repeat the condemnation. Astonished by the international concern over such an insignificant vote—after all, Ukrainian democracy had seen many such frauds in the past—Kuchma eventually asked the "winning" candidate, Ernest Nuser, to step aside so fresh elections could be held.

As October 31 approached—and after a series of pro-Yushchenko "warning" protests that drew crowds in the tens of thousands—the increasingly nervous regime began targeting Pora directly. Some 150 activists were detained and interrogated, and the apartments of Kaskiv and other leaders were routinely searched. On October 15, police raided a Pora office in Kiev, hauling away a load of explosives that it claimed Pora had been hoarding in preparation for an election-time terrorist attack. Given that Pora was largely a creation of Western embassies and NGOs—and especially given its careful observance of Gene Sharp's non-violent principles—most Ukrainians believed the charge to be ridiculous. The more the regime attacked Pora, the more sympathetic to the youth group the public became.

The desperation of all those opposed to regime change peaked when someone poisoned Viktor Yushchenko. Two years after the incident, little is known about it beyond that Yushchenko barely survived a huge dose of TCDD, a highly toxic dioxin best known as a key ingredient in the U.S. Army's Vietnam-era chemical weapon Agent Orange. According to specialists familiar with the case, Yushchenko received the dose on or around September 5, 2004.

That night, Yushchenko had been invited to a secret dinner with Ihor Smeshko, the head of the SBU, Ukraine's successor agency to the KGB. They dined outside Kiev at the dacha of Volodymyr Satsiuk, Smeshko's deputy. Besides Smeshko, Satsiuk and Yushchenko, the only other person there was David Zhvania. Yushchenko's normal security detail was instructed by the SBU not to attend. The dinner of boiled

crayfish, a salad of tomatoes, cucumbers and corn, and some beer pre-
ceded a round of cold meats and vodka, and then cognac as a nightcap.
Yushchenko went home feeling fine afterward, although his wife later
told reporters that she tasted "something metallic" on his lips when she
kissed him that night.

The next day, Yushchenko began suffering from waves of nausea, as
well as severe head and stomach pains. Within a matter of hours, he was
doubled up in agony. As the poison spread through his body, his once-
chiselled face bloated into a purplish mass of lesions and cysts. His wife
told me later that the same markings covered much of his back. When
Ukrainian doctors offered nothing but shrugs, he was finally rushed on
the night of September 10 to the exclusive Rudolfinerhaus clinic in
Vienna. Doctors at the clinic—which first issued a statement saying
poison had been ruled out as a cause of Yushchenko's illness, then
retracted it, and only months later confirmed the prescence of TCDD—
said that by the time Yushchenko reached Vienna, he only had another
twelve hours to live. "The poison hit his body first, then the skin, then
blood, then the bones," Yushchenko-Chumachenko told me two
months later. "He's still suffering quite seriously."

The plan to kill Yushchenko backfired. After three weeks in hospital—a critical campaign period during which he was unable to work—
he returned from Vienna possessed with a new inner fire. "Look at my
face; listen to my voice," he said to a rapt audience in the Rada on
September 21, shortly before being readmitted to Rudolfinerhaus.
"These are small indications of what happened to me. Look hard at
me. This is not caused by cuisine or food, as some might say . . . This
has been caused by a political regime in this country. We are talking
about political cuisine that kills. Don't ask who is next. It could be any
one of us."

If there were any lingering doubts among his foreign and domestic
backers that Yushchenko was the right man to lead the coming revolt,
that performance erased them. While doctors in Vienna struggled to
identify the exact dioxin they were dealing with, Ukrainians took one
look at Yushchenko's blistered face and instinctively knew that this
was no accident, and that it had likely been done by his political opponents. After Yanukovych's brief lead in opinion polls, Yushchenko
surged ahead once more.

While guilt has yet to be established, 5th Channel's hard-hitting investigative program *Forbidden Zone* obtained a tape that it claims is of a conversation between an unnamed SBU officer in Kiev and an FSB operative in Moscow discussing the poisoning and the possibility that Pavlovsky was the one behind it:

KIEV: They will put the blame on Russia.

MOSCOW: In general, that's totally crazy.

KIEV: Not only that, the Americans will also blame it on Russia.

MOSCOW: I'll say. Although, as far as I understand, they too are sick of Yushchenko.

KIEV: Possibly . . .

MOSCOW: And more likely than not, whoever did that, it was them.

KIEV: Alexander Ivanovich [the Russian speaker's name]. There are several options. The moment Russia says that it had nothing to do with this, there are people with significant evidence. And that Pavlovsky will have to run quite far.

MOSCOW: What's the connection of Pavlovsky's people?

KIEV: In this matter?

MOSCOW: With Yushchenko? Could they have poisoned him?

KIEV: No, [he's] the author of the idea. The author of the idea and the organizer. The inspiration for the idea, do you understand?

MOSCOW: No way! That asshole came up with such an idea?

KIEV: Absolutely.

MOSCOW: And there are people who can confirm this?

KIEV: Yes, who can confirm this. Not in the press, but in prosecutor's . . . well, with depositions.

MOSCOW: Really?

KIEV: Absolutely, what did you think?

MOSCOW: Are you saying this seriously?

KIEV: Absolutely. Not only that, the people [who did it] are abroad. Shipped out, as required. When I say there was a large-scale operation underway, I'm not making journalistic jokes.

MOSCOW: So right now you are saying serious things about that plan, because up to now all that was like a joke. Nobody knows anything about this.

KIEV: What's humorous about this?

MOSCOW: But absolutely no one knows about these tricks of Pavlovsky's.

KIEV: The point was to make his face ugly, to disfigure the messiah, and to brand him with the mark of the beast.

MOSCOW: Lord, my God! So he gave this assignment to someone?

KIEV: Yes.

MOSCOW: Mamma mia!

KIEV: As for details, I don't know whether he hired retired or active special operations operatives to prepare this.

MOSCOW: Probably retired.

KIEV: Now that I cannot say.

MOSCOW: It's totally crazy![10]

In an apparent attempt to win back public sympathy in the wake of Yushchenko's rousing speech in the Rada—or at least to muddy the waters about who were the heroes and who the villains—Yanukovych was rushed to hospital on September 24 after being struck in the chest by what was originally described as a "heavy object" when he stepped off a bus for a rally in the western city of Ivano-Frankivsk. Television footage showed Yanukovych clutching his chest and collapsing to the ground after being hit by a small white object. Unfortunately for the prime minister, television replays, gleefully shown all day and all night by Poroshenko's 5th Channel, showed that the "heavy object" was only an egg, turning Pavlovsky's candidate into an object of ridicule. Jokes about egg bombs made the rounds of Kiev.

Still, the Russian Club spin doctors believed they had at least one ace in the hole that had never failed them: the mysterious appeal of Vladimir Putin. Opinion polls over the previous few years had consistently showed that nearly as many Ukrainians as Russians craved a "strong leader" who could turn their country around, and many Ukrainians admired the *stabilnost* that Putin seemed to have brought to their neighbour. Putin frequently placed ahead of even Yushchenko—who was seen as well intentioned but not tough—as the most popular politician in Ukraine.

Five days before the October 31 first round, Putin landed in Kiev to throw his support behind Yanukovych in an hour-long address that

Medvedchuk ensured was carried on all three of the country's major television networks. Though Putin said during the broadcast that it would be "dangerous" and "counterproductive" for him to endorse one candidate over the other, he nonetheless made a point of praising Yanukovych's prime ministerial record as a strong partner for Russia, and credited him for Ukraine's strong economic growth in 2002 and 2003. Two days later, Putin's support became more overt and seemed to include a clear warning to those already planning to take to the streets following the election, by bringing soldiers into the centre of Kiev.

In a further attempt to cash in on the Russian president's popularity, the government hastily rescheduled a holiday marking the liberation of the last corner of Ukraine from Nazi occupation in 1943, from November 6 to October 28, so the military parade marking the date could be held before the election. Putin stood beside Yanukovych and Kuchma on a reviewing stand as some eight thousand goose-stepping soldiers, carrying the standards of the Red Army and accompanied by a vintage T-34 tank, filed past on Khreshchatyk Street. Even the normally impassive Putin, however, couldn't hide his dislike of the man Pavlovsky was charged with selling to the Ukrainians. When Yanukovych nudged Putin and tried to hand him a stick of gum while lines of World War II veterans filed by, Putin shot the prime minister a look of disgust and astonishment that was caught by television cameras.

That night, a massive Western-funded exit poll conducted by the Democratic Initiatives Foundation (backed by $100,000 from NED and $25,000 from Soros's Renaissance Foundation, plus money from the Eurasia Foundation and several Western embassies) showed Yushchenko leading with 44 per cent of the vote to 38 per cent for Yanukovych. Yushchenko announced to a sweaty press conference in Kiev's bohemian Podil neighbourhood—where I found myself sitting on a floor beside Zubr's Vlad Kobets, who had come to join the expected protests—that a parallel vote tabulation showed him winning outright in the first round, with 50.3 per cent of the vote, though they would later adjust the figure down closer to the exit poll result. Pavlovsky's poll, conducted by the Russian Public Opinion Fund, showed almost the exact opposite result, with Yanukovych ahead 43 per cent to 38 per cent.

As the official results began coming in, showing a narrow lead for Yanukovych, Tymoshenko stormed into the press conference room.

Seeing myself and the *Guardian*'s Moscow correspondent, Nick Paton Walsh, Tymoshenko effectively announced that the opposition would take to the streets that night. "Viktor Andreyevich is president of Ukraine," she told us curtly, using Yushchenko's patronymic. "There will be no second round."

After filing a story that would unfortunately be titled "Ukraine's Opposition Ready to Take to Streets over Vote" on the front page of the next day's *Globe and Mail*, I waved down a car and asked the driver to take me to the revolution. He looked at me as though I had just said something in Finnish, so I told him to take me to Maidan, Kiev's central Independence Square. When we arrived to see nobody but some orange-jacketed street cleaners sweeping the square with brooms made of long twigs tied together, I asked the driver to take me to the Central Election Commission, the other spot where I believed the opposition might focus its initial protests. The streets there were empty, too, but I got out of the car anyway. As I stood on the dull concrete expanse of Lesia Ukrainka Square, scratching my head and wondering how I could have been so wrong in my reporting, an old babushka scanning the dial of a handheld AM/FM radio and wearing an orange T-shirt emblazoned with the *Tak!* ("Yes!") of Yushchenko's campaign came up to me and asked, "Where's the revolution?"

Back at the campaign headquarters, Yushchenko—who I had wrongly assumed would immediately follow Tymoshenko's declaration with a call for his supporters to go into the streets—had still not appeared and was now many hours late for a scheduled 10 p.m. press conference. He was working the telephones, talking to his staff, to Washington, to Kuchma's office, to Moscow, trying to decide whether to agree to a second-round showdown with Yanukovych or to do as Vojislav Koštunica had done four years earlier and declare that he had won decidedly in a single round.

After massive manipulation by what became known as the Zoriany team—a group of Yanukovych allies who directed the official vote count from their headquarters inside the Zoriany movie theatre on Kiev's Moscow Street—the "official" figures left Yushchenko in a bind. With just 40 per cent of the vote, if the exit polls and parallel vote tabulation were to be believed, he had been robbed of tens of thousands of votes. At the same time, the count left him just ahead of Yanukovych, although neither man had passed the 50 per cent threshold needed for a first-round victory. If Yushchenko took immediately to the streets, he risked looking like a sore winner not confident of his ability to hold on to his lead in a run-off with Yanukovych.

While Tymoshenko and Pora fumed, the more cautious Yushchenko decided to let the electoral process play out. At 3 a.m., he held a press conference announcing that he would run in a second round scheduled for November 21.

Embarrassed by my front-page headline gaffe, and not yet knowing all that was going on behind the scenes, I started to believe the conventional wisdom in the Western press corps that Ukrainians, who were so much more passive by nature than Georgians or Serbs, couldn't and wouldn't stand up en masse to the authorities. My next stop was Tbilisi, where Mikhail Saakashvili agreed to talk to me about the progress made in the year since the Rose Revolution. At the end of the interview, I asked him what was different about Georgia, and why there had been no revolution in Ukraine under similar circumstances.

He told me to turn my voice recorder off. "I'm in contact with Viktor Yushchenko all the time," he told me with a wide smile and a direct stare. "Don't worry. It's going to happen."

ELEVEN

ORANGE KIEV, BLUE LITTLE RUSSIA

Kiev, Donetsk and Sevastopol

Voting at Kiev's polling station no. 57 was slow but steady as the end of Sunday, November 21, 2004, approached. Then a bus pulled into the parking lot and chaos erupted.

Twenty-five people, mostly senior citizens, all from the city of Cherkasy, a Yanukovych stronghold three hundred kilometres to the southeast, had arrived in Kiev and were loudly demanding to be allowed to cast ballots. They were, one told me, simple tourists who had come to Kiev for the weekend to see the capital and tour its signature golden-domed St. Sophia Cathedral.

"This is what's been happening all over Ukraine," Boris Bespaly, a parliamentary deputy in Viktor Yushchenko's Our Ukraine faction, sighed as the "tourists" were allowed to vote after a long and at times heated argument that seemed to involve everybody in the polling station. "The government of Kuchma and Yanukovych has carried people all around the country in busses so that they can vote more than once." I didn't have to go far to find evidence of this. A few minutes later, at polling station no. 58, just a few blocks away, another busload of "tourists" from Cherkasy arrived, looking to vote.

Pavlovksy and his team had learned a lesson from round one. With so many eyes on the exit polls and parallel vote tabulations, they couldn't just fudge the numbers, not even a bit. They needed physical ballots to be marked and counted in favour of their candidate so that anyone looking to add the numbers polling station by polling station would conclude a narrow Yanukovych victory as the actual result. Pavlovsky's politologists at the Russian Club would also make sure that there was at least one exit poll that supported such a result. So ballot boxes in the east, particularly in the Russian-speaking coal-mining regions of Donetsk and Lugansk (where Yanukovych's support was strongest), were stuffed with almost one million more votes than had been cast in the first round, while buses ferried paid voters from eastern Ukraine, like the ones I encountered in the suburbs of Kiev, to multiple polling stations in the same day.

To a certain extent, the strategy succeeded. The Committee of Ukrainian Voters, which had received $70,000 from the National Endowment for Democracy as well as $380,000 from Soros's International Renaissance Foundation (much of it to a subsidiary NGO, New Choice 2004) and money from Freedom House, had produced a parallel vote tabulation that showed Yushchenko winning handily in the first round. Meanwhile, the numbers compiled by the Committee of Ukrainian Voters were seen as so improbable that the organization never released its count. The NGO sheepishly put out a press release eleven days later that said only that violations had been recorded on such a scale that it was "impossible" to determine how many ballots had been falsified or cast illegally. Unlike in Slovakia, Serbia and Georgia, there would be no parallel vote count in the second round. By playing dirtier than anyone had expected, Pavlovsky's team had neutralized one of the key weapons in the revolution-makers' arsenal.

But the media had also caught them in the act. Pora activists lay down in front of several buses long enough to draw press attention to the voter merry-go-round. Other abuses didn't need such theatrics to highlight them; the number of ballots cast in Donetsk and Lugansk was so large as to defy credibility (in Donetsk it was recorded at a Saddam Hussein–esque 96.7 per cent).[1]

Another tape, this one posted by the *Ukrayinska Pravda* website, seemed to catch the regime's officials discussing the rigging of the vote. The website claims the conversation is between Yuri Levenets, a Yanukovych campaign manager, and another man identified only as Valery:

VALERY : We have negative results.

LEVENETS: What do you mean?

VALERY: 48.37 for opposition, 47.64 for us.

VALERY *(later):* We have agreed to a 3 to 3.5 per cent difference in our favour. We are preparing a table. You will have it by fax. [Yanukovych's official margin of victory was eventually announced at 2.9 per cent.][2]

After holding back on October 31, nothing would keep Yushchenko, Tymoshenko and Pora off the streets on November 21. A giant stage already stood on Kiev's Independence Square (Yushchenko's aide, Roman Bezsmertnyi, had applied well in advance for permission to hold a "concert" there that night), and even before the first official results were released, Pora members began heading for Khreshchatyk Street. They had all the evidence they needed to believe Yushchenko had won the vote: an exit poll by the Democratic Initiatives Foundation showed Yushchenko ahead, 58 per cent to 39 per cent. Those numbers, of course, were sharply at odds with the official figures the Central Elections Commission would later release—which was precisely the point.

"In Ukraine's election, it was the ready availability of independent exit polling data that provided incontrovertible evidence of fraud and brought hundreds of thousands of people into the streets of Kiev to demand a fair vote in what has been called Ukraine's 'Orange Revolution,'" NED wrote in a puff piece on its website promoting the work of the Democratic Initiatives Foundation. The article went on to cite the poll's wide coverage on 5th Channel and the exit poll's role in allowing Ukrainians "to demand a full accounting of the fraud that had taken place."[3]

The man who led the polling operation was even more direct. "U.S. aid help for the poll was absolutely important—the poll results after the second round made people go to the street," said Anatoliy Rachok, director of the Razumkov Ukrainian Centre for Economic and Political Studies, one of the main partners in the Democratic Inititatives Foundation. His own institute was directly supported by NED and the USAID-backed Eurasia Foundation.[4]

With the poll released, Yushchenko finally called his supporters into the streets. "I believe in my victory, but the government today has staged total fraud in the elections in the Donetsk and Lugansk regions," Yushchenko told a press conference in his Podil headquarters before heading to Independence Square, which the demonstrators simply called Maidan, Ukrainian for "the square." With a light snow falling and the world's media gathering (the Orange Revolution, as with the Rose Revolution, would benefit from the fact that little else was deemed newsworthy in the world at the time), a crowd of ten thousand gathered to hear Yushchenko speak. "We must defend every chestnut tree, every tent. We must show to the authorities that we are here for a long time . . . There must be more and more of us here every hour," he told them. The crowd cheered long and lustily in response. The orange *Tak!* banner was everywhere, as was Pora's yellow flag, along with the red and white emblems of Georgia and Belarus. Kmara's Giorgi Kandelaki, Vlad Kaskiv from Zubr and Otpor's Marko Markovic moved through the crowds, helping Pora keep emotions high.

As I walked downhill toward Maidan on the night of November 21 with my friend Ira Sandul, I was stunned by the sea of orange stretched out before me. Ira was agape. An ethnic Russian from the southern Ukrainian city of Mykolaev, she had moved to Moscow several years before in search of better work. She had returned to Ukraine for the elections but was skeptical that she would see anything but the same old games and lies that had marked Ukrainian politics ever since independence. As we walked through the crowd, chatting with jubilant protestors and soaking up the excitement around us, Ira was transformed. "My people! My people! I can't believe it!" she said several times, laughing out loud. It was the first time in my years of knowing her that I could remember her speaking of herself as Ukrainian.

It was hard not to get swept up in the moment. The crowd stretched all around us, waving orange scarves and hoisting aloft a large banner that read "Freedom can't be stopped." "We're here because we're not slaves—because we're for Yushchenko, for the freedom of our country and because we want it to prosper," a thirty-four-year-old English teacher named Anna Turchinova told me as the crowd around her chanted the three syllables of Yushchenko's name. "Right now, nothing in this country works. We export nothing. Villages are dead. Ninety per cent of industry is in the hands of Russian capitalists." A laser show and fireworks paid for by David Zhvania entertained the crowd until their heroes, a weary-looking Yushchenko and Tymoshenko, the latter's hair done up in her trademark thick gold braid (though her intention was to recall the style of Ukrainian peasants, many remarked that she looked like Princess Leia from *Star Wars*), took to the stage to give fiery performances. While the state-controlled channels did their best to ignore what was happening—and to downplay the size of the crowd when they did report on it—5th Channel broadcast the whole thing live, albeit only to the 40 per cent of the country who could get the channel.

Though there were city police on and around the square, they seemed to lack direction as the opposition took over the centre of the city. Nick Paton Walsh of the *Guardian* and I hopped in a cab and drove over to the Central Elections Commission. In the parking lot behind the building we saw at least a thousand Interior Ministry soldiers and special forces troops gathered before three armoured personnel carriers. An Interior Ministry spokeswoman told us she knew of more soldiers around the city. However, they had orders only to protect government buildings and had not yet been asked to disperse the demonstrations. It's not clear how the soldiers would have responded to such orders anyway. When I leaned into one of the troop carriers and asked how the men inside had voted, one piped up, "Like everyone else." When I asked if that meant for Yushchenko, several nodded their heads solemnly.

That night, despite sub-zero temperatures and a light snow, Vlad Kaskiv and a handful of other Pora members planted the first few green, grey and blue all-weather tents, giving birth to what would eventually grow into a mini-city of 1,546 tents with more than 15,000 off-and-on residents. Looking back, Kaskiv said the morning of November 22 was the most nerve-stretching for him. He awoke to see just a few hundred people gathered on the square that morning and briefly worried that the carefully planned revolution had fizzled out in just one night.[5]

"I saw about three hundred people only, and I was very emotional . . . Maidan was empty, it was a very big crisis for me," he remembered later. "I was standing there waiting . . . and then I heard the first column of people coming from Kiev-Mohyla Academy. It was a very cold morning, and they were shouting, so I could hear them coming from afar . . . And then there was another group of people coming from Kiev Polytechnical Institute and from other parts and, then, like in thirty minutes, you had thousands of people on the square and then after that I knew it would be okay."

By the evening of the twenty-second, protestors had bathed Kiev in orange. A much larger crowd, in the tens of thousands, came out, apparently encouraged by the lack of a crackdown the night before and enraged by a phone call that day from Putin to Yanukovych, congratulating him on his victory even before the final official results were in. The official tally was moving much faster than in round one, and with nearly all the votes counted, the pro-regime networks began announcing that Yanukovych led with 49 per cent of the vote to just over 46 per cent for Yushchenko. While monitors from the Organization for Security and Co-operation in Europe slammed the conduct of the vote, observers from the Moscow-led Commonwealth of Independent States gave it their stamp of approval— unsurprisingly, given that some of those giving it the thumbs-up hailed from the outright dictatorships of Belarus and Central Asia.

But as outrageous as the CIS's election monitors were, some Westerners made statements equally rash. Borys Wrzesnewskyj, a Canadian member of Parliament of Ukrainian descent who was an official observer for the election, left impartiality at home in Toronto when he took the stage on Independence Square on November 22 to tell the crowd that he considered Yushchenko to have won the election. "It's quite clear to me that Viktor Yushchenko is, in fact, president of Ukraine," he said to tumultuous applause. It's difficult to see how he could have made that judgment after visiting just a few polling stations the previous day. The OSCE was considerably more restrained, commenting that the vote "did not meet a considerable number of commitments for democratic elections."

But Wrzesnewskyj had said what the crowd wanted to hear. From that day onward, Canadian flags could be seen waving in the crowd alongside Ukrainian ones. "The whole of Kiev will be here tomorrow and the next day, and we will not leave until Yushchenko, our choice, is president," Vyacheslav Kuznetsov, a twenty-eight-year-old railway worker, told me, confessing that he risked losing his job to take part in what had already evolved into a non-stop demonstration. "We are not afraid anymore. It doesn't make sense to live like this." Again, Yushchenko left his normally flat personality at home when he addressed the crowds that night. Yanukovych and Kuchma, he told them, were planning a *"coup d'état."*

His face was still a deathly grey and pockmarked from his poisoning, but he put on a determined expression and called for a campaign of civil disobedience. "Remain where you are . . . From all parts of Ukraine, on carts, cars, planes and trains, tens of thousands of people are on their way here. Our action is only beginning." After he left the stage, speakers pumped out a hastily written hip-hop song that would become the revolution's unofficial anthem: "*Razom nas bahato. Nas ne podolaty*"— "Together we are many. We won't be defeated."[6]

As the revolution spread, the authorities began to panic. In the western city of Lviv, which I had visited on the eve of the vote to find it draped in orange and even more pro-Yushchenko than the capital, simultaneous demonstrations had brought the city to a standstill. Feeding fears of a split between the Ukrainian-speaking west and the Russian-speaking east, Lviv city council declared on the twenty-second that it already recognized Yushchenko as president.

After not reacting for much of the first twenty-four hours, the regime began looking for a counterstrategy. Yanukovych—a street fighter by nature—favoured violence. In a dark parking lot near the Tsarskoye Selo restaurant on the edge of the downtown sat twenty-six buses, filled with bored, rough-looking men—miners from eastern Ukraine who were waiting for unspecified orders. Nick and I counted more than eight hundred of them. "We are not against the people from the west of Ukraine," said one of the men, who gave his name as Boris Savenko, "but I can demonstrate, too." When their presence became known, fears spread that the men would be used to provoke violence on Independence Square, giving the authorities an excuse to clamp down on the demonstration. But in the coming days the expected clash never materialized. Outside of a few drunken fist fights and heated street arguments, the Yanukovych men were content simply to sit outside the Central Election Commission and roast kebabs. They were there, several told me, not out of conviction about the election's fairness, but because they'd been promised ten dollars a day above their regular wages if they took the bus to Kiev.

The next day, as I tried to get into the Rada for an impromptu parliamentary session called by the opposition, the look on the security guard's face made it clear that he wasn't sure who was in charge anymore.

Under the old rules—which had applied even three days earlier, when Kuchma and Yanukovych were clearly in charge of the country—Western reporters weren't allowed into the Verkhovna Rada without a special pass. And for a short while, as I argued with the guard and then with his boss and then with the guard again for upwards of ten minutes, it seemed nothing had changed. They wanted to see a fax from my editor confirming that I'd been specifically assigned to cover the Rada, and then, maybe, I'd be given a pass and allowed inside.

Then the heavy wooden door behind me swept open and Viktor Yushchenko and his entourage hurriedly pushed by. Seeing my chance, I called out to Yulia Tymoshenko as she swept past. Somehow, amidst the kerfuffle, she heard me and with a stern look and a wave of her arm made it clear to the guards that I was to be allowed through. The guard looked at his boss, who shrugged. They grasped very quickly that the old rules were out and that it could well be Yushchenko and Tymoshenko who wrote the new ones.

We swept up the ornate staircase into the round chamber of the Verkhovna Rada, which was decorated with chandeliers and with a blue and yellow map of Ukraine over the Speaker's chair. I found a seat in the packed visitor's gallery, not far from where Russian opposition leader Boris Nemtsov sat, an orange scarf draped around his neck. A circle gathered around Yushchenko as he sat at one of the deputies' desks, debating what to do next. With all the opposition deputies present but none of Yanukovych's backers or the Communist Party deputies in the hall, they had the numbers to force Speaker Volodymyr Lytvyn to call a special session but not enough to pass any legislation.

As one deputy after another got up and gave speeches condemning violations in Sunday's vote, I could see the feisty and fearless Tymoshenko trying to convince Yushchenko to once more abandon his reserve. After a long moment, in one of the more ill-advised steps of the uprising, Yushchenko took the Rada's podium with a sixteenth-century copy of the New Testament in hand, read the oath of office and declared himself president of Ukraine. "We won," Yushchenko told the assembled deputies, a stern look on his blistered face.

Cheers of "Bravo, Mr. President!" followed his declaration, and a massive ovation erupted when he opened a window to address the tens of thousands of supporters who had gathered outside on the streets surrounding the parliament building. The only dissenting voice came from Lytvyn, the Speaker, who called the process a farce. "There will be no oath for you," he told Yushchenko before cutting live transmission of the session.

But Tymoshenko, who wanted to see Yushchenko borrow more directly from the revolution playbook and seize power the way Koštunica had in Serbia and Saakashvili had in Georgia—after a storming of Parliament—wasn't done provoking just yet. She went straight from the Rada to Independence Square, where she urged her followers to march up the icy hill of Institutska Street and lay siege to the Presidential Administration building, to which Kuchma and his entourage had retreated. "Either they will give up their power, or we will take it," she said to a crowd that eagerly followed her instruction, Pora members marching at the front. From somewhere in the crowd, my friend Yuriy Shafarenko of the International Committee of the Red Cross sent me an excited text message that read simply, "Is it victory?" It sure felt like something had to give.

The regime, however, proved to be more firmly entrenched than either Milošević's or Shevardnadze's had been. Hundreds of black-clad policemen, riot helmets on and metal shields linked in a long, unyielding line, stopped the protestors' triumphant march in front of the Presidential Administration. In front of them, blocking the protestors' route, were parked two dump trucks covered in snow.

Undaunted, Pora members scaled the trucks, waving yellow flags and chanting *"Yushchenko—nash president"* ("Yushchenko is our president") and *"Militsia so narodom"* ("The police are with the people"). The latter was a call for the police to stand aside, but they held firm. Caught off guard by the sudden change in the protest's venue, Jeremy Page of the *Times*, photographer Luke Tchalenko and I tried to push our way forward through the mass of people for a better view of whatever was going to happen next. Unable to make much progress in the dense crowd, I pulled out my press accreditation and presented it to a random protestor, hoping he would direct us to a quicker route. "Journalists!" he yelled out to my mixed delight and dismay. "Let the foreign media through!"

Never before have fifty thousand people parted so neatly for three scruffy-looking journalists. As the sea of people opened up, the crowd

took up a new chant of "*Journalisti so narodom, journalisti so narodom!*"—
"The journalists are with the people! The journalists are with the people!"
Caught up in the moment, we laughed and played along until we found
ourselves thrust past the trucks and right into the metal shields of the riot
police, who looked unimpressed by the arrival of these new VIPs. We
turned around and saw that the sea of people had closed behind. The
chant had stopped. Whether we liked it or not, the journalists were with
the people, whatever happened next.

The next parting of the crowd was to allow a more graceful figure
through. Tymoshenko, in a carefully staged scene, moved through the
adoring crowd as flashes went off all around her. She looked very much
like the "people's princess" she longed to be, carrying a single rose that
she presented to the police line as they opened to let her pass. The opposition was betting that with tens of thousands of people massed outside
his office, Kuchma would see no way out and would capitulate as
Shevardnadze had. Tymoshenko had arrived to talk terms of surrender.

In the long, tense period that followed, the crowd tried out new
chants while I tried to make eye contact with the policemen opposite
me, hoping to reach an unspoken understanding with them that if they
got the order to charge, they'd spare at least one Canadian journalist
the baton. I relaxed when I realized that many of them weren't paying
attention to the crowd at all but were busy typing out text messages on
their mobile phones to friends on the other side of the two-truck barri-
cade. While we waited for Tymoshenko to return, I struck up a conversation with a twenty-eight-year-old protestor named Leonid Listovshik,
who, like me, had gotten himself stuck at the front between the police
and the masses, with nowhere to go until the standoff ended. He was
much more sanguine than I was. "This is our first chance in thirteen
years since independence to have a normal country," he said. "If we
don't seize it now, we won't have freedom for another decade."

But just as I was about to phone my foreign desk to tell them to
hold the front page because I thought Kuchma would have to resign
that night, Tymoshenko returned from her meeting with him, ashen-
faced. The protest was illegal and there would be no surrender by the
regime, she had been told. Sensationally, she told her aide (who
repeated it to me) that she had seen Russian *spetznaz* (special forces
soldiers) behind the Ukrainian policemen. "Our people won't shoot,

but there are Russian *spetznaz* in there with automatic weapons who will," her aide shouted to me above the roar of a cheering crowd that was expecting their heroine to tell them of Kuchma's imminent resignation. As word spread that Tymoshenko had been rebuffed, the crowd started to thin out, worried that things were about to turn ugly. I took advantage of the moment and slid back through the crowd, with much less fanfare than when I had arrived. (Although Russia has always denied the presence of its *spetznaz* outside the Presidential Administration that night, Tymoshenko clearly saw something that convinced her to back down fast from her demands that Kuchma capitulate on the spot. Several Western diplomats later told me they believed Tymoshenko was telling the truth, though the Russian soldiers weren't seen by anyone else.)

Almost unnoticed, the Russian Foreign Ministry released a statement complaining of Western interference in Ukraine's affairs. "These demands aimed at destabilizing the situation have not only been supported but also provoked by representatives of certain foreign countries, including those across the ocean, and international institutions," the statement read. The Russians, of course, didn't see themselves as foreigners when it came to Ukraine.

Ukraine's Orange Revolution almost dissolved into bloodshed a second time, on the night of November 28, 2004, after the Central Elections Commission declared Viktor Yanukovych the winner of the election. Some ten thousand soldiers, many armed with live ammunition, the rest with tear gas, were mobilized and given orders to clear Independence Square.

Acting on a tip we had heard, I sat up all night with two of the most adrenaline-driven members of the British press corps, Nick from the *Guardian* and Julius Strauss of the *Daily Telegraph,* keeping warm with a succession of espressos and cognacs in an Italian café with a view of Maidan. We (and the coffee) kept each other awake until nearly 5 a.m., when we finally decided we'd been misled and headed back to our hotels. Concerned, though, that the crackdown would happen the moment we went to sleep, Nick and I walked through the Pora tent camp handing out our business cards to anyone still awake, with instructions to call if anything happened.

Nothing did happen that night, but only because of a massive diplomatic effort combined with what appears to have been a mini-mutiny within the regime. According to a well-sourced story written by C. J. Chivers of the *New York Times,* the secret service had for some time been moving closer to the Yushchenko camp, and the Interior Ministry troops that were moving on the capital backed down and returned to base when they got word that SBU units positioned around the square would use force to defend the demonstrators. Who gave the order for the troops to move and who ordered them back to base remains in dispute. The official version is that Lieutenant-General Sergei Popkov gave the order alone and then rescinded it, an account widely dismissed as improbable, but it seems likely that one or more of Kuchma, Yanukovych and Medvedchuk had to make the call. Kuchma denies a role, while Medvedchuk and Yanukovych, who refused repeated requests to be interviewed for this book, remain mum on the subject.[7]

What is known is that a flurry of phone calls were exchanged that night. The SBU tipped off Oleh Rybachuk, Yushchenko's chief of staff, who then called U.S. ambassador John Herbst. Herbst called Kuchma's son-in-law, Viktor Pinchuk, and warned of serious consequences if soldiers attacked the protestors. Pinchuk called Medvedchuk, while U.S. secretary of state Colin Powell tried to ring Kuchma, though his call was apparently refused.

One oft-reported exchange between Kuchma and Yanukovych on November 27 may provide some clues to what happened the next night. At a meeting of regime officials and eastern Ukrainian politicians, Yanukovych demanded that Kuchma take steps to confirm his victory, specifically to declare a state of emergency, lift the opposition's siege of government buildings and schedule his inauguration as president. Kuchma, who in other comments already seemed to be distancing himself from his one-time protégé, is said to have responded, "You have become very brave, Viktor Fedorovych, to speak to me in this manner," adding that "it would be best for you to show this bravery on Independence Square."

Without knowing how close the Orange Revolution had come to being physically crushed, I accepted an invitation on November 29 to the opposition's campaign headquarters to meet again with Yushchenko. The man I met that day was shockingly different to look at than the Yushchenko I had interviewed two years before. His face looked much worse up close than it did from afar, or on television, for which he evidently applied a lot of makeup to keep himself somewhat presentable. The area around his nose had turned grey. His strong Slavic cheekbones had almost disappeared, lost in the pimply puffiness caused by the poisoning.

His aides told me that Yushchenko, who had previously been a remarkably handsome man, hated to look at himself in the mirror. He was taking painkillers all through the day—at one point he had been on a morphine drip injected into his spine—and his wife confided to me that his nightly appearances were an enormous strain on him. But at the same time, this Yushchenko, dressed in a dark striped suit and orange tie, was far stronger and more determined than the uninspiring central banker I had first met. When he told us that the revolution would prevail and that threats of separatism from Yanukovych's strongholds in the east were a bluff, he spoke with the authority and firmness of a leader. Clearly, those who had tried to kill him had instead created a newly impassioned character for the country to rally around. He paused and dithered only once, when I asked him whether he'd consider granting immunity to Kuchma.

"That's not an issue today, the status of the Ukrainian president and his safety," he finally responded. "Now the issue is will we go the way of dictatorship or be a democratic state. In answering this, we'll find all the other answers."

The behind-the-scenes dramas were scarcely felt on the streets, where the Orange Revolution–cum–endless rock music festival continued unabated. As November drew to a close, a biting December chill set in, accompanied by an even thicker blanket of snow.

Each day, it seemed, the protest machine took over another government building in Kiev. Perhaps the most crucial to the revolt's success was Ukrainian House, a squat grey building at the eastern end of Khreshchatyk Steet that had served as the Lenin Museum in Soviet times. During the late fall and early winter of 2004, it became the office and warehouse of Vitaliy Melnichuk, head grocer of the Orange Revolution. The thin-faced, mustachioed thirty-eight-year-old, who usually sold telephone cards, had quit his job and volunteered for the task of taking in donations of foodstuffs from all over Ukraine (including local grocery store chains that were dropping off supplies by the truckload) and the world, and getting the goods out to the makeshift kitchens and sleeping quarters around the city centre.

For all the work going on inside Ukrainian House, it had the feel of an overpopulated youth hostel. Melnichuk told me that between five thousand and twenty thousand people showed up each day looking for somewhere to sleep. Many would end up on the floors of the building, sleeping in shifts on the foam mattresses that covered all four of its floors. Walking through the building meant hopping over snoring bundles of orange. The whole building stank of sweat, and keeping the toilets unplugged was clearly a full-time job.

Outside on the streets, the demonstrations continued without pause. The dense shoulder-to-shoulder crowd not only filled the broad expanse of Independence Square itself, but stretched west through the dense Pora tent camp along Khreshchatyk Street as far as the eye could see, and up the hill at the south end of Maidan. The pedestrian passage under the square was filled with *babushki* selling clothes and trinkets—anything with the colour orange. The police—unsure of how to handle the unfolding spectacle—effectively disappeared from the city centre, leaving the city's homeless to sleep unbothered in the underpasses that were usually cleared out at night. A newspaper appeared, simply titled *Maidan,* reporting daily on domestic and international reactions to the elections. It was printed on presses purchased by the International Renaissance Foundation.

The Orange Revolution had not only captivated Ukrainians, it had grabbed the attention of the world. With CNN and the BBC broadcasting live from Independence Square, the *Globe and Mail* flew Carolynne, a freelance journalist, in from Moscow so that we could produce multiple stories every day. Though the life of a foreign journalist is sometimes perceived as glamorous, it also can involve two people sharing a five-foot-long single bed in a Soviet-era hotel while cars drive by outside the frosted window honking *beep beep BEEP* (for "Yu-shen-KO!") all night long.

As the protests grew in size—at one point some media outlets were reporting estimates of a million protestors in downtown Kiev—there was a jubilant sense in the city that the regime's hours were numbered.

In one of the bravest acts of rebellion, Nataliya Dmytruk, a sign-language presenter with Ukraine's state-owned television channel UT-1, poked her finger in the regime's eye during a regular news broadcast when she decided to ignore the *temnyki* and tell what she believed was the truth. "The results announced by the Central Electoral Commission are rigged. Do not believe them," she signed, an orange ribbon tied around her wrist. Her Ukrainian-language colleagues carried on, oblivious to the meaning of her gestures. "Our president is Yushchenko. I am very disappointed by the fact that I had to interpret lies. I will not do it anymore. I do not know if you will see me again."

Though Dmytruk was initially understood only by a few who know sign language, the next day much of the rest of UT-1's staff quit and joined the protestors on Maidan. The journalists' revolt spread. To keep Inter and 1+1—the other main state-controlled stations—on the air in the face of threatened mass resignations by their editorial staffs, the networks had to agree to start broadcasting the pro-Yushchenko demonstrations.

But even this journalists' uprising had American fingerprints on it. In early 2004, respected Ukrainian journalist Natalya Ligacheva converted the website she had founded three years earlier—*Telekritika*—into an NGO and began receiving grants from the U.S. embassy, NED and the Soros Foundation; she puts the amount received at about $100,000 for that year. Ligacheva had since been working to convince her media colleagues to come out from under the regime's thumb. According to USAID's website, she "helped spearhead the Orange Revolution's journalist movement in which 42 journalists from six of the most popular national TV channels publicly denounced censorship and political pressure and vowed to follow professional principles. With more than 350 signatures from over 20 regional TV companies, *Telekritika* published letters of support from other print and radio journalists, information agencies, and citizens. In the end, the united, active, and democratic participation of journalists triumphed over political and financial manipulations."[8]

While anyone watching the ongoing events on television couldn't help but think that Ukraine's media had gone overnight from submissive pawns of the state to defiant Woodwards and Bernsteins, their transition was in fact the fruit of a long process that had started during the Cold War, in 1982, when an NGO called Internews was founded in California. Funded primarily through USAID, over the next two decades Internews would train two thousand Ukrainian journalists in Western standards of reporting.

Another, even more critical, reversal came next from the judiciary. On November 25, the normally compliant Supreme Court broke ranks with the regime and agreed to hear the opposition's complaints about the conduct of the elections, agreeing to block the Central Election Commission's certification of Yanukovych's victory until the case was heard. First the journalists and much of the police had deserted the regime; now it seemed the judges were thinking of doing the same. It was right out of Gene Sharp's textbook: the regime's pillars were crumbling.

Though Putin called again to congratulate Yanukovych, the United States, Canada and the European Union all announced that they would not recognize the November 21 election as valid. "This is only the beginning," Yushchenko told the biggest crowd to date on Independence Square that night. "It is proof that it is society that always wins. It is small compensation for the suffering that we have endured."

But as photogenic and uplifting as the revolution seemed in Kiev and Lviv, the Russified east and south of the country were not taking part in the celebration. In the coal-mining heartland of eastern Ukraine, where many arguably felt closer ties to Moscow than Kiev, there was no revolution to report on.

The Donetsk-Lugansk-Kharkov triangle in the east was the country's most resource-rich and economically developed region. Many there viewed the revolt happening in the poorer west of the country as some sort of plot designed to force the predominantly Russian-speaking east to learn Ukrainian and share the wealth. Foreign NGOs had barely penetrated the east—no Soros, no NDI—and big Ukrainian organizations like Freedom of Choice had only token representation. Nor could 5th Channel be seen there, and few cared. Most tuned in instead to Gleb Pavlovsky and Marat Gelman's carefully controlled newscasts from Russia. In other words, even as late as November 2004, the revolution-makers had made no inroads there. If western Ukraine, with its vibrant civil society and free media, had proved itself fertile ground for a repeat of Serbia and Georgia, the east had more in common with Belarus.

Indeed, many eastern Ukrainians I met believed what they saw on Russian television: that a small group of demonstrators, all on the payroll of the United States, was causing havoc in central Kiev—and that consequently, blocked government offices might not be able to make pension and social security payments on time. Understandably, there was a lot of resentment toward anyone who might cause such disorder.

Despite the well-founded concern in Kiev and the west of the country that the east and south were being misled about the nature, intent and causes of the Orange Revolution, most people I met in Donetsk and on subsequent trips to Kharkov in the east and to Simferopol and Sevastopol in the Crimea claimed they didn't feel they'd been tricked into voting for Yanukovych. They admired his economic track record as prime minister, and they genuinely supported his policy of moving Ukraine closer to Russia and making Russian a second official language. They didn't trust Yushchenko, and they especially didn't trust Tymoshenko. "I don't know where these stereotypes [that the east was tricked into voting for Yanukovych] come from. I think the intelligentsia in the west looks down on us working people from the east," a twenty-four-year-old marketing executive named Sergey Smagin complained to me. "They think we're all bandits and mafia, but we're just normal hard-working people, and we really chose Yanukovych because we think he'll be better for us." Others used the term that I had heard so often in my travels through Russia and Belarus: they wanted a period of *stabilnost* after so many years of chaos and change. Yanukovych was the candidate for those who didn't want to rock the boat.

As the revolt in Kiev dragged on, a very real sense of anger developed in Donetsk. Many saw the uprising as an attempt to steal the election from their native son, who most residents believe won fairly. Donetsk at the end of November was covered in billboards that stated simply "Yanukovych—President," and hostility toward foreigners was rampant. When I ducked (inadvisably) into a biker bar near the centre of Donetsk in search of some "man-on-the-street" opinions about the elections, I was grabbed by a burly, leather-clad man who squeezed me in a bear hug until I squeaked out a few words of admiration for Yanukovych. Satisfied, he let me go and offered to buy me a round. I declined and quickly retrieved my jacket from the coat check.

Furious politicians in Moscow—led by Putin's ally, Moscow mayor Yuri Luzhkov—began to agitate for the Kremlin to pull out all the stops. Luzhkov flew to the eastern town of Severodonetsk to lend his star power to a conference of governors from the east and south of the Ukraine who were threatening to seek autonomy, independence or even union with Russia if Yushchenko was made president. Boris Gryzlov, the Speaker of the Russian Duma, grimly warned from Moscow that the situation "is heading toward a split or toward bloodshed. I see no other way the situation could develop." Yanukovych, in attendance, also spoke of the potential for civil war: "There is one step to the edge. When the first drop of blood is spilled, we will not be able to stop it."

While political analysts in Kiev dismissed such talk as nonsense, there was enough popular sentiment behind it to worry Yushchenko's friends in the west. In the Crimean capital city of Simferopol, I met a man named Stanislav Kompaniets who was rounding up signatures for the Crimea's unification with Russia, undoing Nikita Khrushchev's fifty-year-old "gift" of the peninsula to what was then the Ukrainian Soviet Socialist Republic. As we spoke on the city's main square, near yet another statue of Lenin, caravans of cars drove by, drivers leaning on their horns and waving the white, blue and red flag of the Russian Federation out their windows. Citizens declared a "Yushchenko-free zone" in the city.

Yanukovych and Luzhkov weren't the only ones raising the rhetorical stakes. In a speech to the American Enterprise Institute in Washington, D.C., in late November, Zbigniew Brzezinski, formerly the national security adviser to the Carter administration, put a decidedly Cold War spin on things: "The stakes are of truly historic proportions," he said. "If Ukrainian democracy prevails, Russia has no choice but to go to the West and to be a democracy," he told the gathering. "If Ukrainian democracy fails, Russia and imperial ambitions are awakened."[9]

Russia's ham-handed interventions in Ukraine's presidential election were driven, beyond pipelines and fading dreams of empire, by fear of losing what clout they still had in international affairs. A pro-Western Ukraine might eventually join the European Union and NATO, encircling Russia and cutting off its access to much of the Black Sea. These fears came to a head around the matter of the Russian

Black Sea Fleet, which lay slumbering in harbour in the Crimean port of Sevastopol—vicious-looking destroyers, thin frigates and sleek black submarines, with their cannons pointed at both sea and shore. The ships still managed to look menacing, even as rust crept farther and farther up their aging hulls.

To Ukrainian nationalists, these warships—and the white, blue and red Russian flag that flies over them and many buildings in this historic port city—represented an unending irritation and one of the most stubborn vestiges of Russia's postcolonial hold over their county. Under the terms of an agreement Kuchma signed with Boris Yeltsin in 1997, the ships will remain until at least 2017, costing $6.4 million in annual rent. Under a pro-Western government, Yushchenko's allies repeatedly signalled, the fleet would stay not a day longer than the agreement specified.

Losing its hold on Sevastopol would be a crushing blow to Russia's lingering ambition of being able to project itself militarily beyond its borders, yet another humiliation after having already been forced to accept the stationing of NATO troops in the Caucasus and Central Asia. Preparing for the worst, in 2004 defence minister Sergei Ivanov ordered the construction of a new naval base at the southern Russian port of Novorossiysk. However, Novorossiysk doesn't have Sevastopol's large, sheltered bay and likely couldn't accommodate all 130 ships that are believed to make up the Black Sea Fleet.

For residents, the fleet also represented their remaining ties to Russia, which many told me they considered their real homeland. Khrushchev's decision was still the object of curses, five decades on. "I will never bend down to America . . . If Yushchenko is made president, I will personally go about and start collecting signatures for union with Russia," said sixty-four-year-old Tatiana Zvolak, who was manning the ticket window at the city's Officers' Club. Behind her in the office, a portrait of Vladimir Putin hung on the wall.

On the morning of December 3, 2004, it looked like the Orange Revolution might run out of juice. Russian-sponsored talk of separatism and civil war was fraying nerves, and protestors' spirits were starting to sag. It was the twelfth day of the uprising and demonstrators on the streets—many of whom had quit or taken unpaid leave from their jobs to travel to Kiev from all corners of the country—were wondering aloud for the first time about where the political transition was heading.

While protestors slept in tents on the snow-covered streets, demanding nothing less than the resignations of Kuchma and Yanukovych and the installation of Yushchenko as president, their leaders were negotiating with the regime behind closed doors about the possibility of fresh elections. Disillusionment grew, as many protestors believed that any compromise deal with Kuchma would tarnish the revolution and its lofty goals of putting an end to the corruption and the criminalization of politics. When I dropped by Pora's street-side headquarters—on the second floor of a Khreshchatyk Street pub called Chateau, which had wisely handed over its tables to the revolutionaries who were occupying the sidewalk in front—the mood bordered on despondent. "Seeing the national leader getting involved in negotiations with criminals could discredit him in the eyes of the people," the normally cheerful Pora spokesperson Nina Sorokopud told me curtly. In other words, cutting a deal to save Kuchma's bacon is not what she and the others had risked their lives and careers to do. She and others mused whether Tymoshenko approved of Yushchenko's decision to negotiate a way out. Pora even suggested it might not follow Yushchenko's orders if he called off the protest.

One suggestion put forward by the regime, designed to seem magnanimous but in fact an obvious trap, was for both Viktors—Yushchenko and Yanukovych—to stand aside in any new election. This would have been a lopsided arrangement in favour of the authorities, since not only would they be able to run someone new, but the opposition would likely have put forward Tymoshenko, who didn't have the same broad base of support as Yushchenko. It would also have tarred the opposition as equally culpable in the November 21 shenanigans and left Kuchma in office until further notice, something many worried was his plan. "He was still hoping to hang around as a compromise figure," said Dan Bilak, a Ukrainian-Canadian lawyer who had once advised the Kuchma government and would later work for Tymoshenko. "It was a measure of how divorced he'd become from Ukrainian reality."

Fortuitously for the opposition, an unexpected source broke the deadlock: the Supreme Court. When the opposition brought its hundreds of individual complaints of election fraud to the court, the regime paid no notice; judges on the top bench were political appointees who owed their careers to Kuchma and his chief of staff, Medvedchuk. As a result, when Polish president Aleksander Kwaśniewski suggested during the round-table talks that the Supreme Court hearings should be televised, Kuchma agreed. But the instant Poroshenko's 5th Channel started broadcasting the hearings to the crowds on Maidan, the judges became as accountable to the people outside as they were to Kuchma and Medvedchuk.

There was another factor at play as well. In the months proceeding the election, the American Bar Association ran a $400,000 program, funded by USAID, to train Ukrainian judges and lawyers on election law (Ukraine's 1996 constitution is based largely on the American model). Among those who took part in the program—which involved U.S. Supeme Court justice Sandra Day O'Connor—were all twenty members of the Ukrainian Supreme Court, including chairman Anatoliy Yarema. Yarema presided over the hearings on the November 21 vote and announced the judges' verdict: because of "the impossibility of determining the actual will of the voters," the election would have to be done over. They put the blame squarely on the authorities, and a rerun, between Yushchenko and the now thoroughly discredited Yanukovych, was set for December 26. It was a near-complete victory for the opposition (Yushchenko had unsuccessfully demanded that the court declare him the winner of the election based on the results of the first round).[10]

With Yushchenko ahead by sixteen percentage points in the polls, his victory was by now certain. In Moscow, Vladimir Putin could only writhe in frustration as he watched the biggest and dearest chunk of Russia's near abroad slip away. The day before, he had summoned Kuchma to Moscow for a forty-five-minute scolding, during which the two men never left Vnukovo Airport. Afterward, Putin complained bitterly about foreign interference in the election (he obviously didn't consider Russia to be a foreign power where Ukraine was involved) and poured scorn on the very sort of election rerun that the Supreme Court in Kiev was about to endorse. "A re-vote could be conducted a third, a fourth, twenty-fifth time, until one side gets the results it needs," Putin said.

But his outrage came far too late. He and his politologists had already been thoroughly outplayed. During the televised court proceedings, the Ukrainian justices occasionally referred to a document dubbed the "Bench Book," a reference guide on how to interpret

Ukraine's electoral laws, written with the assistance of the American Bar Association and produced with American money.

Beyond the training of judges, the legal trainers—with the International Republican Institute—also educated sixty political party lawyers on the election law, including many of those who would later put the opposition's case before the Supreme Court. And USAID money, managed by these trainers, was used to set up voter complaint hotlines for the reporting of election-day irregularities.

"I can't say that myself or other people who were watching this closely were terribly surprised. We were just extraordinarily heartened, and this is, I think . . . the landmark decision coming out of any judiciary in the former Soviet Union in the last thirteen years. This is really an extraordinary event," Michael Maya, deputy director of the legal trainers gushed on NPR, bizarrely comparing the ruling to the O. J. Simpson case in America. "I think judges throughout the entire former Soviet Union and perhaps even beyond will take heart at this decision."

Oblivious to such background, the crowd that had gathered—at Tymoshenko's urging—outside the Supreme Court exploded in joy. In one of the iconic moments of the revolution, thunderous applause greeted Yarema's announcement and morphed into a deafening chant of "Yulia! Yulia!" as the glamour-queen revolutionary, sporting a brown fur coat and high-heeled black boots, clambered on top of a yellow minibus in the middle of the crowd. A microphone and speakers appeared as Tymoshenko gave yet another virtuoso performance. "You did this! You, the people!" she shouted, with billionaire Petro Poroshenko standing at her side on the bus's roof. "Glory to you! Glory to Ukraine!" As the bus continued down the slope of Hrushevskovo Street, slowly making its way to Maidan and the main stage, the crowd never stopped chanting her name. I sent a text message to Yuriy Shafarenko, returning the question he had asked me a few long days earlier, "Is it victory?" His response was an unequivocal "YEESSSSSSS!"

So great was Tymoshenko's popularity that at times during the Orange Revolution it seemed to eclipse Yushchenko's. That night on Independence Square, she took her customary place at Yushchenko's side as he hailed the arrival of "justice, democracy and freedom" in Ukraine. But privately, the two frequently found themselves at odds, particularly over Yushchenko's willingness to negotiate with Kuchma and Yanukovych. The Supreme Court's decision left the regime with few, but still substantial, options for sabotaging Yushchenko's march to victory. They could pull Yanukovych out of the December 26 re-vote in protest or arrange a large-scale boycott of the vote in eastern Ukraine. Either would have denied Yushchenko the legitimacy he sought. Tymoshenko was less concerned with such niceties.

She would fume in private, and more and more often in public, over the next few days while Yushchenko negotiated with the regime. On December 8, the date many view as the end of the revolution, Yushchenko agreed to a package of constitutional reforms that Kuchma had long sought—including a dilution of the presidential powers Kuchma had gathered to himself, in the expectation that his allies could retain control of Parliament. Tymoshenko could not contain her disgust. "This is a victory for Kuchma," she told journalists. "This vote helps reduce the powers of a President Yushchenko . . . We could have won without it."

She was likely correct, but Yushchenko won key concessions from the regime as well, including a reformed Central Election Commission and guarantees that the December 26 rerun wouldn't be marred by another mass falsification effort. Yanukovych's camp was despondent. "We knew it was lost," Anna German, his press secretary, complained to me. "Everybody knew [the third round] would bring Yushchenko to power. The West wanted a marionette."

Yushchenko called off his nightly speeches on Maidan, which drew the largest crowds of the protest, although Pora decided to maintain its tent city on Khreshchatyk through the December 26 vote and until Yushchenko was inaugurated. Delighted with the outcome, the West gladly forked out more cash for an unprecedented level of election monitoring. The Organization for Security and Co-operation in Europe sent 1,000 monitors and the government of Canada another 400, while the Ukrainian Canadian Congress sent 400 on its own tab. In total, a staggering 12,184 foreign observers were registered to witness the process.

Though all came under the banner of non-partisanship, many of the Westerners hailed from the vast Ukrainian diaspora and made no secret of which way they leaned. Several had to be asked to remove orange Yushchenko scarves so as to at least maintain the appearance of neutrality.[II]

Russia had seen the Orange Revolution coming, but somehow had failed to prevent it. "It was a well-organized street rally which had been based on the experience of the Serbian and Georgia revolutions," sighed Sergei Markov, a member of the notorious Russian Club.

"I call them NGO revolutions. Serbia, Georgia, Ukraine, all of them," he said, putting most of the blame on Soros, the chief "ideologue" behind them. "He is a fighter for freedom," Markov added, his voice dripping with sarcasm. Disingenuously, Markov said the mistake he and his team had made was to spend too much time trying to win the election and not enough on preparing to thwart the revolt.

Pavlovsky, embarrassed and furious, charged in an appearance on Russian television that the West had staged a "political invasion" of Ukraine and had manufactured a revolution "the colour of children's diarrhea." Sounding more than a little unbalanced, he even compared Yushchenko to Hitler. Like Markov, he said the defeat could not be blamed on the Russian Club, which had done all it could to help a bad candidate. "I can't see any failure from our side," he told the *Komsomolskaya Pravda* newspaper.[12]

Marat Gelman, the Moscow art gallery owner who was also the author of the notorious *temnyki,* was more honest in his analysis. While he also gave credit to Western NGOs working on the Belgrade-Tbilisi model, he placed much of the blame at the feet of Kuchma and Yanukovych, who failed to understand that the public was fed up with the cynical machinations of the past. "The main responsibility for what happened in Georgia and Ukraine belongs to the authorities. By treating democratic procedures as a formality, they gave moral right to the other side," he told me. "If the authorities didn't give the people reason to be dissatisfied with the democratic procedures, then all the American money and efforts would be in vain."

Unlike Pavlovsky and Markov, however, Gelman could be smug. While he helped Kuchma and Medvedchuk implement the *temnyki* system of media control, he says he bailed out of the election campaign shortly after he learned Yanukovych would be the pro-regime candidate. Gelman knew a loser when he saw one. "I met him once and decided not to prolong my contract," he explained.

David Dettman's analysis is closest to Gelman's—and a scathing indictment of the Russian Club's efforts. The NDI country director, a veteran of dozens of political campaigns from the U.S. to Iraq, said that while Pavlovsky and his team were busy trying to force Ukrainians to accept Yanukovych, Dettman and his colleagues were figuring out what the public wanted and making sure Yushchenko and his message matched those desires. While the Kremlin was futilely trying to shape the public, the Western team was shaping its candidate."They just don't get it. They don't get democracy," Dettman said, shaking his head. "Elections flow from the people. They don't get it, and they're going to get their asses kicked every time."

And to the victors go the spoils. After handily winning round three, one of the first acts of the new Yushchenko government was to order the flow of the Odessa-Brody pipeline to be reversed. Once more, it would carry Caspian crude to Europe. Russia's ambition of tightening its stranglehold on Europe's energy supply was punctured again. Talks about bringing Ukraine into NATO—and later, perhaps, the European Union—accelerated. Members of the new government openly questioned the future of the Black Sea Fleet at Sevastopol. Within eighteen months, American warships were docking in nearby ports on the same Crimean peninsula, to protests from the region's pro-Russian residents.

The new government also contained many faces the West knew and liked, beyond President Yushchenko and Tymoshenko, who was quickly appointed prime minister under the terms of the secret pact NDI had helped the two hammer out. Though Soros's organization played a much quieter role in Ukraine than it had in Georgia, the foundation's people, as with Open Society–Georgia, would take key positions in the next government. Boris Tarasyuk, a member of the foundation's supervisory council, was made foreign minister. Hryhoriy Nemyria, the head of the foundation's executive board, became an adviser to Tymoshenko and later a Rada deputy in her party. Another member of the executive board was Yulia Mostova, an outspoken journalist whose husband, Anatoliy Gritsenko, became defence minister. And when I next met Vlad Kaskiv, the former Soros employee who led Pora during the revolution, his business card identified him as an adviser to the president of Ukraine, Viktor Yushchenko.

TWELVE

UNMANAGEABLE DEMOCRACY

Beslan, Russia

Vladimir Putin's *annus horribilus* actually began not in Kiev, but two months earlier on the muddy lawn of the red-bricked Middle School No. 1, in a previously anonymous town in southern Russia called Beslan.

On September 1, 2004, the children of Beslan had gathered on the front lawn of the school for a ceremony. The first day of the new school year is akin to a holiday in Russia, and the children were wearing their best clothing. Many parents accompanied them. Suddenly bursts of gunfire interrupted the song that was playing and men with Kalashnikov rifles and masks were running toward the school, surrounding the children and adults on the lawn and herding them inside the building. A military truck pulled up and more masked men jumped out. Families and school staff panicked; the attackers shot and killed a man carrying celebratory flowers. The armed men—militants from the Chechen rebel movement and sympathizers from the neighbouring strife-torn republic of Ingushetia—forced everyone inside the school's gymnasium. Thus began fifty-two of the longest hours in modern Russian history.

Once inside the gym, the gunmen hung explosives from the rims of the two basketball nets, and then from a wire strung between the hoops. While the students and teachers sat on the gym floor watching in horror, the Chechens hung more than a dozen bombs in all, some of them attached to the wire only with tape. The largest bomb was connected to a pair of foot pedals on the floor; the gunmen told their hostages that if pressure was ever removed from either pedal, the bomb would explode. Then the men and the older male students were taken from the room and made to set up barricades around the school hallways. When they finished, they gunmen took them upstairs to a classroom and murdered them all, then hurled their bodies from a window.

From the first hours of the siege, the authorities lied to the public, first about the number of hostages—claiming there were just 354 when they knew the number was over 1,300—and then about the nature and aims of the hostage-takers. The Kremlin said 10 Arabs and an African were involved, in a shameful attempt to portray the hostage-taking as the work of al-Qaeda and thus part of the global "war on terror," rather than Putin's dirty war coming back to haunt him. Subsequent reports of so few hostages annoyed the gunmen, recalled Margarita Komoyeva, a teacher who was huddled in the gym with her three daughters. "They told us that if the authorities are saying there's just this number of people inside, they will be storming—get ready for the storm," she told me after the siege. In other words, the Chechens believed that the Russian government was preparing to cover up how many people died if they stormed the school.

On the second day of the crisis, after a visit by the former president of Ingushetia, Ruslan Aushev, the militants released some of the youngest children and their mothers. But shortly after 1 a.m. on Friday, they fired a rocket-propelled grenade at government forces surrounding the school, injuring one police officer. By morning, after nearly two full days of fruitless negotiations and bursts of gunfire, the tension had reached the boiling point. Petrified hostages watched after daybreak as the gunmen began rearranging the explosives, placing more of them near the gym windows in apparent anticipation of an attack. They forced small boys to stand in the windows as human shields. Children stopped their cries for water, sensing the new, more dangerous mood. Survivors recalled trying to inch closer to the exits, hoping to save themselves and their families from whatever came next.

Negotiations that had been suspended that morning resumed early in the afternoon. At 12:45 p.m., the hostage-takers agreed to let rescuers retrieve the men's corpses, which had been rotting in the sun since being thrown from the window early in the siege. As four men wearing uniforms of the Ministry of Emergency Situations approached the school, one gunman, dressed in brown trousers and a camouflage shirt, came out to supervise.

Just then an explosion that could be heard throughout the entire town rocked the gym, followed seconds later by another, larger blast. Many of the hostages I spoke to later believed that one of the mines suspended from the wire between two basketball hoops came unglued and fell into the crowd below. Others claimed that one of the gunmen stepped off the foot-pedal detonator. In another version, floated by the Kremlin, the hostage-takers quarrelled just before the explosion, with one group wanting to escape while others planned to fight to the death.

Soslan Beteyev, age twelve, was stationed by a window as a human shield when the shockwave hit him. "I was just about to step down from the window and there was an explosion, and I fell on some children," he said. "I tried to get up again and there was another explosion. There was panic and everybody tried to get out." When I walked with him through the ruins of his school a few days after the siege's bloody ending, he spoke so quickly that he was almost incomprehensible, his words spilling into each other without pause, as if he had gone over the story a million times in his head.

After the blast, Soslan climbed out a window and dashed across the courtyard to a store on the edge of the school property. He escaped, along with Komoyeva's two older daughters, who had been forced to stay behind when their mother was allowed to leave on the Thursday with her youngest child. "They were shooting at our backs," Soslan said robotically. Tiny shrapnel wounds covered his arms and back, but it was his mind that seemed to have suffered the most damage. When I asked why he had returned to the school, where I met him wandering through the rubble, he broke into tears. "I don't know," he said. "I thought maybe I could help find some of the missing."

The chaos spread outside the gym after the initial explosion. The hostage-takers, apparently believing it was the beginning of a police effort to storm the building, fired on the emergency workers and then on hostages trying to escape. Security forces outside had ruled out using force to free the hostages and had no set plan for seizing the building, but with the shooting, they had no choice but to move in. "When they started killing civilians, there were no other options," said Vitaly, an Interior Ministry officer who was crouching behind a tree about fifty metres from the gym door when the order came. He asked, for obvious reasons, that I not use his last name. The operation, he said, was made up as it went along. "It was a total mess."

After the two explosions just seconds apart, the remaining militants searched the smoke-filled gymnasium for survivors. They rounded up everyone still moving and took them down the hall to the cafeteria, planning to make a final stand. Several hostages fled upstairs in the confusion and hid behind a curtain on the stage of the assembly hall. They were discovered and also taken to the cafeteria. "The terrorists were shouting, 'Hurry up—walk quickly or we will kill you,'" said Ruslan Margiyev, a short-haired twelve-year-old who by this point was bleeding from a shrapnel wound to his hand. "But we were afraid to step on the corpses."

Bullets were pouring into the cafeteria from outside, he said. He took cover behind an oven, but the hostage-takers ordered the children toward the window. "They said, 'If you do not wave a cloth in the window, we will kill all of you.'" One woman got up on her knees and was hit in the chest by two bullets fired from outside. Eight-year-old Zaur Bitsiyev, whom Ruslan recognized, was killed at the same time—shot in the back by someone in the cafeteria. A Russian *spetznaz* officer stepped through the window and told Ruslan to run; then a Chechen who had been hiding in the kitchen shot and killed the officer, who fell on top of the boy. Ruslan said he hid under the body until the shooting ended, protected by the soldier's bulletproof vest.

Vitaly, the Interior Ministry officer, was among the first of the troops to reach the blackened shell of the gym. "I saw a sea of blood and corpses—adults and children—all over the gymnasium," he said, his husky voice dropping low. "Everything was burned. It was impossible to recognize anything." Despite the gruesome aftermath—not to mention the fact that it was the scene of a major criminal act—Russian officials sealed off the site for barely thirty-six hours. For days after that, journalists and grieving relatives stepped gingerly through the shattered gymnasium, with its cratered floor, covered in blood, dirt and melted shoes, and through the blackened and bloodied hallways that stretched out from it.

It was the most horrifying scene I've ever had to endure, something unrivalled during my time covering the wars in Iraq, Afghanistan and Chechnya. There were bits of hair and streaks of blood on nearly every wall. I fought tears as one woman picked up a girl's knit sweater that was caked in dirt and dried blood and sniffed it, hoping to encounter the scent of someone she'd obviously lost in the firefight. Other local residents stepped sadly over a tie, packed into the mud on the gymnasium floor, which must have belonged to a small boy.

As horrifying as the actions of the Chechen rebels were (and the hostage-taking was part of a string of bloody attacks, including the simultaneous downing of two planes just weeks beforehand), it was nearly as galling to see the Kremlin's reaction to the tragedy. After seeming to have rejected every avenue for a negotiated solution that might have saved many of the children's lives, Putin knew he wouldn't be popular in Beslan. He visited a hospital in nearby Vladikavkaz after the siege and told victims that "all of Russia grieves with you." Television cameras captured the moment for consumption in the rest of the country, but Putin was gone before daybreak, never having set foot in Beslan.

It was only a small part of the deception the Kremlin would resort to after an attack that shocked his country and the world. As the first explosions rocked the inside of the gymnasium on September 3, Russia's state-controlled television stations kept broadcasting old movies, even as CNN and the BBC were broadcasting live from the scene. An hour later, when the Russian networks eventually did start reporting on Beslan, the flagship Rossiya channel stated that the fighting was over and no one had been injured or killed—even as gunfire continued at the scene. Four years of Putin's steady attacks had reduced Russia's television media to what it had been at the time of Chernobyl: an organ for repeating the state's lies to a people once more used to being lied to.

When Putin finally addressed the nation a day and a half after police stormed the school, he did not discuss the war in Chechnya or the massive failure of his alma mater, the FSB, to prevent the whole bloody episode. He blamed the "unfortunate" end of the Soviet Union for making Russia "weak." And the weak, he said, borrowing from Stalin, "get beaten."

"Today we live in a time that follows the collapse of a vast and great state, a state that, unfortunately, proved unable to survive in a

rapidly changing world," he said gravely. The ensuing chaos had made
events like Beslan possible, he continued, glibly leaving out his own
role in starting the second Chechen war. Over the next few weeks he
unveiled a plan that astonished even his supporters: in the name of
fighting terrorism, he would roll back democracy in Russia. The
country's eighty-nine regional governors would no longer be elected
by the residents of their regions; they would be appointed by Putin.
After the failures of the local leadership at Beslan, he wanted the
governors to be people who were loyal to him and whom he could
trust in a crisis. There would be no more directly elected Duma
deputies either, only candidates chosen from party lists. It was all in
the name of his beloved "vertical power structure."

I knew the Kremlin was consumed by a new and destructive paranoia
when I became part of the story.

   Wanting to fill in the blanks in the version that the Kremlin had
spun, I did two things after Beslan that would eventually get me
branded as a hostile journalist by Putin's underlings. One was to
break the Kremlin's embargo on unsanctioned trips to Chechnya so
that I could report on how the Russian army was exacting revenge
for Beslan through *zachistki* in towns where pro-rebel sentiment was
believed to exist, and summary executions of those with even a
rumoured link to the forces of Shamil Basayev, the Chechen warlord
who claimed to have masterminded the Beslan siege. My other
"offence" was to send an e-mail to Basayev, through the Kavkaz
Centre website on which he posted occasional statements. I actually
sent two e-mails, one to Basayev and one to Aslan Maskhadov, the
more moderate Chechen leader. Only Basayev responded.[1]

   The key bits of the interview went as follows:

MM: The international public was shocked by the events in
Beslan. Do you consider yourself to blame for the outcome, or
do you blame President Putin for it all?
SB: [after giving thanks to God, whom he said favours Muslims
and "our jihad"]: I admit some responsibility, but do not consider myself to blame for such an outcome. I am responsible for
having made Putin show the world his true face . . . The

Russians have been holding the entire Chechen people hostage for five years, and nothing has happened! Yet we had only to take a thousand people hostage in order to stop the genocide of the Chechen people, and "the whole world is shocked." If that is not hypocrisy, what is?

мм: Did you hope for the repetition of the Budennovsk scenario whereby the Russian leadership asked for peace?[2]

sb: I did. In fact, I was shocked by what happened in Beslan. I did not expect that kind of outcome. I believed that if we did not give the Russians even a chance of storming, they would not kill children, especially as those were the children of Ossetia—the empire's main outpost in the Caucasus. And especially at this moment, when the Russian leadership is in the deadlock in its attempts to solve "the Chechen problem" and when the war is spilling over to the rest of Russia on a daily basis. I thought that I was doing the Russians a favour by showing them the way out of the deadlock. But Putin is a revenge-seeker who cares only about the strengthening of his own power and also suffers from the inferiority complex. Look at the measures he took immediately after Beslan—he strengthened his own power and not a single Russian objected to this.

What is a link between the appointment of governors and "the war on terror"? One could think that it is not him who has appointed most of the governors and senators. Or look at his law-enforcement ministers: how can one say that FSB Director [Nikolai] Patrushev is a professional and irreplaceable. He is doing the job only because of his personal loyalty to Putin. That's all! Can you imagine having a security minister in Canada who would allow dozens [of] sabotage actions, which claimed thousands of lives, to happen for five years in the territory under his supervision? I think not. But it is possible in Russia, as it is in a gang where everybody has blood on his hands.

мм: Don't the bombings on the metro and attacks on aircraft go beyond the limits of what is permitted in war?

sb: What kind of war are you talking about? There is no war, according to Putin, there is "a counter-terrorist operation" where no rules exist against "terrorists" and where everything goes.

Even doing an interview is seen as "assistance and propaganda of terrorism." Incidentally, by definition you are already "an associate," and you may even go missing in Russia . . . If Putin begins to abide by international law, then automatically we will do so. But we do not want to fight in such a way unilaterally. I said this in January this year and I am saying this now. I would also say that had Putin announced at the time his intention to abide by international law and "the shocked international community" demanded that from him, then neither Beslan nor the explosions on the underground [nor on the] planes would have occurred.[3]

The answers from "Basayev" went on at some length, as though whoever was writing to me either had plenty of time on his hands or hadn't had much contact with the outside world recently. He even went into what kind of salves he liked to use on his wounds, and spoke of always carrying honey with him.

"Basayev" discussed his time at al-Qaeda training camps in Afghanistan but said Westerners overestimated the reach of Osama bin Laden's organization when they blamed it for attacks in every corner of the world. He talked about his time hiding in Georgia's Pankisi Gorge but said that he and his fighters had been anxious to leave and return to Chechnya and that none remained there now, despite Russian contentions to the contrary. He denied responsibility for the 1999 apartment block blasts in Moscow that had provoked the latest Chechen war, blaming them on a Kremlin bent on returning its soldiers to Chechnya. He said the Chechens were ready for another ten years of war, "if Putin doesn't want peace," and even discussed his recent movements in Chechnya and southern Russia, which sounded relatively hassle-free for one of the world's most wanted men, with a famous face and with a pronounced limp since having lost a foot to a land-mine blast. He said he was writing to me from the Zavodskoy neighbourhood of Grozny, adding almost apologetically that he could not give me his exact address.

Of course, I had no way of knowing if it was actually Shamil Basayev who had responded to my e-mail. But when I told the Kavkaz Centre that the *Globe and Mail* wouldn't publish the interview until we were sure of its authenticity, the website's staff simply gave my material to the wire services. Reuters, the Associated Press and the BBC, along with much of the Russian media, all immediately published. The Russian Foreign Ministry turned its fire on me for being an "aide to terrorists," sending me a formal complaint that it gave to the news wires and posted on the websites of its embassies around the world. It strongly suggested that my accreditation wouldn't be renewed at the end of the year.[4]

The response exemplified the way the Kremlin had handled the entire Beslan affair: don't ask why a foreign journalist could make contact with Basayev when the entire FSB apparently couldn't—just threaten him with expulsion. The media, like the elected governors, were to be the culprits: Raf Shakirov, the editor of the *Izvestia* newspaper, which had been known for its independence despite being owned by Kremlin-friendly oligarch Vladimir Potanin, was fired under heavy Kremlin pressure for running large pictures of the carnage and chaos at Middle School No. 1. Radio Liberty's Andrei Babitsky, who had earned a reputation as one of the Kremlin's harshest critics for his reporting from Chechnya, was arrested at the Moscow airport after strange men suddenly picked a fight with him.

Meanwhile, Anna Politkovskaya, a reporter for the feisty *Novaya Gazeta* newspaper who was Russia's best-known, and most fiercely independent, investigative journalist, fell sick with a mysterious poisoning before she even reached Beslan. Two years later, in October 2006, she died in a contract-style hit in the elevator of her apartment building, a killing investigators believe was tied to her work in and around Chechnya.

The Kremlin wasn't going to conduct a proper investigation into the disaster at Beslan, perhaps worried about what it might find, and it certainly didn't want a bunch of foreign and Russian journalists trying to fill that gap. The siege wasn't to be blamed on Russia's inept security services, and certainly not on the president's ill-advised and horrifyingly prosecuted war in Chechnya. Beslan, as Putin's political adviser Vladislav Surkov explained, was the fault of unnamed foreign enemies who aspired "to destroy Russia and to populate its vast expanses with numerous ineffective quasi-states." Journalists and opposition politicians who said otherwise belonged to a "fifth column," he said, that threatened the survival of the nation. "They have the same sponsors of foreign origin and the same hatred for Putin's Russia, as they put it, but, in fact, for Russia per se."

Such tough, seemingly patriotic talk had worked in the past to rally Russians around the president. But not this time, and certainly not among those who'd experienced the school siege first-hand. The Kremlin's arrogance and lies were so great that the residents of Beslan finally decided they'd had enough.

The mourning Ossetians found a surprising new target for their anger: their own government. Their first act of defiance was to establish a website, beslan.ru, run from a computer gaming club a few blocks from the school many of the dead children had once frequented. Working in a near silence punctured only by the soft clicking of keys, a small group of teachers and parents, including three survivors of the siege, began compiling a factual record of the event, something their government obviously wasn't interested in doing. What they produced was a stark challenge to the official version of events: they named 1,338 people who had been inside the school, when the government was still insisting there had been fewer than 1,200. On a black web page, under the simple heading "Tragedy in Beslan," they named all 333 dead, at a time when the Russian government was still announcing lower and constantly changing figures about the number of people killed.

"We know what's true and what is a lie. It happened to us, and they can't lie any more about what happened here," said Vissarion Asayev, the former Internet café manager who launched the beslan.ru project. His forehead was covered with purple scars from shrapnel wounds he received during a gun battle with hostage-takers on the first day of the siege, when he ran toward the scene and engaged the Chechens with his own rifle. The teachers working with him on the website project, he said, had a better handle on what had actually happened during those three terrible days than the government, since they know first-hand who was in the school and who wasn't. "Since the first day, I didn't have any questions about what happened here. I don't need some government official to tell me. I saw it."

Next the residents of Beslan directed their fury at the local government. Protestors massed repeatedly outside the offices of South Ossetia's president, Alexander Dzasokhov, demanding his resignation for disappearing during the crisis and for refusing to meet with the hostage-takers when they demanded to speak with him. In the wake of the Orange Revolution, the protests escalated. Hundreds of residents blocked a major highway for days on end, holding pictures of their dead relatives. In a breakthrough example of people power forcing the authorities to bend, Dzasokhov eventually quit.

While the teachers and mothers of Beslan were blocking highways in the North Caucasus, thousands of pensioners were taking to the streets from Siberia to St. Petersburg, blocking roads and protesting outside regional legislatures, demanding that the government drop plans to cut key benefits such as free medicine and public transport for seniors, benefits that had been in place since Soviet times. In response to what some quickly dubbed the "babushka revolution," Putin quickly hiked pensions to compensate the angry old-timers, and his government postponed plans to scrap a student exemption from military service, fearing that crowds of students and soldiers might join their grandparents in the streets.

At a rally in early February on Moscow's Pushkin Square, many in the crowd of several hundred waved orange scarves and banners. "We need an Orange Revolution here," Igor Tulmanov, a twenty-three-year-old student, told reporter Fred Weir of the Canadian Press. "Our authorities are too arrogant, too authoritarian. They should be reminded that the people exist." At a later rally on the same square, I spotted something I thought I'd never see so close to the Kremlin walls: a white clenched fist on a black background, the one made famous by Otpor and Kmara. It seemed Beslan and the Orange Revolution next door had opened a crack in the facade of Putin's *stabilnost.*[5]

THIRTEEN

THE NEW GREAT GAME

Baku, Almaty and Tashkent

[O]n the morning of May 25, 2005, to loud cheers, crude oil finally started flowing west from British Petroleum's gleaming Sangachal Terminal on Azerbaijan's Caspian Sea coast into the Baku-Tbilisi-Ceyhan pipeline. U.S. energy secretary Samuel Bodman, on hand to observe the occasion with the presidents of Azerbaijan, Georgia, Turkey and Kazakhstan, called it a "day that will change the world." It was certainly a great victory for U.S. diplomacy, and a day the Kremlin had desperately hoped would never come to pass.

President Bush had been in the region just a few weeks earlier to dine with Mikhail Saakashvili and to tell a cheering crowd in Tbilisi that Georgia was a "beacon of liberty" to the world, one the U.S. would defend. But on May 25, when the State Department cheered the pipeline's opening as a boost to the sovereignty and prosperity of both Georgia and Azerbaijan, no one mentioned that Azeri president Ilham Aliev had sent riot police to smash a pro-democracy rally in Baku just a few days beforehand. The American thirst for oil had trumped the quest for freedom. Nonetheless, an astonishing fact marred the hoopla around the pipeline's opening: there wasn't nearly enough of the black stuff to fill it.

Back in the 1990s, the State Department had been the lead cheer-leader behind Azerbaijan's oil boom, telling analysts and oilmen that there were up to 200 billion barrels of crude under the choppy black waters of the Caspian Sea, a figure comparable only to the 262 billion barrels believed to sit beneath the sands of Saudi Arabia. No less a personality than Dick Cheney, then the chief executive officer of the Halliburton oil services giant, weighed in. "I cannot think of a time when we have had a region emerge as suddenly to become as strategically significant as the Caspian," he said in 1998.

But instead of the 200 billion barrels predicted in 1995, estimates a decade later put the Caspian reserves at somewhere between 17 and 32 billion, most of it on the other side of the sea from Azerbaijan, in the waters off Kazakhstan. "I think that there were some people that did exaggerate the amount of oil reserves in the Caspian. That is without doubt," Michael Townsend, executive director of BTC, the BP-run company managing the pipeline, told me as we sat in BP's sprawling Baku headquarters, a former Communist Party office now known locally as the Villa Petrolea. "It's not another Middle East. It's more similar to another North Sea, or Algeria, or Norway."

To fill the pipeline (and ensure its profitability), as well as to meet the post-9/11 aim of diminishing America's reliance on Middle Eastern energy, the oil majors couldn't rely on just pro-Western Georgia and pliant Azerbaijan. They needed the countries of post-Soviet Central Asia, predominantly Kazakhstan, to agree to ship their crude across the Caspian by sea to Sangachal, rather than overland via the competing pipeline to Russia's Novorossiysk port, or via a proposed new pipeline through Iran. And they had to get the Central Asians on board quickly; Kazakhstan's other neighbour, China, has turned an increasingly interested eye on the region because of its own enormous and growing appetite for energy.

"The Great Game continues," Nadia Diuk of the National Endowment for Democracy told me, using the words Rudyard Kipling had used for what had once been fought between Britain and czarist Russia across Central Asia. Although oil and gas interests were "far away from what NED does," she said, the Kremlin was putting them at the centre of the growing U.S.–Russia conflict through its use of Gazprom and Lukoil to control and influence its neighbours.

After Tbilisi and Kiev, there was talk that an "orange" wave was about to wash over the entire post-Soviet space. Opposition parties in such far-flung corners as Moldova, Belarus, Armenia and Kazakhstan began to talk bravely of revolution, and even Gleb Pavlovsky seemed to believe all was lost. He openly despaired that the "orange contagion," as he called it, would eventually spread to Moscow. Then, in February 2005, the contagion seemed to strike one of the most remote outposts of the former USSR, the Central Asian republic of Kyrgyzstan.

Kyrgyzstan, a ruggedly beautiful country of five million mostly Muslim people bordered by China in the east, Kazakhstan in the north and Uzbekistan and Tajikistan to the south, had gained increasing strategic importance to the United States in its "war on terrror." Already seen as one of the most pro-American states in the former Soviet Union, since 2001 it had hosted, outside the capital city of Bishkek, a major American airbase that supplied the war effort in nearby Afghanistan. Kyrgyz president Askar Akayev was hailed as a pro-Western reformer who could help spread democracy in the Muslim world. To the delight of American ears, he told an interviewer in 1991 that the economic revolution had been launched not by Karl Marx, but by Adam Smith.

Like Shevardnadze, however, Akayev would later anger the White House by taking a half-step back into Moscow's orbit. In 2003 he invited the Russians to take over a military airfield just thirty kilometres from the American base. Allegations surfaced of corruption inside the regime.

All of which made Kyrgyzstan fertile ground for the revolution-makers. As the West turned away from Akayev, the president himself spoke of an "orange danger" facing his country, claiming that the U.S. was determined to topple him. But in the context of the global "war on terror," concerns were high that opening up the political space too far in Kyrgyzstan might provide an opportunity to Islamists, who were perceived as the best-organized political force in Central Asia, after the regimes. A few preparatory steps were taken in early 2005 toward staging another pro-Western uprising—most notably the formation of a Pora-like youth group called KelKel—but the sort of massive, coordinated effort seen in Ukraine never materialized, because many in Washington feared what a sudden power vacuum in the heart of Central Asia might produce.

In the end, events happened too fast for anyone to fully control them. Working on its own inititiative, an NED-backed NGO called

Civil Society Against Corruption translated and distributed copies of Gene Sharp's "From Dictatorship to Democracy." But few seemed to grasp the non-violent principles behind the movement.[1]

Kyrgyzstan's revolt, made memorable by a lone rioter riding on horseback around Bishkek's central square hoisting a yellow flag, was as chaotic as it was photogenic. Though the deposition of Askar Akayev had many of the outward characteristics of the Belgrade-Tbilisi-Kiev chain and was hailed by the United States as another example of democracy spreading, this time in the Muslim world, the "Tulip Revolution," as it was immediately dubbed, actually had far less in common with the Rose and Orange revolutions than met the eye.

The February 27 election produced clear results in only thirty-one of seventy-five districts, with the rest to be decided in run-offs. The election monitors (which included Western-funded monitors from Serbia, Georgia, Ukraine and thirteen other post-Communist countries) surprised many by concluding that outside of violations "in a few precincts," the election had been "largely free of vote-buying, voter intimidation, harassment of journalists, and massive misuse of administrative resources."

It didn't matter. Demonstrations began before a second round could be held, focusing on the fact that Akayev's son and daughter had both won seats amidst allegations of vote-buying. The protests turned violent from the start; angry mobs carrying sticks and gasoline bombs seized control of the southern Kyrgyz city of Jalal-Abad, then the larger centre of Osh. Several deaths were reported. Though the mobs—who often appeared leaderless and frequently forgot to wear the yellow that was supposed to symbolize their "democratic" uprising—rallied around the ousting of Akayev, he had already promised to step down at the end of his term that October.

To a large extent, the unrest was actually fuelled not by concern over the elections, but by frustration in the predominantly Uzbek south with the north, which was dominated by ethnic Kyrgyz who controlled much of the nation's politics and business. The Akayev family, known for corruption and influence-peddling, had come to represent all that the typically poor Uzbeks in the crowd disliked about their lives. This was more about clans and revenge than it was about democracy.

Osh had seen violent conflicts during the early 1990s, and Akayev, who called for talks and ordered a review of the election results in an effort to appease the crowd, repeatedly warned that the protests could quickly degenerate into civil war. That nightmare scenario never unfolded, but it was too late for Akayev to save his regime. "The situation is spinning out of control . . . [It] cannot be any more explosive than it is," Kurmanbek Bakiyev, a loosely defined leader of the opposition and a former prime minister under Akayev, told reporters in Bishkek. He was speaking to his own powerlessness at that point as much as to Akayev's.[2]

On March 25, 2005, demonstrators stormed and looted the Presidential Administration offices, forcing Akayev to flee to Moscow. An interim government—headed by Kurmanbek Bakiyev—formed swiftly, but little else changed. The looting stopped and the corruption continued. While Akayev complained bitterly that America had backed a coup against him, the new government quickly proved, if anything, more pro-Russian than Akayev had been.

Those who had hoped for a real Tulip Revolution were dismayed. "We did not have an intention to storm the Government House. We wanted to stage rallies days and nights as was in Georgia and Ukraine. What happened in the square [near the Government House] on March 24 was the result of the activities of state power-wielding and criminal structures," said Roza Otunbayeva, a key opposition figure who served as acting foreign minister in the new government. Rather than backing the uprising, the West had let Kyrgyzstan down. "Neither the NDI nor Soros in Kyrgyzstan gave us money. On the contrary, they kept aloof from us. I was disappointed with this aloofness," she said.[3]

When I visited Belgrade shortly after the chaos in Bishkek had come to an end and asked Otpor's Siniša Šikman if he or the other travelling revolutionaries had any hand in Kyrgyzstan, he laughed out loud: "The first thing I said when I saw that happening on television was that 'Oh no, they're going to blame this one on us, too.'"

Kyrgyzstan's Akayev, like Shevardnadze and Kuchma who fell before him, had once been seen as one of the more democratic post-Soviet leaders. He had allowed civil society to flourish and a relatively open media to develop. The country had been remarkably free, at least in contrast to the repression in neighbouring countries like Kazakhstan and Uzbekistan. The leaders of those countries would look at the fall of Akayev and decide, as Lukashenko did in Belarus, that the answer was to clamp down.

Many thought that Kazakhstan, Kyrgyzstan's large and oil-rich neighbour, would provide the scene for the next "colour revolution," as the uprisings were now dubbed. While Kazakh president Nursultan Nazarbayev had held uncontested power since 1990, supported by a substantive cult of personality he and his followers had cultivated, the country was, after Kyrgyzstan, perhaps the most politically open in Central Asia.

That's not saying a whole lot, however, in a region that is home to the despotic Islom Karimov of Uzbekistan, who stands accused by human rights groups of boiling dissidents alive, among other crimes, and to Turkmenistan's Saparmurat Niyazov, better known as "Turkmenbashi" or "Father of All Turkmen." Until his death in 2006, Turkmenbashi's cult of personality might have made Stalin blush. A fourteen-metre-high gold-plated statue of the president, motorized to rotate so that Turkmenbashi is always facing the sun, dominated the centre of the capital city, Ashgabat. In 2002, he renamed the first month of the year Turkmenbashi and decided that the fourth month should now bear his mother's name instead of boring old April.

Kazakh president Nazarbayev, who had ruled the country first as the top Communist in the last days of the USSR and then as its "elected" president following a pair of blatantly fixed votes in 1991 and 1999, possessed an autocratic streak, too. Opposition politicians and overly critical journalists made a habit of dying in strange car accidents or committing suicide. The official version of what happened to them was often ludicrously improbable. Most notoriously, cabinet minister–turned–opposition figure Zamanbek Nurkadilov reportedly took his own life with two shots to the chest and one to the head.

As Nazarbayev's re-election loomed in December 2005, the only uncertainty seemed to be whether he, at age sixty-four, would stand for another term or whether he'd hand the reins of power to his daughter, Dariga Nazarbayeva, whom he had groomed for the post by giving her control of the country's largest media company. She also headed the country's second-largest political party, which stood in theoretical opposition to the government but in fact supported everything her father did. "I can't say never. I can't swear it will never happen," she told me when I asked her in 2004 at her office in Almaty, the largest city in a sprawling, thinly populated country, about the possibility of succeeding her father as president.

In such a democratic desert, however, it was easy to look like an oasis, especially if you opened your doors to Western oil firms like Chevron and Exxon Mobil, as Kazakhstan did in the 1990s. That oil money gave Kazakhstan some stability and made it the wealthiest republic in Central Asia. By 2005, Nazarbayev's fiefdom had 15 billion barrels of provable oil reserves, or 2 per cent of the world's known supply. Drawn like moths, Western and, later, Chinese investors poured in, and average wages rose to become the best in the region, nearly on par with those in Russia.

Kazakhstan's political system was closer to Russia's "managed democracy" than to the outright dictatorships of its neighbours. There were opposition parties, though they complained of "administrative resources" being used against them and of unequal access to the media. NGOs, notably the local offices of the Soros Foundation, the Eurasia Foundation, Freedom House and the International Republican Institute, were permitted limited space in which to operate.

But in the wake of the Orange Revoluton, paranoia reigned inside Nazarbayev's regime. One day after the third round of voting in Ukraine, tax authorities launched a tax evasion investigation into the Soros Foundation–Kazakhstan, warning that the NGO might have to be closed down if the books weren't in order. The foundation survived, but the crackdown continued. Democratic Choice of Kazakhstan, one of the two main opposition parties not headed by a member of the Nazarbayev family, was banned a few months later over revelations that it sent a delegation to Kiev to study how the uprising there had come about. In April 2005, a parliament dominated by Nazarbayev's allies passed a law banning street demonstrations during and after the election period. After consulting with the Kremlin—and hot on the heels of a visit by George Soros to Almaty—Nazarbayev introduced legislation restricting the foreign financing of NGOs and authorizing tax inspectors to seize banking data on the origins and purpose of NGO funding. Dariga Nazarbayeva made it clear that her father was worried. "[A revolution] is quite possible," she said in a speech at a special congress of her Asar party. "We have witnessed many examples of this, from Serbia to Kyrgyzstan."[4]

The opposition was indeed actively investigating the possibility of bringing the Georgia-Ukraine model to Kazakhstan. A key Pora activist, Mykhailo Svystovych, as well as Kmara's Giorgi Kandelaki and others, helped establish the latest Otpor knockoff, a Kazakh youth group called Kakhar, or "Anger." A new, unified opposition movement dubbed For a Just Kazakhstan emerged and nominated a single candidate, Zharmakhan Tuyakbai, a one-time leader in the main pro-presidential party who claimed he had defected to the opposition after witnessing official corruption.

Similar preparations were also being made in the Caucasus republic of Azerbaijan in the spring and summer of 2005. A youth group named YOX (Azeri for "No") planned to take to the streets around the November 2004 parliamentary elections in support of a new opposition coalition, with orange as its campaign colour. But just as opposition hopes were building in Kazakhstan and Azerbaijan, the dangers of pushing a dictator too far made themselves known in another rarely heard-from corner of Central Asia.

It was an argument I'd been having with my colleagues since the day we watched Mikhail Saakashvili lead the final charge on the Georgian parliament building. All of us believed that the West had played a significant role in what happened. Did the end—overthrowing an unpopular semi-autocratic leader—justify the sometimes underhanded means?

The answer was yes, we agreed, if the measuring stick was bettering people's lives in the country in question, and the majority of Serbians, Georgians and Ukrainians I met supported the ouster of an unpopular leader. Many felt they were better off since then. But the question gets more complicated if you widen the lens and take a look at the former Soviet area as a whole. Is it a good thing to topple two of the least repressive leaders in the region (Shevardnadze and Kuchma) if autocrats like Lukashenko and Nazarbayev react by cracking down on the opposition and civil society in their already less open states? Is bettering the lives of Georgians for the best if its ripple effect includes a crackdown on dissent and the closing of political space in Russia?

In some places, the ripple effect was more like a tidal wave. As in Kazakhstan, NGOs across the former Soviet space started coming under incredible scrutiny. Many closed entirely. In no place was the fallout worse than in Uzbekistan, where the cruel regime of Islom Karimov was one of the fastest to recognize the threat posed to it by the growth of civil society and the first to hit back with everything it had. Shortly after the Rose Revolution and the subsequent election of Saakashvili, Uzbek authorities introduced legislation forcing all NGOs, foreign and domestic, to re-register, and subsequently closed the Uzbek offices of the Open Society Institute for funding anti-regime election materials. "The main goal [of OSI] was to select from among the young talented Uzbek intelligentsia those who could become a supportive force for them, to fool and brainwash them against the constitutional order," charged Karimov. When he said "the constitutional order," he meant himself, having ruled the country with an iron fist since 1989.[5]

The purge cast a chill over the entire NGO community. When I visited Uzbekistan in the fall of 2004, in part to investigate the allegations of boiling of dissidents and other torture in a place that was seen as an ally in America's "war on terror," my hardest task was finding anyone to speak with me. Though Freedom House still had an office in the capital city of Tashkent, and even though her own organization had repeatedly slammed the country in its annual report as being less free in 2004 than it was in the last years of Soviet rule, I couldn't drag a bad word about Karimov out of the office's director, Mjusa Sever. (It's worth noting that in its dealings in Uzbekistan, Kazakhstan and Azerbaijan, the Soros Foundation distinguished itself from the other main democracy-promotion groups. Unlike those funded by NED or USAID, Soros's foundations are remarkably consistent in the application of their declared principle of promoting "open society," caring little if a repressive regime is a friend of the current White House or whether the opposition has an Islamic bent.)

One of the few people in Tashkent who openly criticized the government was Surat Ikramov, a fifty-nine-year-old human rights activist who joked that he'd had the fear beaten out of him. Weeks before we met at his apartment, a group of much younger men had attacked him. They put a plastic bag over his head, drove him to the bank of a canal and beat him within an inch of his life, leaving him, bloodied, under a pile of twigs. When he arrived in hospital with a concussion and two broken ribs, he refused treatment for fear the doctors would give him an injection to finish him off. He believes the thugs were Karimov's secret police.

"One of them said, 'If you keep silent, you will stay alive,'" he recalled. Then he smiled impishly through his thin grey-going-on-white beard and added, "But I'm still talking. Every day I'm alive after that is a gift, and I'm going to keep talking." Quick-witted and full of energy, he was deeply dismayed at Freedom House's seeming support for Karimov and at what he saw as the U.S.'s abandonment of its principles when it came to Uzebekistan's air base and the war on terror. True to his word, the incredibly likable Ikramov sent me e-mails about the happenings in his forgotten country every week, without fail, for years after.[6]

At the time, criticism of Karimov was still rare in the U.S. since he, like Askar Akayev in Kyrgyzstan, had allowed the Americans to use his country as a staging point for the war in Afghanistan—and, unlike Akayev, he hadn't invited the Russians to move in down the road. The Western foreign policy establishment also tended to believe that much of Central Asia was fertile ground for radical Islam—thinking bolstered by the occasional suicide bombing in Tashkent—and that if Karimov's regime were to collapse, something like the Taliban would take its place. So the U.S. and Britain (which recalled its ambassador to Taskhkent, Craig Murray, in 2004 after he spoke out about the Karimov regime's use of torture) turned blind eyes to the repressions, believing the alternative was a greater evil. "Because Uzbekistan is now an ally of the United States after September 11, the U.S. closed its eyes to the human rights situation here," Ikramov sighed.

For a while, Karimov, like Akayev and Nazarbayev, made enough changes—liberalizing parts of the economy and letting groups like Open Society and Freedom House in—to gloss over his image in the West. But after seeing the string of revolutions, he realized the danger he had been put in by his flirting with the U.S. and agreeing to more political openness. He soon began to disengage from the West and to rely again on Russia (and, to a lesser extent, nearby China) for support. At the same time, he dropped any lingering pretenses of being a democrat and continued further down the path to outright despotism.

———

Despite Karimov's stepped-up repressions, or perhaps because of them, the unrest in neighbouring Kyrgyzstan started to spill over the Uzbek border in early 2005. On March 25, a small crowd of about sixty people gathered outside the U.S. embassy in Tashkent to show their support for the Kyrgyz uprising. They unfurled orange flags and chanted "Democracy!" Most of the crowd was made up of women and children, in hope of lessening the odds of a crackdown. "We, members of the Uzbek opposition and rights activists, have welcomed the victory of Kyrgyz democracy with great pleasure. It is indeed an historic event since peoples of Central Asia have gained their independence. The Kyrgyz people wanted freedom and achieved it!" activist Yelena Urlayeva said, reading out a statement on behalf of the protesters. The irrepressible Surat Ikramov was in the small crowd as it marched to the Kyrgyz embassy to deliver a message of congratulations to the ambassador.[7]

Whether that pro-democracy demonstration had anything to do with what happened next in a previously unheard-of town called Andijan, in the east of Uzbekistan, is a matter of hot debate. On May 10, a crowd of about a thousand demonstrators gathered outside a prison to demand the release of twenty-three jailed businessmen who the regime claimed were tied to Islamist groups but who others say were simply political opponents of the regime. After authorities did nothing to either disperse the crowd or meet its demands, a larger crowd, of four thousand people, gathered the next day. Again, nothing happened.

On the third day, armed men stormed the prison and released everyone inside—the twenty-three businessmen and about two thousand other prisoners. After that success, a rumour spread through the jubilant but nervous crowd that Karimov was on his way to Andijan to hear the complaints of the protestors and to negotiate a solution. The expectant crowd, estimated at ten thousand, massed on May 13 on the city's central Bobur Square.

Instead of Karimov, they were met by tanks and soldiers who opened fire on the crowds—fighting terrorism, by the dictator's definition, killing indiscriminately by anyone else's. Galima Bukharbaeva, a reporter for the Institute for War and Peace Reporting, was in the crowds when it began. "The eight-wheeled armoured personnel carriers, APCs, appeared out of nowhere, moving through the streets at speed, past the people on the outer fringes of the rally," she wrote. "The first column of vehicles thundered past without taking any aggressive action. But a second column arriving five minutes later suddenly opened up on the crowds, firing off round after round without even slowing down to take aim . . . People on the square, who were unarmed and included women and children, started screaming and trying to run away." Bukharbaeva herself narrowly escaped after a bullet pierced her backpack.[8]

The government claims 173 people were killed in a battle between police and Islamic extremists. Most other accounts, supported by photographs of lines of corpses awaiting identification, put the number of dead somewhere between 400 and 1,000, all of them civilians. Thousands more fled over the border into Kyrgyzstan.

Where the Rose Revolution eighteen months earlier had illustrated just how precariously the region's rulers were clinging to power, the Andijan killings reminded giddy democracy-promoters with their eyes on Central Asia of the stakes involved and of what could happen if a paranoid dictator decided to use all the means at his disposal to cling to power. Though there's little indication that the revolution-makers were at work in Uzbekistan, the events in Georgia, Ukraine and Serbia were almost certainly high in the paranoid Karimov's mind when he gave the order to shoot. The revolution-makers had seen their Tiananmen Square.

After several long days of silence, the U.S. State Department reluctantly condemned the Andijan killings. On the global chessboard, the U.S. lost a prized if unsavoury ally. Karimov would eventually expel the U.S. military from his country and sign a $1.5 billion deal that gave Gazprom complete control of the export of Uzbek gas. Afterward, Karimov spent the first anniversary of the massacre at the Russian Black Sea resort of Sochi, in the company of Vladimir Putin. "We know what happened in Andijan better than you," Putin coolly told a press conference with foreign journalists in early 2006. "We do not need any revolutions there."[9]

In the aftermath of the bloodshed, talk of an uprising cooled considerably in Kazakhstan, in large part because the opposition itself was suddenly no longer sure that bringing people into the streets to challenge the regime would succeed. The Americans' double standard, which Ikramov complained so bitterly about, once again came sharply into play. During an October 2005 visit to the Kazakh capital of Astana,

Condoleezza Rice—who earlier in the year had named Belarus and five other countries as "outposts of tyranny" where the U.S. would actively seek regime change—said nothing about the need for reform. Instead, her message contained *de rigueur* comments about America's commitment to democracy, with a preamble that suggested she really favoured the status quo as far as Nazarbayev's regime was concerned. "While we do have interests in natural resources and in terms of the struggle against terrorism, we have in no way allowed those interests to get in the way of our open and clear defence of freedom," she told reporters. It was a bald-faced lie. America, fearing that elections could bring Islamists to power and threaten American oil interests, had decided it could live with the regimes of Central Asia. As elections approached in Kazakhstan and Azerbaijan, NED would basically stand down in its support for the opposition.

That opposition, which had hoped Rice would use her visit to pressure the regime for change, was crushed to hear her instead praise the progress being made in Kazakhstan. Tuyakbai, the For a Just Kazakhstan candidate, was clearly staggered by the wide gap between Rice's commitment to democracy in Belarus and the flat statement she delivered in Astana. "Unfortunately, we have to acknowledge the other challenges and interests which the United States has in this region," he said later. "That makes them accept the current state of affairs and partly sacrifice their democratic statements about this region."[10]

The December 2, 2005, election went the same way elections always do in Kazakhstan. Nazarbayev was elected for another seven-year term, with an improbable 91 per cent of the vote. The OSCE complained of ballot-box stuffing, intimidation of the opposition and media bias, but there were no protests. And the president received a congratulatory phone call from Vladimir Putin.

The non-revolt in Kazakhstan provided an interesting counterargument to those who have claimed that the revolutions in Serbia, Georgia and Ukraine came about because the circumstances were right for the opposition to pounce, rather than because of a Western-led effort. The NGOs, so this argument goes, only give tools to the opposition— they don't tell them how to use them. While partly true, Kazakhstan showed how little this well-funded toolbox can do without heavyweight diplomatic support for the opposition and foreign pressure on the regime. In Kazakhstan, many of the revolution-makers' planks were in place: the Soros Foundation backed independent media, there was an Otpor-like group, election monitors revealed fraud, and the opposition united behind a single candidate. But the U.S. administration determined it needed oil and stability in Kazakhstan more than another victory for democracy, so there was no pressure on Nazarbayev to clean up his act or to allow the opposition to express its displeasure on the streets. The protest ban remained in place, and nothing happened.

The travelling revolutionaries had experienced a similar disappointment a month before in Azerbaijan, another post-Soviet state dominated by oil and Islam where the regime had bought favour with the White House by opening its doors to Western energy companies and, of course, to the Baku-Tbilisi-Ceyhan pipeline (interestingly, most of the oil that would eventually go into the pipeline came from Kazakhstan). Kmara and Pora members had been working closely with YOX in the run-up to the November 2005 parliamentary elections, preparing to take to the streets following a vote that they expected would be just as tainted as the 2003 presidential elections. But, as in 2003, the opposition faced a regime that was willing to use force to suppress demonstrations—and that had the backing of the United States. In a message delivered to the Azeri government ahead of the elections, President Bush noted President Ilham Aliev's "commitment to a free and fair election" and concluded, "I look forward to working with you after these elections."[11]

Though observers slammed flaws in the election process, and though tens of thousands of opposition supporters staged a series of peaceful rallies under orange banners in the centre of Baku, the protests had more in common with 1996 and 1997 Serbia's anti-Milošević demonstrations or the 2001 Ukraine Without Kuchma campaign. Both had been impressive displays of people power, but in both cases—Milošević in 1996 was still considered a "force for stability" in the Balkans, while Kuchma still had Yushchenko as his prime minister in 2001—the West hadn't been quite sure it wanted rid of the regime yet.

FOURTEEN

WHERE ROSES DON'T GROW

Minsk

kraine's Orange Revolution wasn't even over yet when Denis Buinitsky began recruiting for what he dearly hoped would be the next uprising. Standing outside the tent on Khreshchatyk Street that had been his home for much of the past five weeks, he waved his arms and tried to draw a crowd. "Who's coming to the revolution in Belarus?" he shouted with the strained voice of someone who had done a lot of yelling lately. Though only two days had passed since the third round of voting that would eventually propel Viktor Yushchenko to the presidency, a line of enthusiastic orange-clad revolutionaries quickly formed. Buinitsky handed a red pen to the first in line and encouraged them to sign their names, e-mail addresses and mobile phone numbers on a list he had fastened to a Styrofoam sheet outside his tent.

"People in Kiev have freedom now; this isn't the case in Minsk," Buinitsky, an organizer from the Zubr youth group that had tried to topple Lukashenko in 2001, told me as he watched dozens of Ukrainians volunteer to help his cause. "Lukashenko has made it impossible to hold such a demonstration there because people know if they go into the streets they will go to prison. But maybe it will be possible some day soon." He and a group of other Belarusian activists had taken part in the Ukrainian revolt from the beginning. They'd waved the white-red-white flag of pre-Lukashenko Belarus at nearly every demonstration in Kiev. "This has given us hope," Buinitsky said simply.

Buinitsky wasn't the only one hoping. I had spotted Vladimir Kobets, Zubr's de facto leader, several times during the Orange Revolution, usually conferring with the Pora leadership or sitting in the Yushchenko campaign headquarters taking mental notes. His close friend Vlad Kaskiv told me that since Zubr had helped Pora, Pora would certainly do its best to help Zubr bring down Lukashenko. Having grown up in the Soviet Union, Kaskiv compared the new democracy-spreading network to the old Comintern—Communist International, the organization Lenin had founded to spread the Bolshevik revolution worldwide. "I would say this millennium has seen the forming of a sort of a Democracy International, a Demintern," he laughed.

Kobets and Kaskiv weren't the only people dreaming about an orange-flavoured uprising in Belarus. The U.S. and Polish governments, marvelling at the success their democracy-promotion programs had wrought in Kiev, quickly decided to try for a repeat in Minsk, around the presidential elections scheduled for 2006. In early 2005, U.S. secretary of state Condoleezza Rice designated Belarus—along with Iran, Cuba, North Korea, Burma and Zimbabwe—an "outpost of tyranny" (an expansion of the "axis of evil" that the Bush administration initially sought to defeat). Shortly afterward, she told reporters in Lithuania that Belarus "is really the last dictatorship in the centre of Europe, and it's time for a change in Belarus."[1]

U.S. Congress passed the Belarus Democracy Act, authorizing $23 million in spending aimed at destabilizing the regime, which Lukashenko memorably responded to by labelling Congress a bunch of "dumb asses." The push to topple Lukashenko through a post-election uprising in early 2006 would be America's biggest and most overt effort at peaceful regime change in Eastern Europe since the ouster of Slobodan Milošević in 2000. "They're throwing way, way more money at this than they ever did at Ukraine," said one staff member at a major American NGO who asked that his name not be used because he was not authorized to talk about it.

"But it's not going to work," he added, because Lukashenko's regime was much more willing to crack skulls than Kuchma's or Shevardnadze's had been. And, unlike Milošević, whose "pillars of support"—notably the security services—had stopped believing in him after a decade of near-constant warfare, Belarusians supported their president after a decade of *stabilnost*. Many saw that as preferable to free-market democracy, which had failed them spectacularly once before.

Any attempt at revolution in Belarus would suffer from another key difference: the Bush administration would take the controls, not the revolution-makers. While the Clinton administration, and in particular Madeleine Albright, had become deeply involved in the anti-Milošević efforts, the Georgian and Ukrainian revolutions had been largely prepared by the local offices of the NGOs, who took money from the U.S. and other Western governments and spent it as they saw fit. Then they called in diplomatic support from Washington when the time was right. George W. Bush didn't send Mikhail Saakashvili to Belgrade or Alexander Maric to Tbilisi or David Dettman to Georgia. The NGOs did that on their own, believing that taking on corrupt and repressive regimes was within their mandate and their funding. Few in the field believe the White House knew or understood what the NGOs were up to until they'd already done much of the groundwork for the Rose and Orange revolutions.

But with Belarus, Bush and Rice would lead from the front, hoping to show the world that their commitment to "spreading freedom" wasn't applicable only to oil-rich parts of the globe. Many who played an active role in Ukraine also believe Bush was looking to further attach his administration's name to the telegenic success of the Orange Revolution.

Ahead of an increasingly rare one-on-one meeting with Putin in Bratislava in February 2005, Bush brashly attached his administration to what Mikhail Saakashvili had dubbed Europe's "third wave of liberation" (after the fall of the Berlin Wall and the collapse of the USSR), handing out twenty-one "Champion of Freedom" medals to Eastern Europeans, including Pavol Demeš of OK'98, Ivan Marovic of Otpor, Vlad Kaskiv of Pora, Vlad Kobets of Zubr, Ukraine's Nataliya Dmytruk (the subversive sign-language translator) and two key Georgian revolutionaries, the Liberty Institute's Giga Bokeria and Tinatin Khidasheli of the Georgian Young Lawyers' Association.

But this strategy also carried risks. Many argue that openly attaching the Bush administration's name to the Orange Revolution instantly made life more difficult in places where similar efforts had yet to pay off. Lukashenko's regime seized upon Bush's and Rice's proclamations that they were allied to the democrats in Belarus, claiming them as proof to the Belarusian public that groups like Zubr and politicians like Anatoly Lebedko, the eloquent leader of the opposition United Civil Party, were little more than U.S. agents. Shortly after Kobets received his award from Bush, a documentary on Belarusian television ridiculed him as a marionette in the hands of the White House. He became such a controversial figure that he handed the leadership of Zubr to younger activists and spent much of his time in quasi-exile in Kiev.

Even if the White House seemed to poorly grasp the differences between Kuchma and Lukashenko, Zubr understood well what it was up against. I visited Minsk in October 2004 to cover a referendum to amend the constitution, which currently limited the head of state to two consecutive terms. The amendment would allow Lukashenko to stand for a third term in office. Though many of the revolution-makers' pieces were already in place—a leftover from the 2001 effort to depose Lukashenko, with a fresh injection in 2004 of $1.1 million from NED—the activists held little hope as referendum day, October 17, approached. Nikita Sasim, a young Zubr member I had planned to meet with, was arrested before I got the chance and sentenced to fifteen days in jail for the crime of swearing in public. Kobets, when I saw him, still spoke optimistically but had a haunted look about him as he tried to organize demonstrations. "Every person that goes into the streets knows they will be arrested. There's not a 60 per cent chance or a 70 per cent chance; it's a 100 per cent certainty," he told me. "That's why most people won't protest. People are scared for their jobs and for their families."

Voters openly admitted to being scared. "This is 100 per cent a dictatorship. He's created a situation where there's no alternative to him," said Vladimir Kuzuro, a forty-two-year-old information technology worker who said he voted against the constitutional changes, even though he believed there was little chance of stopping them. "It's difficult to take part in demonstrations when they beat you on the head with batons," he said.

Others were too frightened to give their names to a reporter. "You could be KGB," said one woman, a grade-school teacher sitting in a cafeteria sharing coffee and sandwiches with her colleagues. "It's easy to fake press accreditation and nice English." She hinted that she, too, had voted against the amendments. "You can't say there is stability—you see how we live," she told me, nodding out the window at the blocks of shabby apartment buildings that surrounded the school.

When the official results came in, Lukashenko's amendments had passed with 79 per cent support. "It's a convincing victory. I consider it an elegant victory," exclaimed the sycophantic chair of the country's Central Election Commission, Lidiya Ermoshina. The West disagreed. The Organization for Security and Co-operation in Europe declared that the vote "fell significantly short of [international] standards," while an exit poll conducted by the Vilnius office of Gallup/Baltic Surveys tried to demonstrate that Lukashenko had in fact lost.

It was the oddest of exit polls. While the headline number was that Lukashenko's proposal had received only a 48.7 per cent "yes" vote, the methodology showed it could in fact have been far higher. According to Gallup's own data, 53.1 per cent of the 18,000 people they polled said they had voted yes, versus 28.55 per cent who voted no. To get the support level below 50 per cent, Gallup took the 53.1 per cent and put it against their estimated turnout of 87 per cent (the Central Election Commission said 90 per cent had voted) to come up with a figure that fewer than half of eligible voters had backed Lukashenko. Startlingly, Gallup had concluded that the 17 per cent of those they polled who refused to answer their questions had voted "no" but were afraid to say so. While this could well be true given the atmosphere of fear Lukashenko had created in Belarus, it was hardly a standard way of analyzing polling data. In its eagerness to bring regime change to Minsk, the Bush administration had deserted the high-minded ideals adhered to by the NGOs that had taken part in Serbia, Georgia and Ukraine. The exit polls weren't being conducted simply to catch the regime in a fraud; they were conducted to provide justification—real or concocted—for what was to come next.[2]

While nearly all the Western ambassadors in Minsk, including the American, Polish and British representatives, turned out for a press conference at the opposition's headquarters to hear Gallup read out the results of the poll they had funded, the numbers had little effect on the Belarusian public, given the regime's total control of the broadcast media. A crowd of just one thousand people—most of them Zubr members—gathered in the shadow of the Presidential Administration building on the capital's central October Square that night to chant "Lies!" and "Lukashenko lost!"

The feeble protest lasted only a few hours before riot police moved in, using batons to disperse the crowd and arresting several dozen. They chased opposition leader Anatoly Lebedko into a nearby pizza restaurant and beat him so badly he was hospitalized. In a hospital-room interview with the Russian news agency Interfax, Lebedko concluded that Belarusians couldn't topple Lukashenko on their own and that the international community would have to do even more than it had been doing if it wanted to see change. "We need a much bigger involvement from the outside to introduce democracy here," he said.[3]

BINGBINGBINGBINGBING!

I was deep in thought, typing an article about a gathering of Belarus's beleaguered political opposition that I had attended that night in central Minsk, when I was jolted by the sound of someone repeatedly hammering on the doorbell of my apartment. This wasn't the single polite ring used by Federal Express or a neighbour needing to borrow sugar.

In fact, I had no neighbours that I knew of. My translator, Ilya, had handed me the keys to the apartment the previous day and told me there was no one living in the facing unit, leaving me alone on the sixth floor of the drab apartment block that overlooked a phallic World War II monument in the middle of the capital. The flat itself belonged to a friend of Ilya's who, like many talented young Belarusians, had gone to Moscow in search of work, having exhausted his limited employment options at home. While one of President Alexander Lukashenko's most often repeated claims is that he has brought the country economic stability after the post-Soviet collapse of the 1990s (officially, the unemployment rate is just 1.9 per cent), the 80 per cent state-run economy hardly encourages the young and the entrepreneurial. According to the World Bank, per capita income in 2004 was just $1,590.

Ilya's friend had left a long time ago. No one had lived in this apartment for six months.

I crept to the door, flipped up the piece of metal covering the peephole and peered into the corridor. I could feel my heart start to beat faster as I surveyed the empty hallway. I hadn't heard anyone run down the nearby staircase—whoever had rung seconds before was either calmly walking away or carefully staying out of sight. I called my wife, Carolynne, who could sense something was wrong from as far away as Moscow. We both remembered the warning signs I had noticed but ignored before this trip to Belarus. When I'd sent in my application for a visa to cover the October 2004 referendum, Ilya had told me it was a hopeless cause. "They hate you," he said. He and I were both sure there would be no visa.

Six months earlier, I had visited the country and written a four-part series about Lukashenko's Belarus. The articles were, inevitably, negative, since finding positive things to say about political life in the oppressive, backward dictatorship was nearly impossible. The series had highlighted the repressive human rights situation, featured interviews with dissidents who weren't supposed to be talking to the press and called the country a "living Cold War museum." After the pieces appeared, Andrei Savinykh, the normally articulate spokesman for the Belarusian Foreign Ministry whom I had interviewed to get the government's side of the story, went around Minsk telling the few journalists who were based there that my articles were full of lies.

Ilya and I were thus shocked when the visa for a return trip in October was approved. But Ilya still had a queasy feeling about the trip, one that was reinforced when he went to pick up my accreditation card on the day I was supposed to land in Minsk: the woman at the Foreign Ministry who handed the card over recognized my name and ominously told Ilya, with a smile, that they had been "waiting" for my return.

THWOCK! THWOCK! THWOCK! THWOCK!

Now the bell wasn't being used anymore. These were four door-slamming knocks, so forceful that they shook the thick wooden door and made me wonder later if a fist or a foot had been used. Working hard to keep my voice from betraying my escalating fear, I yelled out "Who's there?" in Russian, then English, then Russian again. No answer. I peered again into the hallway. Same as before: nobody.

I called Ilya at home. He told me that I was right to be scared. The apartment had been empty for too long for someone to just be dropping by looking for the previous tenant. His advice was the same as

Carolynne's: Stay inside; don't open the door. "This is what they do," he said. By they, he meant the real authority in this country frozen by fear—the KGB.

The knocks ceased, but the pounding in my chest didn't. I lay awake in bed for hours, trying to convince myself that I was crazy, with my tiny Swiss Army knife—useful only if I were attacked by slow-moving rabbits—on the bedside table.

The next day I heard that Pavel Sheremet, a prominent Russian journalist with state-controlled Channel One television who had once before been jailed in Belarus for criticizing President Lukashenko, had been drawn into a fight, badly beaten and then charged with hooliganism that same night. He said later that he had been ambushed outside his apartment.

"Liberating" Belarus had become almost a matter of honour for the Bush administration. Between 2004 and 2006, it directed more than $25 million of American taxpayers' money toward toppling Lukashenko.[4]

"Each time [Lukashenko's] government has held an election, it seems those who have been pushing for democratic reform take a step forward," NED's Rodger Potocki, who was heading the Belarus effort, told me optimistically when I met him in Washington on the eve of the 2006 vote. But, he added, "it's certainly true that Lukashenko is afraid of coloured revolutions and he's cut off [the NGOs] so that they won't happen in Belarus. But he has been on the offensive against civil society there since he took power."

That Lukashenko, despite knowing beforehand that the West would use the election process to try to pry him out of power, went ahead with the vote anyway, as he had with the constitutional referendum, signalled both how confident he was in his ability to withstand the revolution-makers and the power of the very idea of democracy. In post–Cold War Europe, even an outright dictator like Lukashenko believed he needed at least the mirage of popular approval.

Nonetheless, Lukashenko's scorched-earth policy toward NGOs had left the democracy-promoters at a severe disadvantage, as it forced them to do their work from offices in Kiev, Vilnius, Bratislava and Warsaw. Many key players in the NGO sector could no longer get visas to travel to Belarus. Trygve Olson, director of IRI's Belarus program, had been banned from travelling to the country since his involvement in the 2001 effort. Otpor's travelling trainers, including Miloš Milenković, who had made twenty previous trips to the country to work with Zubr, were on the *personae non gratae* list, though Siniša Šikman told me he was able to slip into the country.

That distance likely can be blamed for some severe mistakes that crippled the anti-Lukashenko effort, including a strange willingness to trust an assertion by Lukashenko that the presidential vote would be held in the summer of 2006. Organizers consequently spent money on programs—such as a new youth group called Khopits (the Belarussian word for "Enough") that was funded by IRI's Vilnius office—that were caught ill prepared when Lukashenko switched the date to March 19. Khopits received substantive backing from NED, as well as from Britain's Westminster Foundation and the German foreign ministry, but had no effect in the election or its aftermath. "Khopits were a bunch of nice guys, but they didn't really have much of a campaign. They were planning for an election in July," said Zubr's Vlad Kobets, whose more experienced group didn't make the same mistake.

After 2001, Lukashenko had taken other measures to curb opposition to his rule. Before the 2004 referendum, he decreed that rallies could be held only at a single remote location on the outskirts of Minsk. Those who took part in unsanctioned demonstrations not only risked their jobs but faced fifteen-day "administrative detention" and fines of up to $2,500—a prohibitive amount not far off the average annual wage. Almost one hundred NGOs were forced to close or leave the country.[5] The KGB arrested Mikhail Marynich, a leading opposition politician and former cabinet minister who many believed might pose a formidable challenge in the 2006 presidential election, for allegedly stealing computers from his own NGO; he was jailed until after the elections. Lukashenko also strengthened his already formidable popularity by pushing through a massive pay hike for civil servants, a category that included a sizable chunk of the population.

The wily dictator had tripped up his opponents, again. But despite all the disadvantages—as well as a widespread belief that Lukashenko's regime was impermeable—their campaign (the third, after 2001 and 2004) began in earnest in the fall of 2005 when Nikita

Sasim, the oft-jailed twenty-one-year-old Zubr activist, gave the opposition a new symbol to rally around.

Tall and good-looking, with light brown hair, Sasim was taking part in a small demonstration on September 16 in central Minsk that featured youths bearing pictures of missing opposition leader Viktor Gonchar and of businessman Anatoly Krasovsky, who had disappeared on that date six years earlier. As security officers moved toward the protest, Sasim was struck by inspiration, took off the denim shirt he was wearing and tied it to a wooden pole, turning it into a flag. To the officers already keeping a close eye on him, he may as well have been waving red in front of a bull. They charged the demonstration and beat him so badly he was hospitalized.

Western-funded polls had been showing that many Belarusians had grown tired of the commotion caused by the opposition and believed the regime's allegations that Lebedko and Zubr were foreign-sponsored saboteurs. Sasim's run-in with the police allowed the opposition to reinvent itself and try once more to win the sympathy of an apathetic people. With help from the German Marshall Fund of the United States, notably Pavol Demeš, now the head of its Bratislava office, they devised the Jeans Solidarity campaign, which brought groups as disparate as Zubr and the Charter 97 human rights network together under the same umbrella. It was a clever idea—Belarusians as far back as the Soviet era associated jeans with the West and with freedoms they didn't enjoy.

The money came flooding in. The European Union awarded a two-year, $2.4 million contract to a German organization, Media Consulta, to give Belarusians alternative news sources to the state-run broadcasters. NED handed out $2.2 million in election-related grants. Terry Nelson, the national political director of George W. Bush's 2004 re-election campaign, was dispatched by the administration to oversee matters from Lithuania.

As Sasim left the hospital and went directly into hiding, the opposition asked supporters to light a candle in their window on the sixteenth of each month, supporting solidarity, and the revolution-makers went to work. First came the unified candidate, a little-known fifty-eight-year-old physics professor without much political background named Alexander Milinkevich, chosen precisely because of his lack of notoriety. State propaganda had been so successful in performing character assassinations on Lebedko, Stanislau Shushkevich and other potential candidates that in the eyes of most Belarusians, who watched only state-controlled television, they'd become "fascists" and Western agents.

"Lebedko is a strong leader, a hero, but in this situation everybody in the opposition understood we needed a single candidate," Kobets explained. "All the political parties' leaders were well-known people who had been called fascists in television programs. Milinkevich was a new person, a guy nobody knew anything about." Lebedko fell into line and became the opposition's campaign manager.

At regular meetings in the IRI offices in Vilnius, the opposition plotted a strategy to get them on the map against Lukashenko. The data was disappointing. When Milinkevich assumed leadership of the opposition in the fall of 2005, only one-quarter of Belarusians said they knew anything about him. Six months later, as election day approached, he had tripled his recognizability, but his support level had barely broken out of the single digits. A poll in January by Gallup/Baltic Surveys found that only 17 per cent of Belarusians planned to vote for Milinkevich, while nearly 55 per cent supported Lukashenko. Lukashenko's stranglehold on the flow of information remained largely unbroken. An old woman I met at a restaurant outside of Minsk told me that she would vote for the president because life in Belarus was better than in Germany and Poland. When I asked her why she believed that, she told me she had seen it on television.[6]

With Russian help, Lukashenko was making life very difficult for the would-be revolutionaries. With tensions high in the wake of the Orange Revolution, Gazprom needed to ensure that even if Ukraine decided to play its trump card—blocking the flow of Russian gas through its pipelines to Europe—the route via Belarus would remain open. More than ever, the Kremlin needed Lukashenko as much as he needed the Kremlin.

The decision to move up the election date appears to have been devised at a Putin–Lukashenko meeting in Sochi in the fall of 2005, and there's evidence that the Russian analysts who had watched the revolutionaries up close in Ukraine were now advising the Belarusian strongman. A second "democratic" candidate, Alexander Kozulin, stepped forward, denouncing Lukashenko and splitting the opposition vote. Though he stood on October Square beside Milinkevich after the vote and would be eventually be beaten and jailed by the authorities, many in the opposition wondered if he wasn't a Kremlin pawn.

When a group of Belarusians met at a Minsk movie theatre in October 2005 to form a new election-monitoring organization called Partnership (Western-funded and linked to the Committee of Ukrainian Voters and its equivalents in Georgia and Ukraine), police found out ahead of time and simply arrested all seventy participants. As Milinkevich began to speak more and more openly about calling people into the streets after March 19, Lukashenko warned an already cowed population that it would be unwise to take part. "Any attempt to destabilize the situation will be met with drastic action. We will wring the necks of those who are actually doing it and those who are instigating these acts," he said on live television in January 2006. "Embassies of certain states should be aware of this. They should know that we know what they are up to. They will be thrown out of here within twenty-four hours."

On election day, the authorities declared a predictable 83 per cent victory for Lukashenko, versus a farcical 6 per cent for Milinkevich. That night, a crowd of more than ten thousand people massed on October Square, many of them with strips of denim tied around their arms and waving blue flags alongside those of pre-Lukashenko Belarus and the European Union. Some pitched tents in a conscious imitation of Kiev. It was—given the likelihood that almost everyone there would face some kind of punishment at their workplace or school—a stunning, though certainly only partial, show of force by the opposition.

"I think everybody was surprised [by the size of the crowd]," Kobets smiled when I saw him later. "Before election day, on Belarusian TV, the head of the KGB had said that people on the square would be treated as terrorists, meaning they could be killed. I think that provoked people. People who were not going to go, but couldn't believe they were hearing this speech in the twenty-first century, decided to go to the square."

But one successful demonstration wasn't enough. After letting it continue for almost a week—during which the number of demonstrators shrank, rather than grew—police moved in during the early hours

of Thursday, March 23, 2006, arresting more than two hundred protestors who had spent the cold night in their tents, including Milinkevich,
Kozulin and Zubr leader Nikita Sasim.

The slaughter in Andijan had been followed by somewhat less violence in Minsk, but both uprisings had failed. The autocrats had found
an antidote to the "wave of liberation" in the form of heavy-handed
repression.

————

FIFTEEN

THE KREMLIN STRIKES BACK

Moscow and Kiev

Sergei Markov was in a hurry. We met at his office in Moscow's Polyanka neighbourhood but he didn't have time to talk there. The Kremlin tactician had to catch a plane to Kiev.

Barely a year before, Markov, with Gleb Pavlovsky and the other Kremlin spin doctors who were supposed to deliver the presidency to Viktor Yanukovych, had all but been chased out of Ukraine as the streets turned an angry orange. Yanukovych blamed his loss on bad advice from the Russians, while the opposition held up Markov's and Pavlovsky's very presence in Ukraine during the elections as proof that Kuchma and Yanukovych took their orders from Moscow and not from Ukrainian voters.

It was an embarrassing defeat. And had Viktor Yushchenko and Yulia Tymoshenko proved able to rapidly deliver on some of the promises they'd made during the uprising, Markov and Pavlovsky might have been forced to stay out of Ukrainian politics forever. But by the fall of 2005, the "orange" coalition had already dissolved like the bad marriage it always was. After Yushchenko fired Tymoshenko from the prime minister's job, the mood of Ukrainian voters turned sour. Improbably, the opinion polls showed that Yanukovych's popularity was actually recovering. On the afternoon I went to see Markov, he was heading back to Kiev to see, once more, if he couldn't "manage" Ukraine's stumbling democracy.

Because of the hurry, I offered to ride with him to the airport so we could talk in his car. As we whizzed through Moscow's streets, he gave me a small demonstration of the power he held in Russia, directing our driver into a lane reserved for traffic heading in the other direction, then through a barrier at a railway crossing. When a bewildered policeman finally signalled for us to pull over, Markov simply waved his identification card at him. "Presidential Administration" was the only explanation he offered for the myriad and dangerous traffic violations. The policeman nodded and waved us on. In Putin's Russia, the rules don't apply to those who write them.

Markov was ebullient about the fallout between Yushchenko and Tymoshenko. "It's exactly what we expected. The program of the Orange Revolution was unrealistic—they prepared for a revolution but had no strategy for running the country after they won," he said, directing the driver to turn left despite a red light. "The majority of the nation of Ukraine wants to have geopolitical orientation toward Russia because Ukraine, ethnically, it's connected to Russia," he continued, sounding relieved that after a year of being ridiculed for such statements, he could make them again. "Yushchenko is not the leader of the nation, he was imposed . . . He was a puppet the whole time and still is—a puppet of the United States."

The Orange Revolution was over, Markov said, and he and his colleagues were back in business in the near abroad. Moscow had long since lost Serbia, but the fight was far from over in Ukraine and Georgia. And Kyrgyzstan's confused new leaders had already tumbled back into the Kremlin's orbit on their own.

Things were indeed going poorly for Yushchenko. The coalition that NDI had so carefully crafted between him, Tymoshenko and Socialist leader Oleksandr Moroz had dissolved into mutual recriminations. Yushchenko's people blamed Tymoshenko and her populist economic policies for the country's recent slide—GDP growth had slid to 2 per cent from the lofty 11 per cent achieved the previous year under Kuchma and Yanukovych. Meanwhile, Tymoshenko and Petro Poroshenko, the owner of 5th Channel and a key financial backer of the revolution, who had been rewarded for his support by being named head of the National Security Council, had fought an ugly struggle for influence that ended with each publicly accusing the other of corruption. Yushchenko ended up firing them both. "It had to end," said Dan Bilak, the Ukrainian-Canadian lawyer advising the new government. "The tension just kept building up internally. The president didn't want to just stand around resolving disputes between kids in a sandbox." Yushchenko and Tymoshenko "were diametrically opposed on every issue, and the only thing that unified them was opposition to Kuchma."

It was a repulsive display of exactly the kind of politics Ukrainians had hoped to end when they had taken to the streets twelve months earlier. On Independence Square, supporters of the politically rejuvenated Yanukovych now erected a large transparent garbage can for disgusted voters to throw away their orange paraphernalia. I saw the metre-high bin one afternoon, half full with discarded scarves and flags.

With fresh parliamentary elections scheduled for early 2006 and Yanukovych's Party of Regions, the long-time political face of the Donetsk clan, suddenly ahead again in the polls, Moscow stepped up the pressure. In the fall of 2005, a year after the revolution, Gazprom demanded that Ukraine begin paying market rates for Russian natural gas—more than a fourfold increase in pricing, which would cripple the country's already struggling economy. If Ukraine didn't pay the new price of $230 per 1,000 cubic metres, instead of the $50 Gazprom had charged Kuchma's government, the gas giant would turn off the taps on January 1.

Since the collapse of the USSR, Russia had provided subsidized gas to most of the former Soviet Union, including Ukraine. Now it was clear that the arrangement had been conditional on those countries' deference to Moscow. Ukraine, Georgia, Moldova and the three Baltic states would all face sharp price increases in 2005 and 2006, while Gazprom would continue to provide cheap gas, at $47 per 1,000 cubic metres, to Belarus and the pliant regime of Alexander Lukashenko.

Though Yushchenko had his own card to play (most of the gas Gazprom supplied to Europe went through Ukraine), he blanched when gas deliveries stopped for twenty-four hours at midnight New Year's Day. He signed a deal under which Ukraine agreed to pay a relatively modest $95 per 1,000 cubic metres but gave Gazprom the option of reopening the price discussion six months later. In the meantime, Gazprom would provide the gas to Ukraine through a mysterious middle company called RosUkrEnergo, which had previously been under criminal investigation. Tymoshenko, back in opposition, noisily slammed the deal as capitulation to the Russians and to organized crime. Many Ukrainians started to recall the era of Kuchma and Yanukovych—and their good relations with Russia—more fondly.

Russia took a beating in the international press for threatening Europe's energy supply, but it achieved its political end. In the March parliamentary elections, Yanukovych capped a stunning political comeback when his Party of Regions finished first with 31 per cent of the vote. Tymoshenko's bloc came second, bolstered by her opposition to the gas deal, while Yushchenko's Our Ukraine stumbled to third, leaving him in the unenviable position of having to rehire his old foe Yanukovych as his prime minister. Though Yushchenko was able to retain control of some key ministries under his deal with Yanukovych, having to invite the man he had publicly branded a crook to form the government was a staggering blow that led many to label the Orange Revolution as over barely eighteen months after it had begun.

Yanukovych quickly put the idea of Ukraine's joining NATO on ice, saying such a drastic move could happen only after a national referendum on the topic, which he made clear would not happen in the near future. When Yushchenko's allies objected, Parliament passed a motion backing Yanukovych.

Russia wielded similar economic weapons against Saakashvili in Georgia and against Moldova's Vladimir Voronin, who, after the Orange Revolution next door, had abandoned his pro-Russian bent and thrown in his lot with the West. On January 27, a mysterious explosion in the North Caucasus cut the gas supply to Georgia, which was in the midst of its coldest winter in years. Though Russia blamed Chechen separatists for attacking the pipeline, Saakashvili charged in an interview with BBC World that the Kremlin was waging economic warfare against his government.

While that sounded sensational, the Kremlin bolstered Saakashvili's argument in April by banning Georgia's wines and brandy, as well as its famous Borjomi mineral water, claiming to have detected unacceptably high levels of pesticides. Moscow banned Moldovan wines for similar reasons, along with Ukrainian milk. Meats from Poland, a country that

Russia blamed for encouraging unrest in Ukraine, Moldova and Belarus, were blacklisted, too.[1]

Each ban seemed designed to hit the country where it would hurt most. Borjomi, perhaps the Georgian company with the best international reputation of all, suddenly faced health questions about its product. Wine is Georgia's biggest export, bringing in about $90 million a year to the teetering economy, and before the ban, 80 per cent of it went to Russia. The same went for Moldova, where wine, three-quarters of which was exported to Russia, had accounted for 30 per cent of the country's GDP. Half of Ukraine's dairy exports went to Russia, while meats accounted for 10 per cent of Russian imports from Poland. Tellingly, the European Union had no problem continuing to import the products that Russia's Health Ministry was rejecting.[2]

In October 2006, relations between Russia and Georgia abruptly worsened when four Russian army officers were arrested along with some two dozen Georgians in connection with an alleged coup plot against Saakashvili's regime. Though proof of a Moscow-backed coup attempt was never offered, few Caucasus observers had any trouble believing it might be true, given the festering acrimony between the Kremlin and Saakashvili.

The arrests of the four officers led to Russia's tightening the screws even further on Tbilisi. Transport and post links were cut, and Russia moved to hit Georgia where it hurt most by targeting the remittances that Georgians working in Russia sent home to their families. Russian embassies were ordered to stop issuing visas to Georgians.

In scenes that recalled for some the early days of Stalin's purges, lists were made of Georgians living in Russia and schools were ordered to submit lists of children with Georgian names. In early October, 132 Georgians living in Russia were put on a plane and forcibly deported as their relatives watched helplessly.

"They're crushing people, they're destroying families. They used to persecute Jews like this. Now it's the Georgians' turn," Inna Bashkirova told the Asssociated Press. She said her brother Shota Georgadze, who was married to a Russian citizen, had been deported on the suspicion of having faked his residence permit, an accusation she said was false. "If Saakashvili did something wrong, why do common people suffer?" she asked.[3]

For Andrei Illarionov, these latest and most obvious examples of what he called the Kremlin's aggressive "neo-imperialism" were the final straw. After four years of working in the Kremlin as Putin's senior economic adviser—a time during which he failed miserably to arrest the country's slide into authoritarianism—he resigned on December 28, 2005, three days before Gazprom switched off Ukraine's gas supply.

Russia, he charged, had become a "corporate state," one that trampled freedoms and bent the economic rules of the game to suit and enrich a powerful few. Russia was a business, he explained, and Putin and the *siloviki* were its only shareholders. Seen as the last pro-Western reformer in Putin's inner circle, Illarionov had ruffled feathers by protesting the Yukos affair—specifically the rigged auction of Yuganskneftegaz—as the "scam of the year." He went on to complain to reporters about the creeping return of an "atmosphere of fear" in the country.

Nonetheless, he had always been seen as personally loyal to Putin, who frequently used him to reassure foreign journalists that the leader was still a reformist at heart. The first time I met the short-haired, round-faced economist was in 2003 at a stylishly furnished Moscow apartment owned by the state-run RIA Novosti news agency, where he spent several hours giving the foreign press corps a spirited off-the-record defence of the Kremlin's economic policies. The next time I saw him, three years later in Washington, D.C., he had become one of Putinism's most damaging and effective critics. In a March 2006 speech to a crowd of foreign and American diplomats at the Cato Institute, a right-wing think tank, he warned that Russia could no longer be considered a "free" country. He recommended that it be expelled from the G8, of which it had just assumed the leadership.

"The reason why I went [to work for the Kremlin] was really very pragmatic—it was a possibility to do something for the country. Having declined twice, on the third offer I decided to give it a try. And I tried," he told me in D.C., sounding genuinely saddened. "The country ceased to be free. It's one thing to work in a country that's maybe not completely free, that's partially free but trying to do its best to be freer. But what we have seen is very persistent efforts to move the country from partially free to not free . . . and it's going to be even less free and they are going to destroy what remnants there are of economic freedom."

It was exactly what the anti-Kremlin hawks at NED had been saying for years, even while the Bush administration clung to its belief that Putin—a man whose "soul" Bush had seen and liked—was at his core the pro-Western reformer that Illarionov had once also believed him to be. But Illarionov's defection and his connections to the right-wing establishment in Washington seemed to win over the remaining doubters in the White House. A bipartisan report on U.S.–Russian relations, headed by former Democratic vice-presidential candidate John Edwards and senior Republican Jack Kemp, found that it "no longer seems realistic" for the U.S. to consider Russia as a strategic partner. They pointed out not only Putin's authoritarian streak but also a foreign policy that was increasingly in direct conflict with Washington's, such as in its support for Iran's nuclear program and for the newly elected Hamas government in the Palestinian Territories. Increasingly, the Kremlin's friends were America's enemies. The report called for increased support to pro-democracy groups in Russia and for swift NATO admission for Ukraine and Georgia.[4]

In May 2006, at a conference in Lithuania that brought together a collection of countries threatened by Russia's new expansionism—the Baltic states, Poland, Ukraine, Georgia and Moldova—Vice President Dick Cheney abandoned all pretence that Russia and the U.S. were allies. He lambasted the Kremlin for using "intimidation and blackmail" against its neighbours and said Russia had "a choice to make" about whether it was going to travel the path to democracy or to authoritarianism. "Actions by the Russian government have been counterproductive and could begin to affect relations with other countries," he warned, clearly meaning with the United States. In his remarks, Cheney repeatedly referenced Illarionov's criticisms, and the *Washington Post* reported that the vice president met in Vilnius with an unnamed leading member of the Russian opposition. The Russian daily *Nezavisimaya Gazeta* reported that it was independent MP Vladimir Ryzhkov.

If there was any doubt in Moscow about whether the U.S. was planning to put its shoulder behind the opposition in the 2007 Duma elections and the 2008 presidential vote, Cheney's speech ended it. The Russian press compared Cheney's attack to the speech Winston

Churchill had given six decades before in Fulton, Missouri, where he spoke for the first time of an "Iron Curtain" dividing Europe. The covert war between Moscow and Washington that had raged for Putin's entire presidency was now in full public view.

"Enemy at the Gates: Dick Cheney Made a Fulton Speech in Vilnius," read the main headline the next day in *Kommersant,* Russia's pro-Western business daily. The article went even further: "U.S. vice president Dick Cheney made a keynote speech on relations between the West and Russia in which he practically established the start of the second Cold War . . . The Cold War has restarted, only now the front lines have shifted."[5] To hammer home the point, the best-selling *Komsomolskaya Pravda* tabloid ran a large map, colouring in the states that convened in Vilnius to show a purple line severing Russia from the rest of Europe. "Yesterday in the Lithuanian capital of Vilnius, like in Yalta in 1945, the map of Europe was redrawn," the article read. "What can Russia do? It would appear it will have to strengthen ties with Belarus and Central Asia. And get close to China, to balance this Western might."[6]

Putin's reaction was more sanguine, as though the end of the overt friendship between Russia and America was something he had anticipated for some time. In his state-of-the-nation address a week later, he made it clear that he would ignore Cheney's advice and would carry on trying to manage democracy. He repeated that he would not run for a third term but suggested he would have a strong hand in choosing his successor. "I think I would be right to express my point of view on one candidacy or another," he said in the televised speech.

He pointedly attacked Cheney for slamming Russia as anti-democratic and then flying directly on to Kazakhstan to talk oil deals with the even less democratic Nursultan Nazarbayev. "Where is all that pathos of the need to fight for human rights and democracy when it concerns the needs to realize their own interests? Then it seems everything is possible. There are no limits at all," he said. And while claiming there would be no return to the Cold War, he noted it was "premature to speak of the end of the arms race"—Russia needed to increase military spending to catch up with that of the U.S., which had a defence budget twenty-five times larger than the Kremlin's. "Their house is their fortress—well done! But it means that we must build our house strongly, reliably, because we see what is going on in the world," he said. "We must always be ready to counter any attempts to pressure Russia in order to strengthen positions at our expense . . . The stronger our military is, the less temptation there will be to exert such pressure on us."[7]

Putin and Cheney had finally brought the behind-the-scenes battle that had been waged since Putin came to office in 2000 out into the open. The U.S. would continue to push for Lukashenko's ouster and would provide more support to anti-Putin forces inside Russia. Meanwhile, the Kremlin would increasingly treat the pro-Western governments that met in Vilnius as hostile and would seek to undermine them using its energy weapon and other economic levers.

Sitting in his flat in Moscow on December 8, 2004, Andrei Sidelnikov had watched television jealously as fireworks exploded over the sea of orange on Kiev's Independence Square. The next day, Sidelnikov called two of his friends and told them to meet him at Zen Café, a trendy sunken coffee spot on Moscow's Kamergersky Pereulok favoured by the city's disillusioned liberal chattering classes. But, that morning, Sidelnikov wanted to do more than just complain about how awry things were going in Putin's Russia. The twenty-something political junkie admired Pora, and had marvelled at how the enthusiasm and dedication of a bunch of youths of his own age and similar background had changed their country. He convinced his two friends, Ivan Potapov and Viktor Morozov, that they could do the same in Russia. That afternoon in the Zen Café, Russian Pora was founded. Its mission would be to bring the Orange Revolution to Russia.

Sidelnikov and his friends represented the kind of Russia that Soros and NED had thought they were helping to build when they had started pouring money into Russia fifteen years earlier. Clad entirely in denim, they sipped espressos and talked about the need for more democracy and freer markets. They were young, hip and extremely Westernized. Sidelnikov had previously worked as a spokesman for Boris Berezovsky, the oligarch and Yeltsin confidant exiled by Putin. Though the young men hadn't yet made any contact with the funders of the revolution-makers (and with Berezovsky's backing, they didn't necessarily need any outside financial help), from the beginning they consciously modelled their efforts on Otpor, Kmara and, of course, Pora, with which they made immediate contact.[8]

"I call it the task of the moment: to change the regime that is now far from democratic principles and that violates human rights and freedoms, the regime under which the mass media has been turned not free and the legal system turned not independent," Sidelnikov told me as we sat in the same café nine months later. "We watched what was happening in Ukraine and just decided that it's time in Russia as well."[9]

In the nervous atmosphere that fell over Moscow following the Orange Revolution and the copycat uprising in Kyrgyzstan, the new group made some easy headlines simply by announcing that it existed and by staging its initial demonstration on Pushkin Square, the same place where tiny anti–Chechen war rallies took place each week. Breaking from the non-partisan tradition of Otpor, they quickly endorsed the not-yet-announced candidacy of former prime minister Mikhail Kasyanov, who had been fired before the 2004 presidential elections after voicing his opposition to the Yukos affair.

The emergence of Russian Pora highlighted the excitement of the country's opposition following Pavlovsky's failure to "manage" democracy during the Ukrainian elections. I went to see Boris Nemtsov, the one-time Yeltsin protégé who, after initially backing Putin in the 2000 presidential race, had re-established himself as one of the opposition's most charismatic leaders. During the Orange Revolution, when I spotted him wearing an orange scarf in the crowd, the Russian media were pillorying him for giving speeches in Kiev about how its uprising was giving hope to democrats in Russia, and later for working as an adviser to Yushchenko. He also allied himself to pro-Western forces in Belarus, quite openly in 2004. When I entered Nemtsov's Moscow offices in early 2005, Anatoly Lebedko, who had recently been released from jail in Minsk, was just leaving after a private one-on-one meeting.

The 2007 and 2008 elections, Nemtsov told me, would be as critical to Russia as the 2004 presidential vote had been to Ukraine. By 2006, all expectations were that Putin would either try to go the Lukashenko route, amending the constitution so he could remain in power, or try a variant of Kuchma's strategy—but find someone much more competent and sellable than Viktor Yanukovych. Either way, Nemtsov said, Ukraine had shown the limitations of managed democracy. If it could happen in Kiev, it could happen in Moscow. The struggle was not just for the old Russian empire, Nemtsov said, but for the Orthodox Christian world.

"The main message from Putin is that the Orthodox world is not ready for freedom and democracy, the Orthodox world is ready for something like managed democracy. If Ukraine will show that we are Orthodox and yet on the other hand we build a European-style Ukraine, this is a very, very great example for Russia . . . The Ukrainian success means that Russia has a hope," he said. And a revolution in Russia didn't even need foreign help, Nemtsov claimed. The Khodorkovsky affair had turned many in Russian business against the Kremlin. While their opposition had so far been quiet, they were willing to fund an anti-*siloviki* campaign.

The liberals, he acknowledged, were still battling to unite their forces, as they had been since the time of Yeltsin. But the search for a Russian Yushchenko was well underway. Grigory Yavlinsky, the head of the social democratic Yabloko party, had already run for the presidency (and lost) twice. Nemtsov's own name often came up in speculation, but after serving as a co-leader of the Union of Right Forces (along with Anatoly Chubais and Irina Khakamada) as they failed to break the 5 per cent barrier in the 2004 parliamentary elections, his electoral track record was not much more impressive than Yavlinsky's.

Former world chess champion Garry Kasparov joined Kasyanov as the two most serious candidates. Shortly after the disaster of the 2004 presidential elections, Kasparov had formed a loose collection of liberals called Committee 2008: Free Choice, dedicated to getting the democrats' act together for the next vote. Kasparov impressed many with a campaign-style tour of the country giving anti-Putin speeches, a tour during which he overcame mysterious power cuts, "booked" hotels and cancelled flights. But his ethnic background (he is Jewish and was born in Azerbaijan), combined with his reputation as a grumpy egghead, meant he appealed to only a limited part of the population.[10]

Kasyanov, meanwhile, had an easier case to make. As prime minister during Putin's first four years, he could claim some responsibility for the *stabilnost* that period had brought, with the added bonus of having quit before the Beslan disaster and the tawdry conclusion of the Yukos saga. A handsome man with a stirring baritone voice, Kasyanov could even compete with Putin on the sex-appeal front.

And he would have no problem raising money. Russian Pora's overt backing was a signal that Kasyanov could count on some of Berezovsky's billions—should he choose to accept such dubious help. On top of that, when I went to see Mikhail Khodorkovsky's old business partner, Leonid Nevzlin, at his home in exile just outside Tel Aviv, he confirmed that he planned to put his remaining political and financial clout behind Kasyanov, hoping he could oust Putin and free his jailed friend.

But those connections to the Yeltsin era and its tycoons also made Kasyanov a tough sell. Many Russians saw Kasyanov—who served under Yeltsin as deputy finance minister and finance minister—as having been chest-deep in the rampant corruption and influence-peddling of that era. His nickname in parts of the Russian press was "Misha Two Per Cent," referring to allegations that he demanded a 2 per cent cut on every deal he approved.

Nonetheless, by 2006, the opposition had all but decided on Kasyanov as the man they would put forward in 2008 against Putin, or whomever Putin picked as his successor. When I asked Marat Gelman, the Kremlin spin doctor, what Kasyanov's chances were, he gave me an astonishingly frank reply. "To answer that, I need to know what *kompromat* [compromising material] there is against him," he said, referring to the post-Soviet Russian tradition of ruining political careers with scandalous videos and other unsavoury revelations. *Kompromat* had been the end of many promising politicians. "I don't know of any and I don't think [Putin's allies] know. I think it's with the Family."

Russian politics had always been unpredictable, and Gelman said it was possible that if the opposition found its Saakashvili or Yushchenko, the wave of pro-Western uprisings could culminate in 2008 with another Russian revolution. "They lack a leader. Once a leader appears, all the mistakes the authorities have made will become critical," he said. Gelman, who had been instrumental in Project Putin back in 2000, hinted to me that he was hedging his bets this time around. His publishing house had produced the Russian edition of Gene Sharp's revolutionary "From Dictatorship to Democracy," complete with an orange cover.

Despite Cheney's speech in Vilnius, the time was far from ripe to bring the Orange Revolution to Moscow. Soros's 2003 decision to quit Russia, combined with the attack on Khodorkovsky and his

Open Russia project, left NGOs operating in an environment that was increasingly unlike Ukraine or Georgia and more comparable to Belarus. And the pro-Western opposition weren't the only ones thinking of taking to the streets around the 2007 and 2008 elections. Dmitri Rogozin, the charming leader of the xenophobic Rodina party that the Kremlin had created ahead of the 2003 Duma election, was also scheming. Still perceived by many as a Kremlin pawn, Rogozin told me in his corner Duma office that he genuinely opposed Putin following the disastrous handling of Beslan. Rogozin hoped to unify his nationalist party with the remnants of the Communists before the elections but expected that the election results would be falsified and the matter decided, as in Ukraine and Georgia, in the streets.

"I don't think about a revolution in Russia, but I'm sure that the fate of those in power will be decided in the streets and not in Parliament . . . and I'm convinced that we have a real chance to gain power," he said. Putin's popularity would keep a lid on social discontent for the time being, but Rogozin expected that to change if and when Putin stepped aside in 2008. And if change came, Russians would be more likely to embrace Rodina and the Communists than those associated with the Yeltsin years.

Every opinion poll that came out about Russia backed up Rogozin's assessment. A 2006 study by the Levada Centre, for example, found that 52 per cent of respondents agreed with the ultranationalists' slogan "Russia for the Russians." Liberals realized that their biggest liability would be their being perceived as pro-Western in a country that was becoming increasingly hostile to foreigners. Even as he sat in his office and talked revolution, Nemtsov admitted that if the opposition took to the streets of Moscow, the demonstrations might not have the happy ending that they did in Kiev and Tbilisi.

"The most difficult question for Russia is what kind of revolution you will get—orange or brown or red. There is a very big danger for Russians and for the world because unfortunately nationalists and fascists are very popular in this country," Nemtsov told me. "It's why I'm afraid that a revolution will be a different colour."

Sergei Markov, like Marat Gelman, understood Russia's vulnerability to what he called an "NGO revolution." While managed democracy had been successful, Russia had not completely eliminated the opposition, as had been done in Belarus and Turkmenistan. Putin had brought the national television channels under control, but, as Beslan had demonstrated, the print press could still be feisty. And while Soros had largely withdrawn from the country and Khodorkovsky's Open Russia had been effectively neutralized, other NGOs that had been key supporters of the coloured revolutions—particularly the National Democratic Institute and the International Republican Institute—maintained large offices in Moscow.

"It could happen here," Markov said, and went on to list the reasons why. Russia, he said, had social problems similar to Ukraine's, specifically official corruption and a massive gap between rich and poor. And like Ukrainians, Russians had learned over the decades not to trust their government, its courts, its media or its election results. "We have a political system in which all these NGOs can work very freely. And we have a group of politicians who dream of Russia becoming more Westernized . . . So what is the difference, why hasn't it happened yet? Because we have a strong and popular leader named Vladimir Putin."

So, looking ahead to 2008, the Kremlin faced a massive conundrum. Who, if anyone, could succeed Putin? While many of Russia's liberals believed that Putin planned to amend the constitution so that he could stay on in the name of *stabilnost,* Putin himself regularly rejected the idea. He did, however, leave open other possibilities for himself, such as taking the prime minister's job—which skeptics pointed out could be constitutionally made more powerful than the presidency—or moving over to head the ever-expanding Gazprom. Another scenario that liberals feared was a Russia–Belarus *Anschluss,* which Putin could use to argue that he could run again, since it would be a new country with a new constitution.

In November 2005, Putin seemed to narrow the field of potential successors (if there was to be a successor) to two main contenders: Dmitry Medvedev, his long-time ally from St. Petersburg and the head of Gazprom, and Sergei Ivanov, the defence minister who had known Putin even longer, having risen along with him through the ranks of the KGB. Putin made both men deputy prime ministers, theoretically reporting to Prime Minister Mikhail Fradkov but in reality far outranking him in power and influence. The Russian media dubbed the *siloviki's* hand-wringing over how to replace Putin "Operation Successor," and even insiders like Gelman claimed not to know how it would turn out. "There is a split within the *siloviki*," Gelman said obliquely.

With a dangerous power vacuum looming, the president tasked Pavlovsky and top political adviser Vladislav Surkov with making sure revolutionaries never pitched tents on Red Square. A close colleague of Pavlovsky's, a spin doctor named Modest Kolerov, became head of a new presidential department on "inter-regional ties" dedicated to halting the tide of colour revolutions in the former Soviet space.

"Orange technologies," as Surkov called them, posed a threat to the country so great that he spoke of them in the same breath as international terrorism. "We know how this is done: values are undermined, the state is declared inefficient and domestic conflicts are provoked. The 'orange' technology has shown this explicitly," he said in a speech posted on United Russia's official website. "If [revolutions] have succeeded in four countries, why not to do the same in a fifth?" The answer, he said, was to form a "nationally oriented" society.[11]

The rise of angry nationalism was one of the saddest things I observed during my time in Moscow. Almost daily, it seemed, there were small stories in *The Moscow Times* about foreign students being beaten or stabbed on the metro or skinheads trashing a market run by traders from the Caucasus. There was certainly a rise during the time I was there in the amount of hateful graffiti and spray-painted swastikas. When I visited the capital's People's Friendship University—famous in Soviet times for welcoming students from all over the world—I found African students afraid to leave their dorms after dark because gangs of skinheads were known to wait for them on the edge of campus. The students distrusted and feared the police. The hostility got so bad that by 2004, when the satirical English-language newspaper the *eXile* published a long list of ways Putin's Russia was comparable to Weimar Germany, nobody laughed; members of the foreign press corps pored over the list at an American-style diner one morning, nodding their heads in agreement with the substance underpinning the *eXile*'s humour.

To combat the threat of a pro-Western uprising in Russia, Surkov and Pavlovsky decided to harness this xenophobia. In July 2005, Pavlovsky gathered three thousand young activists at a summer camp at picturesque Lake Seliger outside Moscow and established the Kremlin's answer to Otpor and Pora. The group was called Nashi, meaning "Ours," and at the founding event—closed to all but state-controlled media—Surkov asked the youths to protect Russia from Western influence and promised to "hand over the country" to them if they did. The young people spent the afternoon listening to ideologically charged speeches by Sergei Markov and Vyacheslav Nikonov, as well as by several pro-Putin Duma deputies. Pavlovsky described Nashi's role most directly. "You must be ready to disperse fascist rallies and physically oppose attempted anti-constitutional coups," he told them. In other words, they were to make sure that any non-violent protest organized by the opposition didn't remain non-violent for long.[12]

Next up on Surkov and Pavlovsky's hit list were the NGOs. In January 2006, Putin signed off on a new law that required them to provide the government with detailed reports of their financing and activities. He made it clear that those found to be interfering in Russian affairs would be forced to close. "We do not want them to be led by puppet masters from abroad," he told a press conference with foreign journalists. "States cannot use NGOs as an instrument of foreign policy on the territory of other states."[13]

Back in Washington, staff at NED braced for a crackdown on their grantees. These included groups like Memorial, which was still trying to tell the public about the evils of Stalinism, and the anti–Chechen war Soldiers' Mothers Committee, the group behind the small weekly rallies against the war on Moscow's Pushkin Square, to NGOs more directly involved in the political process, such as Golos ("Voice"), an election-monitoring group styled after the Committee of Ukrainian Voters and its predecessors in Serbia and Georgia. NED also funded the Panorama think tank, which received a $41,000 grant in 2003 to publish a series of books outlining the setbacks suffered by Russian democracy under Putin, and $45,000 the following year in "support of newly emerging democratic groups, movements, and initiatives." Meanwhile, NDI and IRI continued to receive hundreds of thousands of dollars annually from NED to work with the pro-Western opposition.[14]

"I think in the Orange Revolution [the Kremlin] sort of discovered, in a sense, the role that NGOs play in all of this," sighed NED's Potocki. "Before it was limited to restricting the power of oligarchs, intervention with independent media, television and radio in Russia, but now they understand that civil society plays a dramatic role in these efforts and . . . it's time for them to work on these troublesome NGOs."

James Woolsey, the former CIA chief who headed Freedom House's efforts in Ukraine and Kyrgyzstan, called the Kremlin's crackdown on NGOs an "honour" since it meant the democracy promoters were doing their job. "Mr. Putin and his movement toward fascism in Russia are on the wrong side of history," Woolsey told Radio Free Europe in October 2005. "They are not going to succeed . . . Ultimately they will lose."

Shortly after the anti-NGO bill was signed into law came one of the most bizarre episodes in the post–Cold War rivalry between Russia and the West: the Case of the Transmitting Rock. It had all the intrigue and improbable gadgetry of a James Bond film—Russian authorities accused Marc Doe, a staff member at the British embassy who was allegedly a member of the spy agency MI6, of hiding a transmitter inside a fake rock left in a Moscow park. The fake rock, according to the Kremlin, hid a wireless device that could transmit and receive data with devices brought into the park by other British agents.

It was bizarre stuff, but the subtext put democracy promoters on edge. The Russian authorities made it public that Doe—an alleged spy—had also been responsible for handling grants to democracy-promotion groups, including the Eurasia Foundation, a supporter of independent media, and the Moscow Helsinki Group, a human rights watchdog that had prominently criticized Russia's conduct in the Chechen war. Significantly, both groups were also funded by NED. The Moscow Helsinki Group's feisty chair, Lyudmila Alexeyeva, said she believed the government was preparing public opinion ahead of a move to shut down her NGOs and others that cooperated with the West.

"Today, we are having a clash of two concepts of democracy," Pavol Demeš, who had helped build Otpor, Pora and Zubr, told me. "This Russian concept of democracy, Nashi, versus the U.S. and EU concept of democracy, and their instruments." After years of struggling for an answer while the West pushed its offensive onto its old turf, the Kremlin had found a way to fight back.

SIXTEEN

AFTERGLOW

Belgrade, Kiev and Tbilisi

The city, with its grey, Stalinist buildings, large town squares and wide boulevards, could be anywhere in the former Soviet Union, or much of Eastern Europe for that matter. I thought it looked like Minsk on one of its endlessly cloudy days. When I told him that, Otpor's Ivan Marovic laughed and said he thought it looked like his native Belgrade, which is just as prone to long sunless stretches.

The city on Marovic's computer screen was actually a fictional place called Grbac, deliberately designed to look like modern Minsk or Milošević's Belgrade or anywhere else in the parts of the world Freedom House has ever pronounced "not free." It didn't quite look like the glitzy centre of Moscow, but it could have passed for one of its drab suburbs. Or Donetsk in eastern Ukraine, for that matter.

Grbac, however, exists only in a computer game—the latest, and most commercial, expansion of the revolution-makers' efforts. *A Force More Powerful* both entertains and instructs: you can play at being Otpor (or Kmara, as both logos appear throughout the game) and organize street demonstrations to topple a fictional dictator as an after-school distraction. Or you can use it as a real-life training tool. "The game contains no secrets, no sure-fire recipes for winning," the user guide reads. "But through active immersion in simulated conflicts—in fictionalized but realistic settings—the game allows you to learn the principles and techniques of nonviolent strategy."

Filmmaker Steve York and Freedom House chairman Peter Ackerman, the same team that had produced *Bringing Down a Dictator,* dreamed up the game. Backed by something called the International Center on Nonviolent Conflict, an American consulting firm seeking to make a specialty out of spreading revolution, the game appeared in early 2006 from BreakAway Ltd., the computer game company that produced *Civilization III* and other well-known strategy games. Marovic provided quality control.

Sitting in the windowless Washington, D.C., boardroom of the International Center on Nonviolent Conflict, the thin-faced, sharp-featured Ackerman—who succeeded James Woolsey as the head of Freedom House in September 2005—first gushed over the potential of the formula he helped to spread from Serbia to Georgia to Ukraine and beyond, then in the next breath denied there was such a recipe. Helping non-violent revolutions move from one country to the next can rid the world of tyranny, he told me, but it was time for governments to get out of the way and to let private foundations like his do the work.

"Whether it's NDI, IRI or NED, these are wonderful organizations doing important work. But they're not in the business of conflict. We [the Center on Nonviolent Conflict] are in the business of conflict," he said. The business of "colour revolutions" was being privatized.

Ackerman described his centre's task as preparing for the moment when regimes like those in Serbia, Georgia and Ukraine stop cooperating with civil society. NED, NDI and IRI, he said, laid the groundwork for peaceful change through decades of painstakingly chipping away at the regimes' "pillars of support." When a regime realizes what's going on and tries to clamp down, that's where non-violent resistance comes in, pushing for the regime's final collapse.

Designing the good guys for *A Force More Powerful* was easy enough. That part Marovic and Ackerman understood intrinsically. The player takes control of a rag-tag bunch of student leaders, independent journalists and election monitors and directs them to raise funds, hold rock concerts and design graffiti campaigns. When the time is right, you rally around a chosen opposition politician and take your people into the streets.

The tough part was convincing the computer to act as erratically as a Lukashenko or a Kuchma. First they had to program the computer-government to be corrupt, since early versions apparently didn't see the logic of wasting money and alienating the government's own people. Later the designers had to tone down the computer's tyrannical streak in order to give the opposition a chance. When I saw an early version of the game in Marovic's apartment, the computer-government cracked down hard on his first tiny rally. "Artificial intelligence is much better than a real government. They always know what you're up to and how to stop you. We had to force the computer to waste money and to stop doing things for the people," Marovic said, with one of the many belly laughs he seems to produce every hour. "You have to keep a low profile or the dictator, which we modelled on [Chile's Augusto] Pinochet, will start shooting."

In Marovic's career as a travelling revolutionary, the dictators haven't shot at the crowds—at least not in Serbia and Ukraine, where he was directly involved. The computer game, he hoped, would help spread Otpor's message and tactics far beyond Eastern Europe, perhaps to the Middle East, where the U.S. was ramping up democracy promotion despite an Islamist backlash sparked by the catastrophe of the Iraq war. The game was launched shortly after Lebanon's Cedar Revolution, during which Marovic had travelled to Beirut on his own initiative to advise those running the pro-Western, anti-Syrian uprising that followed the assassination of former prime minister Rafiq Hariri in early 2005. An Egyptian group called Kifaya (which, like Kmara, means "Enough") had also sprung up and was borrowing Ukraine's orange colour and Otpor's street-theatre tactics in its campaign to oppose the extension of Hosni Mubarak's twenty-five-year hold on power there.[1]

Though Marovic's work in Serbia and Ukraine won him that Champion of Freedom medal from George W. Bush, teaching revolution is not a career that's made him rich, which perhaps explains the move into computer games. Five years after he helped bring down Slobodan Milošević, Marovic was living in a two-room apartment in a working-class neighbourhood of Belgrade. He still dressed like one of the punks he says formed the backbone of Otpor, and he met with me in jeans and sneakers, a large gold earring in his left lobe.

Like many Serbs, Marovic has mixed feelings about his country's progress in the first five years after the revolution. Belgrade in late 2005 still had a revolutionary feel about it, and Otpor's clenched-fist logo could still be found spray-painted on walls, with *Gotov je!* sometimes updated to *Je v Hagu!*—"He's in The Hague"—followed by a triumphant "Ha! Ha!" The dictator was long gone, but Milošević's legacy still haunted his people.

From the moment it began in 2002, every minute of Milošević's trial before the International Criminal Tribunal for the Former Yugoslavia was carried live on B92 television. The broadcasts were funded by USAID, suggesting an understanding that NATO had yet to success-fully justify its bombing of Belgrade to the majority of Serb citizens, However, by year three of the trial many Serbs had stopped paying attention. Most I spoke to believed Milošević was "winning" his tele-vised showdown with the International Court of Justice's lawyers and judges. Polls showed that 50 per cent of Serbs believed the country had not committed any war crimes during the conflicts of the 1990s. Even after a video appeared on television showing Serb policemen executing some of the seven thousand Muslim men and boys who were killed during the 1995 Srebrenica massacre, many simply asserted that the film was a fake. Serbia, like Russia, has yet to face its past.

Even those Serbs who understood the ills of that period and had no love for Milošević saw the whole court case as a made-for-TV charade aimed at justifying NATO's attacks. I spotted several Serbs wearing T-shirts emblazoned (in English) with "Fuck B92," and new posters of a defiant-looking Milošević in a blue business suit were slapped back up on buildings and telephone poles every time the authorities took them down. Each year in July, thousands of nationalists gathered on the capital's Republic Square for a loud rally mourning the anniversary of the government's decision to sur-render Milošević to the tribunal. Milošević's death from natural causes in his prison cell in early 2006—before a verdict could be reached—further fed the minds of the conspiracy theorists. An esti-mated crowd of 100,000 turned out for his funeral.

In many ways, the Milošević era continued long past October 5, 2000. For many of the Serbs who took to the streets that day, the revo-lution ended three years later when Zoran Đinđić, the charismatic opposition leader who had become prime minister under Vojislav

Koštunica, was shot and killed by a sniper on the steps of his Belgrade office. The assassin was a member of the feared Red Berets paramilitary unit, known for its brutality in the Balkan wars, and still loyal to Milošević. Forty-three others were charged in the meticulously planned and executed plot.

Meanwhile, Ratko Mladić, the Bosnian Serb army chief who over-saw the Srebrenica killings, was still on the lam six years after the revo-lution, despite Western intelligence services' belief that he had never travelled outside of Serbia and Montenegro. The European Union had made his arrest and handover, along with that of his political boss, Radovan Karadžić, a condition for the country's further integration into the organization. The EU and NATO held up the Kostunica gov-ernment's inability or unwillingness to arrest Mladić as proof that Serbia had not changed enough to be seriously considered for member-ship in either Western institution.

Still cut off from the rest of Europe, and with the problem of Kosovo still festering in its underbelly, Serbia's feeling of isolation heightened in May 2006 when Montenegro—the last Yugoslav republic still joined to Serbia—voted for independence. "At first people were very angry with the West. Now we just want them to come. We need investment and tourists," said Mosa, a thin, bespectacled cab driver in Belgrade I became friendly with. "People keep saying that things are getting bet-ter, but I don't feel it in my life yet. There's no more money in my pocket than there was five years ago."

While revolution's shortfalls stung, there had nonetheless been sub-stantial progress made. The era of gasoline shortages and of young men being sent off to fight for the dream of a "Greater Serbia" was long past, and the late-night laughter and music that spilled out of Belgrade's packed restaurants spoke to an optimism unheard of under the old regime. Having left the sanctions and war of the 1990s behind it, Serbia was no longer ranked alongside Africa's trouble spots in terms of quality of life, as it had been in the late 1990s. Five years after Milošević's ouster, the country was finally emerging from his shadow. Belgrade now looked and felt a lot like the capitals of nearby Hungary and Ukraine, even if a few bomb-damaged buildings still remained.

Marovic, characteristically, looked at the glass as more than half full. "However disappointed we may be today, we don't have a war, people are not getting killed. There are no economic sanctions," he said. "This is a totally different country than when Milošević was in power."

It's much easier to spot the changes in Saakashvili's Georgia. All you have to do is stand in the middle of Tbilisi and watch them happen. Tbilisi by 2006 was a vastly different place than when I had first seen it four years earlier. Though still poor by Western standards, the city bubbled with a sense that things were starting to move in the right direction. "*Po tikhonichku,*" many Georgians would tell me with a hopeful wink. "Slowly, slowly."

The Old City, which had for decades been sliding deeper and deeper into disrepair, was undergoing a street-by-street overhaul that was not so much a restoration as an attempt to reproduce a tiny bit of Amsterdam or Copenhagen in a corner of the Caucasus. The roads were being repaved, the facades of crumbling buildings were being repainted and swish Japanese restaurants, Irish pubs and French wine bars were popping up on seemingly every corner. The sound of construction filled the air at all hours of the day—even on weekends. The refugees from Abkhazia who had lived for more than a decade in the Hotel Iveria in the centre of the city had been paid $7,000 per family to move out to the outskirts of Tbilisi, clearing the way for German investors to move in and renovate the crumbling eyesore into what would eventually be a sparkling new Radisson hotel. The old house leaning precariously on the iron bar, which had nearly fallen on my head (or so it seemed) every time I walked in the Old City, was gone, the ground cleared for something more stable to be built in its place.

The Kmara kids had got what they wanted. One night in summer 2005, I ran into a table of the revolutionaries hanging out in a jazz bar that was their own private replica of somewhere in the European Union. The place was packed with foreigners speaking English. They were businessmen, mostly—the backpackers hadn't yet discovered the hidden gem of Georgia—and proof that Tbilisi was back on the map. A year after the revolt, after an eighteen-month hiatus, British Airways restored its direct London-Tbilisi flights—a sign that the country was no longer dismissed as simply a region of Russia to be visited only after stopping in Moscow. In 2005, Lufthansa added a Munich-Tbilisi route.

Proclaiming its European desires for all to see, the Georgian government lifted the EU flag alongside the new Georgian one (the red and white flag of Saakashvili's National Movement had replaced the old, detested purplish post-Soviet banner) as if to suggest the country had already joined the EU, even if the news hadn't yet reached Brussels. In another public display of affection that was sure to displease Moscow, large billboards of Saakashvili and George W. Bush clasping hands were erected throughout the city, recalling the U.S. president's 2005 visit to Tbilisi when he hailed Georgia as a beacon for other states in the region seeking their freedom. "You've got a solid friend in America," he'd told a cheering crowd of 150,000 on Freedom Square. Returning the compliment, Saakashvili named one of the roads connecting the capital to its international airport President George W. Bush Street, along which stood a billboard of the smiling president waving his hand.[2]

But three years after the Rose Revolution—and Saakashvili's 96 per cent win in the subsequent election—the country's most startling difference was in the look and behaviour of its police force. Instead of following the post-Soviet tradition of extracting bribes on street corners, they wore new uniforms and cruised about importantly in American-purchased Volkswagen Passats. In one of his first (and most popular) acts of office, Saakashvili had fired the entire force, rehired a third of them and then tripled their pay.

He launched similar assaults on corruption in the judiciary and the customs service. Aided by the boost in revenues gained from the port of Batumi when Kmara chased Aslan Abashidze out of Adjara, the government budget tripled its paltry 2003 tax revenues of $400 million to $1.2 billion the following year. That allowed Saakashvili to take another populist step: doubling pensions from 14 Georgian lari (about $8) a month to a still insubstantial but better 29 lari.

But, as in Serbia, fundamental problems kept the country from its dream of truly joining Europe. The Russian-backed separatists in Abkhazia and South Ossetia still refused, in 2006, to recognize Tbilisi's authority. Russia continued to dominate the economy—as demonstrated by the devastating effects of the wine ban. While Saakashvili regularly spoke of the need to escape the Kremlin's influence, geography dictated that he could not.

The reformist team that swept to power through the revolution was dealt a crushing blow when Zurab Zhvania, Saakashvili's long-time friend and post-revolution prime minister, died in 2005 under circumstances that have never been fully explained. The official version says that he died of gas poisoning from a faulty heater in the early hours of February 3 while visiting a friend, who was also found dead. An FBI team invited to help investigate the case concluded there was no foul play, but Zhvania's family has challenged that version of events, noting inconsistencies in the story of how the bodies were found.

Some of those who had backed Saakashvili's rise to power, meanwhile, had become his sharpest critics. They saw signs that winning 96 per cent of the vote in the presidential election had gone to Saakashvili's head. They worried that, like Shevardnadze before him, the president had become convinced that only he could save the troubled country, and that he might not step aside when the time came. Saakashvili's zealous anti-corruption drive, they complained, had become a tool for punishing political opponents, while the media were now more afraid to criticize the government than they had been under the old regime. On the first anniversary of the revolution, a group of fourteen NGOs, including many of those behind the Rose Revolution, warned that Saakashvili's regime risked becoming "anti-democratic." A disgusted Tinatin Khidasheli, the young lawyer who had been one of Saakshvili's partners in plotting against Shevardnadze, left the Soros Foundation and joined the political opposition outright. Meanwhile, a Moscow-backed opposition movement rose to prominence by targeting not Saakashvili, but his patron. Caling itself simply "anti-Soros," it asked for Georgians to re-evaluate the wisdom of aggravating their giant neighbour in the name of good relations with faraway America.

Surprisingly, one of those who was least critical about the changes in his country was Eduard Shevardnadze. "When I returned back to Georgia, my only goal was to build democracy, and with a few exceptions, we succeeded. It really was democracy without restrictions," he said, walking with me around his green-walled study, which is lined with photographs from his time as a superstar of global diplomacy. There are pictures of him smiling and shaking hands with Ronald Reagan, Jacques Chirac and, somewhat incongruously, Ray Charles.

He looked both like and quite different from the man in the photographs. He was twenty years younger then, but his hair was as white in the pictures as it is now, though it has since receded farther up his prominent forehead. His face was now more lined, and his jowls saggier. But it was his once confident, angular shoulders that had changed the most. The man laughing with Reagan was a comfortable master of the global chessboard who was at home posing with the American president on the White House lawn. The man leading me around his study was slumped, tired and largely forgotten.

The tour was a slow-motion one. At seventy-six, the Silver Fox could hardly lift his feet anymore, forcing his gait into a stiff-kneed shuffle. But his mind was still sharp and he had plenty of time to think—especially since his wife, Nanuli, had died in 2004—about the Rose Revolution and why it happened. He considered it a matter of natural succession: he had served his purpose and it was time for him to go. By choosing not to fire on the crowds (an order Saakashvili still insists Shevardnadze gave) he effectively chose those who would succeed him.

Like Khidasheli, he was worried about declining freedom of the press under the new regime, he said, seeing it as a threat to the country's fledgling democracy. But he had confidence that Saakashvili, Nino Burjanadze and the other "youngsters" would keep Georgia on the right path. "They are very young and talented people who work in very modern ways," Shevardnadze told me. "They'll work things out."

Ukraine's progress was in many ways diametrically opposite to the changes in Georgia. While Saakashvili's forceful personality pushed through radical changes that boosted the economy but raised worries about renewed authoritarianism, Yushchenko's first two years were marked by indecision, poor leadership and economic backsliding, countered by a genuine rise in the freedoms of the people.

Yushchenko and Tymoshenko disagreed sharply on the country's economic model—infighting that cost a chance to capitalize financially on the international interest generated by the Orange Revolution—but their rule saw the birth of the first period of true press freedom in Ukraine's long history. Newspapers and television channels could and did criticize or caricature whomever they wanted. The main story of the parliamentary elections of March 2006 may have been the revival of Viktor Yanukovych's previously moribund political career (though many Ukrainians are quick to point out that the disbanded "orange" coalition of Tymoshenko and Yushchenko still won far more votes than Yanukovych), but the election was also declared the freest and fairest the country had ever had. Gone were the *temnyki* and the ballot stuffing. Managed democracy had retreated back over the border to Russia. When I had dinner with my friend Yuriy in post-revolutionary Kiev, I asked him the same question as he had asked me the first time the crowds moved into the streets: "Was it victory?" After a long pause and a chuckle, he answered that yes, it was. His answer was a lot like the one Marovic had given me in Belgrade. "It's not perfect, and there are a lot of problems, but Ukraine today is a completely different place than it was under Kuchma."

On Independence Square, all the orange graffiti of fall 2004 has been scrubbed clean, save for a single pillar in front of the central post office, where the excited scribblings of that time have been preserved under Plexiglas. But one thing that lingered was the belief that people could change politics—that they didn't have to live with another Kuchma if he came along, that they could throw him out. As a reminder of that, every time an elected official made a decision that went against what was perceived as the people's will, tents would appear. Mayors and cabinet ministers frequently woke up to this reminder that it was the people who had put them there.

Vlad Kaskiv, the Belarusian activist who now spends much of his time in Kiev, says that despite all the stumbles by Yushchenko and Tymoshenko in the first eighteen months, Ukraine had changed dramatically at a fundamental level. "It's an absolutely free atmosphere . . . You can just feel it. My friends here all say the same thing. They never thought Ukraine would ever be such a free place, so dynamic. It's what we want in Belarus."

Kaskiv's appreciation of the "new" Ukraine partially answered a question that had been nagging me throughout. Were the Western-backed uprisings in Belgrade, Tbilisi and Kiev a good thing?

For the people of Serbia, Georgia and Ukraine, the answer was yes. Life in 2006 in all three countries was freer and thus better than it had been under Milošević, Shevardnadze and Kuchma. None (except perhaps the Slovaks and Croats, whose "revolutions" had been less dramatic) had gotten quite what they'd been promised by their leaders, particularly when it came to economic progress and the dream of joining the European Union. But the political sphere was unquestionably more open than it had been—people could complain freely, get useful information from their media and pitch a tent in front of Parliament if they didn't like what was happening inside. But all that is more a condemnation of the dictators and the practitioners of managed democracy than it is a salutation to the work of the revolution-makers. The democracy-builders' work is, in the end, justified because of the nature of their foes as well as the genuine desire for change amongst a large portion of the local population. While the vast majority of the programs supported by groups like Soros and the National Endowment for Democracy are very worthy projects, the ones that dabble in the political systems of other countries by uniting political blocs for opposition supporters to rally around and creating radical youth groups to lead the opposition's charge into the streets are in clear violation of the principle of national sovereignty. It's worth noting that the help that NDI and IRI gave to political parties in countries like Ukraine would have been illegal had a Ukrainian NGO been giving such aid to the Democrats or the Republicans.

There was speculation, too, that Soros in particular had ulterior financial motives for backing regime change in Serbia, Georgia and Ukraine. After the Rose Revolution, Saakashvili raised eyebrows by appointing engineering magnate Kaka Bendukidze, a sometime business partner of Soros's, as the country's new economy minister. And Soros Fund Management did hold more than $600 million worth of shares in Exxon Mobil, one of the main players in the Caspian oil basin and a sure beneficiary of the opening of the Baku-Tbilisi-Ceyhan pipeline. But $600 million is not an enormous amount by the standards of Soros Fund Management, and the billionaire has scrupulously avoided making splashy business investments in the countries that Open Society has helped remodel.

Those who interacted with Soros during his battle with Putinism and Russia's renewed empire believe the billionaire did what he did out of pure conviction. "[Open Society] is a way for him to spend money, not make it. [Bill] Gates does it one way, Soros does it another," said

Andrew Robinson, the Canadian ambassador to Kiev during the Orange Revolution. "If you have the money, philanthropy and ideology are not necessarily different things."

In New York and Washington, at the offices of the Open Society Institute and NED, the excitement over what had been accomplished in Georgia and Ukraine was tempered by the knowledge that the job was unfinished, and about to get a lot more difficult. For all the gains made over a decade of democracy promotion in the old Communist bloc, it was also inescapable that there had also been a giant setback: Russia had become less democratic and more hostile to the West than at any time since 1991. And by turning its fire on Soros, NED and the NGOs they supported, the Kremlin was working at undermining all that had been accomplished in Tbilisi and Kiev. "We're facing a lot of roadblocks," Leonard Bernardo sighed when I asked him about the Soros Foundation's stalled efforts in Russia. "Increasingly so."

What was good for the Serbs, Georgians and Ukrainians arguably came at a cost to Russians, Belarusians and Central Asians, whose leaders predictably cracked down when they saw the threat posed to their regimes by increased political openness. This argument against America's intervention in the former Soviet space would be less damaging if the U.S. government and its democracy-promotion agents had stuck to their stated principles throughout. The Bush administration's failure to show the same commitment to democracy when dealing with the U.S.-friendly autocrats in Kazakhstan and Azerbaijan as it did in Ukraine and Georgia exposed the revolution-makers as a political weapon that served U.S. interests—a way of installing friendly regimes to take care of their energy interests—rather than as a humanitarian effort. Which is why Putin's "Where is all that pathos?" question about Dick Cheney's oil-and-gas-focused trip to Kazakhstan struck a chord.

From a Great Game perspective—examining the chessboard on which all the events from Bratislava in 1998 to Minsk in 2006 were played—it looks like a period of great advances for the U.S., through the establishment of a string of new Western-friendly governments that predictably made their markets more accessible to Western investment. But you can count these changes as victories for Washington only if you accept that Russia was lost as a partner even before Vladimir Putin came to power.

In fact, Russia was not lost. As late as 2003, there was a substantive faction within Putin's Kremlin, typified by Mikhail Kasyanov,
Alexander Voloshin and Andrei Illarionov, who were fighting a running
battle with the *siloviki,* trying to keep the country on a course that was
broadly friendly to America and the West. Many point to the arrest of
Mikhail Khodorkovsky as the moment that faction lost its fight, but
you could just as easily point to the Rose Revolution less than a month
later and the establishment of a vociferous friend of Washington and
foe of the Kremlin in an ex-Soviet republic as the day the pro-Western
faction saw its influence disappear. From that point on, Putin came to
speak more and more often of the West as a force that was opposed to
Russia's interests and that wanted to keep Russia weak. He, like
Komsomolskaya Pravda, saw the drawing of a big purple ring around
Russia, cutting his country off from the Black Sea and Europe and out
of discussions about new pipelines flowing westward.

Siniša Šikman braced for the question even before I asked it. Šikman,
the genial Otpor veteran who had gone on to help train Pora in Ukraine
and Zubr in Belarus, was the one who brought words like "puppet"
and "CIA" into our conversation.

"Do I think the CIA used us?" he asked pre-emptively as we shared
a two-litre bottle of Coca-Cola on a sweltering June day in Belgrade.
He looked more like an accountant than a revolutionary that afternoon, dressed in a golf shirt and sitting in the offices of an institute
that studies educational reform in Serbia. "Well, maybe we used the
CIA for our own interests. If the CIA wanted to bring down Milošević,
and I, who grew up here, wanted to bring down Milošević, who do you
think enjoyed it more?" The CIA, he added with a heavy note of irony,
had called Milošević "a force for stability" in the Balkans in the early
1990s, a time when Šikman and his fellow students were already battling against the regime.

Unlike Ukrainians and to a lesser extent Georgians, who tend to
look on their uprisings and their new friends in the West through rose-
tinted glasses, many of the Otpor veterans are more cynical about their
country's transition to democracy and about the role they played in
helping similar revolutions happen in other countries. They know that
when it suited America's purposes to support Milošević, the White

House did. And they remember vividly that when Milošević became a problem for the U.S., NATO first dropped bombs on Belgrade and only turned to "democracy promotion" to oust the regime when bloodier measures failed. While Ukrainians can get angry if you suggest that their revolt was anything but home-grown, Serbs—including those who took part in the Orange Revolution—generally see things more practically. "A lot of critics say we were working for American money," shrugged Marko Markovic, the Otpor veteran who now lives in Kiev. "I say we brought the American money here."

Still, Markovic is even convinced that he didn't understand the big game he was a part of until long afterward. "It's like a game of Risk sometimes. I think there are some people sitting in a room somewhere, playing Risk with us, saying let's do [a revolution] here, let's do one there . . . I was somebody's little red chip. I'm deeply convinced of that."

Both Šikman and Markovic have a very European distaste for George W. Bush and his administration. They understand, even if they don't like to phrase it just so, that they were part of a machine that topples governments that run afoul of Washington. Both say they do what they do because they understand and care for those trapped—as they once were—under a repressive regime, and want to help them.

Šikman says he admires people like Soros who, rather than squirrelling their fortunes away, use them to try to do good in the world. But he hates the moment when his work grows to fruition—and a Shevardnadze or a Kuchma flees from office—and the next day Bush or Condoleezza Rice appears on television to applaud the regime change, hinting broadly that the people of Eastern Europe did not so much free themselves from oppression as jump on a wave of freedom that originated in Washington, D.C.

That's when Šikman gets cynical again. "Maybe they have some interests in a revolution in Ukraine and a revolution in Georgia, but the people in Georgia and Ukraine also did what they did for their own interests," he says, the rhythm of his speech so slow that it seems each syllable is the end of his answer. Then there's an even longer pause. By this point, the conversation has stopped and Šikman is debating only with himself. "But maybe the CIA did use us. Maybe they did."

ACKNOWLEDGMENTS

Everything that precedes is dedicated to Carolynne, my partner, editor and inspiration. This book would never have happened without her, and her name should be on the front of this beside mine. There's no way to fully express my love, appreciation and gratitude, but for the first time in two years, we're going to take a vacation that my laptop computer is not invited to join us on.

Michael Mainville is an old friend from Canada who fortuitously ended up in Moscow for the three years we were living there. His being there to share it all made the entire experience better. He did the same for the book, giving it a crucial first read and making many helpful suggestions.

The professionalism and enthusiasm for this project of Anne Collins and Craig Pyette, my editors at Random House Canada, made the whole process much more pleasant than I thought it could or would be. The same goes for my agent, John Pearce, who took a wisp of an idea and helped me mould it into what you're holding. The keen eyes of Stephanie Fysh and Gillian Watts during the editing process saved me a thousand minor embarrassments and a few major ones.

Throughout the time I lived and worked in the former Soviet Union, I was lucky to have great colleagues and travel partners, some of whom are named in this book. My friendships with Luke Tchalenko, Nick

Paton Walsh, Jeremy Page and Ellen Pinchuk all survived war, revolution and far too much vodka for anyone's good.

Tatiana Smirnova, the long-suffering translator and office assistant in the *Globe and Mail*'s Moscow bureau, deserves special praise and sympathy for putting up with three years of my strange questions at odd hours, and for answering them with patience and good humour.

My time in Russia, and my understanding of the country, was made richer by friends like Irina Sandul, Kiril Kirsanov, Dimitry Nemirovsky, Svetlana Ivanova and Alexey Sakharov. The same goes for Yuriy Shafarenko and Danilo Bilak in Ukraine, as well as Lika Peradze in Georgia. There are others who live in more repressive countries that I won't name for fear it will cause them trouble. This book is far the better for all their contributions, large and small. It goes without saying that any errors are completely mine.

I have to thank my editors at the *Globe and Mail*—especially my foreign editor, Stephen Northfield—for their support and for giving me time off from my hectic new job in the Middle East to complete this project. John Stackhouse and Paul Knox also deserve applause for allowing me to indulge in my fascination with forgotten corners of the old Soviet Union.

The underappreciated Canada Council for the Arts provided a generous grant that helped me make extra trips during the research and writing.

Last, I'd like to thank my father, Wayne, who instilled in me a fascination with Russia that drove everything I did there. It's he who should be writing books about the country. And though she wishes my job took me to safer places, my mother, Alannah, has always been one of my biggest cheerleaders. Love and thanks to them both.

Finally, when I was a small boy, my grandfather, Thomas Feeney, dedicated a book to me. He died many years ago, but I'd nonetheless like to even the score.

SOURCE NOTES

PROLOGUE

1. Helen Womack, "Did Alexei Stumble across Russian Agents Planting a
    Bomb to Justify Chechen War?" *The Independent,* January 27, 2000.

CHAPTER 1

1. All figures are in U.S. dollars unless otherwise indicated.
2. Details of the Davos Pact are drawn from Chrystia Freeland, *Sale of the
    Century: Russia's Wild Ride from Communism to Capitalism* (Toronto:
    Doubleday Canada, 2000).
3. Yevgenia Borisova, "And the Winner Is?" *The Moscow Times,*
    September 9, 2000.
4. Geoffrey York, "Russian Voters Silent about Signs of Fraud," *The Globe
    and Mail,* October 11, 2000.
5. Vladimir Putin, letter, *Izvestia,* February 25, 2000; translation by BBC
    Monitoring.

CHAPTER 2

1. George Soros, "Who Lost Russia?" *The New York Review of Books,*
    March 2000.
2. If you had invested $100,000 U.S. in Quantum back in 1969, it would
    have been worth more than $350 million thirty years later.

3. See George Soros, "Toward a Global Open Society," *The Atlantic Monthly,* January 1998.

4. Details of Sakharov's warning are drawn from a speech given by Soros in Moscow on the tenth anniversary of the founding of the Soros Foundation–Soviet Union.

5. From a summary of George Soros's spring 2004 trip to Ukraine provided by the International Renaissance Foundation, the Ukrainian branch of the Open Society Institute.

6. George Soros, *Soros on Soros: Staying ahead of the Curve* (New York: Wiley, 1995).

7. Connie Bruck, "The World According to George Soros," *The New Yorker,* January 23, 1995.

8. President George W. Bush doubled the NED's funding in 2004, decreeing that the new money should go to efforts in the Middle East.

9. David Ignatius, "Innocence Abroad: The New World of Spyless Coups," *The Washington Post*, September 22, 1991.

CHAPTER 3

1. Mladen Lazic, ed., *Protest in Belgrade: Winter of Discontent* (Budapest: Central European University Press, 1999).

2. Matthew Collin, *This Is Serbia Calling: Rock 'n' Roll Radio and Belgrade's Underground Resistance* (London: Serpent's Tail Press, 2001).

3. See the 2000 annual report of the National Endowment for Democracy, available at http://www.ned.org.

4. Allan Little, *Moral Combat: NATO at War*, BBC2, March 12, 2000.

5. Chuck Staresinic, "In Love and War . . . ," *Washington Post,* February 10, 2002.

6. Adam LeBor, *Milosevic: A Biography* (London: Bloomsbury, 2002).

7. "How Kostunica Was Chosen," *Der Spiegel,* October 9, 2000.

8. Michael Dobbs, "U.S. Advice Guided Milosevic Opposition," *Washington Post,* December 11, 2000.

9. National Endowment for Democracy, *Annual Report 2000* (Washington, D.C.: National Endowment for Democracy, 2001); available at www.ned.org.

10. Helvey was interviewed by correspondent Steve York for the 2001 PBS documentary *Bringing Down a Dictator.*

11. Dragan Bujosevic and Ivan Radovanovic, *The Fall of Milosevic* (New York: Palgrave Macmillan, 2003).

12. This and the transcripts of the October 5 police conversations are drawn from Bujosevic and Radovanovic, *The Fall of Milosevic.*

13. Madeleine Albright, with Bill Woodward, *Madam Secretary: A Memoir* (New York: Miramax Books, 2003).

CHAPTER 4

1. Many of those in Russia and Belarus nostalgic for the days of the USSR have long complained that Yeltsin, Kravchuk and Shushkevich were likely drunk when they dissolved the union. Shushkevich told me they'd had a bottle of wine "but we were not drunk!" when the decision was made.

2. Richard Boudreaux, "Leader Pushes Belarus Back Towards Russia," *Los Angeles Times,* September 17, 1995.

3. Ian Traynor, "Reign of Terror in a Soviet Time Warp," *The Guardian,* September 7, 2001.

4. Viasna is also a member of ENEMO, the Western-funded European Network of Election Monitoring Organizations, which includes Serbia's Citizens for Free Elections and Democracy (CeSID) and Georgia's International Society for Fair Elections and Democracy (ISFED).

5. Steven Lee Meyers, "Bringing Down Europe's Last Ex-Soviet Dictator," *The New York Times Magazine*, February 26, 2006.

6. Kozak is now assistant secretary for democracy, human rights and labour to Condoleezza Rice.

7. While there's ample suggestion that Wieck, whom Lukashenko called "the opposition's chief of staff," personally shared Kozak's aim of forcing the regime out (he met several times with Zubr leaders in 2001), there's less proof that the European Union was interested in regime change in Belarus. Washington saw toppling the likes of Milošević, Lukashenko and Ukraine's Leonid Kuchma as a chance to create U.S.-friendly regimes and markets while keeping Russia backpedalling, but Paris and Berlin were less than excited at the prospect of millions of former Soviet citizens suddenly "free" and clamouring for EU membership. Jacques Chirac and Gerhard Schröder saw their countries as the centre of the EU. But the Bush White House liked the idea of the centre of gravity drifting east, giving more weight to pro-American countries like Poland,

which is why it consistently dangled the EU membership carrot in front of Belarus and, later, Ukraine.

CHAPTER 5

1. Catherine Belton, "Russia Revising Great Game Rule Book," *The Moscow Times,* April 15, 2004.

CHAPTER 6

1. Currently the main route for getting Caspian Sea oil to the West is a pipeline from Baku to the Russian Black Sea port of Novorossiysk, a route that goes through the bomb-blasted Chechen capital, Grozny.
2. Georgian radio, May 27, 1994; translated by BBC Monitoring.
3. The deal on the two bases, which also called for Russia to train the Georgian military, has never been ratified by either side. Since 1993, Georgia's parliament has passed a flurry of resolutions calling for the bases to be closed, but Russia has refused, saying it would take years and that it should be compensated for the costs of any withdrawal.
4. *Black Sea Press,* February 19, 2002.
5. The Russian case that Chechen rebels used Pankisi as a rear base was proven to have some basis in fact when British freelance journalist Roddy Scott was killed while travelling with a band of Chechen fighters. The video footage on his camera showed that he had met with the rebels on the Georgian side and then crossed into Russia with them.
6. Georgian TV, October 7, 2002; translation by BBC Monitoring.
7. Aliev, a former KGB general, had come to power in Azerbaijan following a bloodless coup in 1993. His government was one of the most repressive in the former Soviet space, but Aliev knew the limits of what his old bosses in Moscow could do for him and instead aligned himself tightly with Ankara and Washington. Allegations later surfaced that BP, the company overseeing the BTC pipeline, played a behind-the-scenes role in the coup that brought him to power.
8. The Soros Foundation has no grant on its books for Kmara but instead funded the Liberty Foundation, which was virtually inseparable from the new group. The head of Open Society–Georgia at the time, Kakha Lomaia, gave the $350,000 figure in an interview with the BBC's Natalia Antelava shortly after the revolution. See Natalia Antelava, "How to Stage a Revolution," http://news.bbc.co.uk, December 4, 2003.

9. George Soros, *The Bubble of American Supremacy: Correcting the Misuse of American Power* (New York: Public Affairs, 2004).

CHAPTER 7

1. Margarita Antidze, "Shevardnadze Bloc Leads Georgia Poll," Reuters, November 4, 2003.
2. Natalia Antelava, "United States Cuts Development Aid to Georgia," http://eurasianet.org, September 29, 2003.
3. "Armoured Vehicles, Soldiers Seen in Central Tbilisi," Reuters, November 14, 2003.
4. Not only Saakashvili but also much of the mainstream media initially called the uprising a "velvet revolution"—the same name that was given the anti-Communist revolution in Prague in 1989. Only afterward did CNN dub it the Rose Revolution, a name that stuck.
5. Interview with Mikhail Saakashvili from James V. Wertsch and Levan Mikeladze, *Enough! The Rose Revolution in the Republic of Georgia* (Hauppage, NY: Nova, 2005).
6. BBC World interview with Mikhail Saakashvili, January 19, 2004.

CHAPTER 8

1. Details of the arrest are drawn from various Russian media reports.
2. While the West and many Russian liberals saw Khodorkovsky's arrest as a clear case of political persecution, the Kremlin often compared it to the arrest of Enron CEO Kenneth Lay and expressed bewilderment at the West's double standard.
3. Details of the Surkov–Saidullayev meeting are drawn from the excellent *Kremlin Rising: Vladimir Putin's Russia and the End of Revolution*, by Peter Baker and Susan Glasser (New York: Scribner, 2005).
4. Melissa Block, interview with George Soros on *All Things Considered*, National Public Radio, November 12, 2003.
5. Putin, while angry over the American role in Georgia's Rose Revolution, nonetheless appreciated that he was better off with Bush in the White House than with Bush's rivals, such as John McCain or John Kerry, both of whom advocated—as Bush once had—a less friendly relationship with the authoritarians in the Kremlin. Putin publicly expressed his support for Bush during the latter's own 2004 election campaign.

6. Michael Mainville, "Poster for Putin Ally Ignites Furor," *The Toronto Star,* November 1, 2003.

7. Interfax news service, December 8, 2003.

8. Vladimir Isachenkov, "Putin's Presidential Campaign Slick," Associated Press, March 9, 2000.

9. Anti-Semitism also played a major role in the attitude of Russians toward Khodorkovsky, Berezovsky and Gusinsky. All three are Jewish, and open anti-Semitism, along with other forms of racism, exploded after the fall of the Soviet Union.

10. Fradkov's appointment was a surprise to everyone but Kremlin spin doctor Stanislav Belkovsky, one of the princes of "managed democracy." Though it garnered little attention at the time, a news website affiliated with Belkovsky announced in December 2001 that Fradkov would succeed Kasyanov.

CHAPTER 9

1. Zbigniew Brzezinski, *The Grand Chessboard: American Primacy and Its Geostrategic Imperatives* (New York: Basic Books, 1997).

2. In 2005, a report by the United Nations' nuclear energy organization, the IAEA, found that just 56 people died from causes that could be directly attributed to the Chernobyl disaster, though another 9,000 will likely die from some form of cancer caused by radiation. However, the report was widely scorned—many point accusingly at the IAEA's mandate to promote nuclear power—and was sharply at odds with evidence compiled by the local Red Cross, as well as with what I saw during my own trip to the region. Greenpeace says at least 93,000 people—and perhaps 200,000 more across Ukraine, Russia and Belarus—died as a result of the Chernobyl explosion. The World Health Organization noted a hundredfold increase in incidences of thyroid cancer.

3. Estimates of how rich the oligarchs are were drawn from *Ukrainian Weekly,* October 31, 2004.

4. Ukraine has a history of suspicious car crashes. In 1999, Vyacheslav Chornovil, the anti-Soviet dissident who was expected to challenge Kuchma for the presidency that year, was killed when a truck suddenly pulled out in front of his car on an otherwise empty stretch of highway.

5. Olga Kryzhanovska, "Opposition Chief Urges U.S. to Stay Engaged: Yushchenko Seen More Democratic," *The Washington Times,* February 11, 2003.

CHAPTER 10

1. The Kuchma government's complaint about Ambassador Robinson's comment regarding the media bias backfired because it gave Robinson's remarks wide coverage in the Ukrainian media, which had been afraid to report his initial comments—inadvertently kick-starting a debate about media manipulation in the country.

2. "Black Pora" was based around the western, and highly Europeanized, city of Lviv and favoured using more radical, Rose Revolution–style tactics to force Kuchma out. "Yellow Pora" was Kiev-based and more partisan from the beginning, regularly coordinating strategy with Yushchenko's political team. However, the split was largely kept out of public sight until after the revolution, when they fractured.

3. George Soros, "Step Aside, Mr. Kuchma," *The Financial Times,* March 2, 2001.

4. From the *Ukrayinska Pravda* website, March 24, 2004; translation by BBC Monitoring.

5. Madeleine Albright, "How to Help Ukraine Vote," *The New York Times,* March 8, 2004.

6. Information about Pora funding is taken from Vladislav Kaskiv with Iryna Chupryna, Anastasiya Bezverkha and Yevgen Zolotariov, "A Case Study of the Civic Campaign PORA and the Orange Revolution in Ukraine," www.pora.org.ua, December 6, 2005.

7. Boris Berezovsky, the exiled Russian tycoon, says Zhvania sought and received financial aid from him, though Zhvania has denied this.

8. Katherine Yushchenko-Chumachenko has repeatedly been called a CIA agent by the Russian and Ukrainian media. She has twice gone to court and won libel cases against journalists who have explicitly suggested that she was charged by the CIA with putting her husband in power.

9. National Public Radio, *All Things Considered* with host Melissa Block, December 23, 2004.

10. Translated from a transcript of *Forbidden Zone,* http://maidan.org.ua. The original transcript, in Russian, is available at http://5tv.com.ua/pr_archiv/136/0/265.

CHAPTER 11

1. According to the Central Elections Commission, voter turnout in Donetsk leapt from 78.1 per cent in the first round to 96.7 per cent in the

second. In the western Ukrainian city of Lviv, a Yushchenko stronghold, turnout rose much more mildly, from 80.8 per cent on October 31 to 83.5 per cent on November 21. The national turnout, including the higher figures in Donetsk and Lugansk, rose from 74.9 per cent to 80.9 per cent.

2. The full transcript can be found at http://www2.pravda.com.ua/en/archive/2004/november/24/4.shtml. Oleh Rybachuk, Yushchenko's chief of staff, told *The New York Times* that he obtained the tape from a source inside the SBU and passed it on to *Ukrayinska Pravda*.

3. The press release highlighting the Democratic Initiatives Foundation in a "grantee spotlight" was posted at http://www.ned.org/grants/04programs/spotlight-eurasia04.html.

4. Rachok's words are taken from a USAID report on its contributions to the Orange Revolution (http://www.usaid.gov/press/frontlines/fl_jan06/democracy.htm).

5. Many in the tent city would stay a few nights in the cold, then trade their spot with someone else so they could go home for a proper night's sleep and a shower. Kaskiv and some others stayed the entire time.

6. The song was written and sung by an Ivano-Frankivsk–based band called GreenJolly.

7. Some in the opposition have poured scorn on the SBU's version of events, noting that the secret services—who are still among the suspects in the poisoning of Viktor Yushchenko—seemed to be trying to cast themselves posthumously on the right side of history. Chivers's story appeared in the *International Herald Tribune* on January 18, 2005, under the headline "The Untold Story in Ukraine: How the Security Service Averted a Postelection Bloodbath."

8. From the website of USAID's Kiev office, http://www.usaid.kiev.ua/accomp_dem.shtml.

9. George Gedda, "Powell Uses Quiet Diplomacy to Induce a New Russian Attitude toward Ukraine," Associated Press, December 1, 2004.

10. Details of the training are drawn from the website of the American Bar Associations's Central European and Eurasian Law Initiative, http://www.abanet.org/ceeli/countries/ukraine/ukraine_2004_elections_activities.html.

11. Carolynne Wheeler, "Eager Canadian Observers of Ukraine Vote to be Armed with Cellphones, Video Cameras," *The Globe and Mail*, December 23, 2004.

12. Pavlovsky made the diarrhea comments on the Sunday morning program *Apelsinovy Sok* (which, ironically, means "Orange Juice"), broadcast on NTV on November 28, 2004.

CHAPTER 12

1. Maskhadov, who condemned the Beslan hostage-taking and called for Basayev to be prosecuted, was systematically ignored by the Kremlin despite his repeated calls for a negotiated end to the senseless conflict. He was eventually killed by Russian soldiers, in the fall of 2005.
2. Basayev led a hostage-taking at a hospital in the southern Russian town of Budennovsk in 1995 that ended after Prime Minister Viktor Chernomyrdin spoke with him personally. Many Chechens believe the attack forced the Russian government to seek peace in 1996.
3. A full transcript of the e-mail exchange was posted at www.chechenpress.org but is no longer available.
4. The full statement released by the Russian Foreign Ministry, and published by nearly all of its embassies, is still available at http://www.rusembcanada.mid.ru/pr/041104_e.html. Britain's Channel 4 and America's ABC would run into similar trouble for broadcasting Basayev interviews the following year. Basayev was killed in 2006 when an explosive-laden truck he was driving blew up. See also http://www.rusembcanada.mid.ru/pr/041104_e.html.
5. Fred Weir, "Ukraine Election Emboldens Opposition in Former Soviet States, Worries Kremlin," Canadian Press, February 20, 2005.

CHAPTER 13

1. Philip Shishkin, "Ripple Effect: In Putin's Backyard, Democracy Stirs—with U.S. Help," *The Wall Street Journal,* February 25, 2005.
2. Michael Steen, "Kyrgyz Protests Spread, President Offers Talks," Reuters, March 21, 2005.
3. "No Foreign NGOs behind Kyrgyz Revolution—Acting Minister," Kyrgyz AKIpress news agency, April 2, 2005; translation by BBC Monitoring.
4. Raushan Nurshayeva, "Kazakh Head's Daughter Decries 'Democratic Pressure,'" Reuters, June 7, 2005.
5. Gulnoza Saidazimova, "Kazakhstan: Soros Foundation Says Tax Evasion Case Is Politically Motivated," www.rferl.org, November 30, 2004.

6. As is the case with Belarus and Turkmenistan, the National Endowment for Democracy doesn't disclose the names of specific grantees in Uzbekistan for fear of endangering them. Despite Ikramov's criticism, however, NED's annual report says it spent a substantial amount, $107,149, in 2004 to "bolster the organizational capacity of Uzbekistan's human rights defenders."

7. "Uzbeks Rally in Support of Kyrgyz Events," www.ferghana.ru, March 25, 2005; translation by BBC Monitoring.

8. Galima Bukharbaeva, "Blood Flows in Uzbek Crackdown," iwpr.net, May 14, 2005.

9. January 31, 2006; transcript by BBC Monitoring.

10. Michael Steen, "Kazakh Leader Set to Win Vote Seen as Flawed," Reuters, December 2, 2005.

11. Graeme Smith, "In Azerbaijan, Opposition Chances Run Straight Uphill," *The Globe and Mail,* November 5, 2005.

CHAPTER 14

1. "Rice: Belarus 'Last Dictatorship in Europe,'" Associated Press, April 22, 2005.

2. For a breakdown of Gallup's exit poll methodology, see an interview conducted by Yury Drakakhrust of Radio Free Europe/Radio Liberty with Rasa Alisauskiene, director of Gallup/Baltic Surveys. A transcript is posted at http://www.charter97.org/eng/news/2004/10/26/interview.

3. Interfax news service, October 19, 2004.

4. As with Uzbekistan, the National Endowment for Democracy doesn't disclose the names of specific recipients in Belarus.

5. See Vitali Silitski, "Preempting Democracy: The Case of Belarus," *Journal of Democracy* 16, no. 4 (2005).

6. Poll figures are taken from Jonathan Steele, "Europe and the US Decide the Winner Before the Vote," *The Guardian,* March 10, 2006.

CHAPTER 15

1. Georgian and Moldovan wines are among the most popular brands in Russia. When I visited one of Moscow's many Georgian restaurants in April 2006, the wine card contained a page marked only "here should be Georgian wines," illustrated dramatically with a sword plunged into a wooden table.

2. Saakashvili tried to claim that the Russian ban on Georgian wines was actually a good thing since it raised the profile of Georgian brands worldwide. One place sales did increase was Ukraine, where advertisements at a Georgian Wine Festival held during the ban read, "Drink the wine that contains too much freedom for Russia."

3. "Russia Deports Dozens of Georgians, Steps Up Pressure on Businesses, Schools," www.mosnews.com, October 7, 2006.

4. "Russia's Wrong Direction: What the United States Can and Should Do," Council on Foreign Relations, March 2006.

5. *Kommersant,* May 5, 2006.

6. *Komsomolskaya Pravda,* May 5, 2006.

7. May 10, 2006; translation by BBC Monitoring.

8. Sidelnikov told me Berezovsky had no tie with Russian Pora, though the oligarch himself said he was putting his wealth behind a campaign to oust Putin and the *siloviki.* Berezovsky also claimed to have helped fund the Ukrainian revolution, though Viktor Yushchenko denied having received the money Berezovsky said he sent.

9. The word *pora* means the same thing in Russian as in Ukrainian: "It's time."

10. Following the murder of Anna Politkovskaya in October 2006, Kasparov said he feared he, too, would be targeted for assassination.

11. "Putin's Aide Outlines Main Threats to Russia," www.mosnews.com, March 4, 2006.

12. "Kremlin Official Pledges Russia to Pro-Putin Youth Movement," www.mosnews.com, July 18, 2005.

13. January 31, 2006; transcript by BBC Monitoring.

14. See the National Endowment for Democracy's annual reports, available at www.ned.org.

CHAPTER 16

1. American efforts at using the revolution model in the Middle East quickly hit a major stumbling block. Most of the positives in Lebanon were undone by the summer 2006 war between Israel and Hezbollah, when the White House's unqualified support for Israel's bombing campaign fed renewed anti-American sentiment. In other countries—such as Egypt and the Palestinian Territories—backing Otpor-style regime change has proved complicated because the ones who can bring the

crowds into the streets are often Islamists. Ayman Nour, the de facto leader of Egypt's beleaguered democrats, once told me in Cairo that some Americans—he wouldn't name them—had offered to stage a Ukraine-style revolution for him around Egypt's 2005 presidential vote. He said he couldn't afford the price they were asking.

2. Disaster was luckily averted on the visit when a twenty-seven-year-old man, identified as a supporter of the ousted governor of Adjara, Aslan Abashidze, hurled a cloth-wrapped grenade in the direction of the stage Bush and Saakashvili were speaking from. The grenade never exploded and the would-be attacker, Vladimir Arutyunian, was sentenced to life in prison.

INDEX

A page number followed by the italic letter "n" and another number indicates a note: e.g., 281*n2* indicates note 2 on page 281.

MARK MACKINNON was the Moscow bureau chief for the *Globe and Mail* from 2002 to 2005, and in addition to Eastern Europe covered the wars in Afghanistan, Chechnya and Iraq. A two-time winner of the National Newspaper Award, Canada's top reporting prize, his latest posting is in the Middle East.